THE BEAR AT THE BACK DOOR

The Soviet threat to the West's lifeline in Africa

BY

GENERAL SIR WALTER WALKER,

K.C.B., C.B.E., D.S.O.

Former NATO Commander-in-Chief,

Allied Forces Northern Europe

First edition

Published 1978
by the Foreign Affairs Publishing Co. Ltd.
139 Petersham Road, Richmond, Surrey, TW10 7AA
England

Printed in Great Britain
by Anglia County Press
63 West End, March
Cambridgeshire

ISBN 0 900380 23 3

First edition

Published 1978
by the Foreign Affairs Publishing Co. Ltd.
139 Petersham Road, Richmond, Surrey TW10 7AA,
England

Printed in Great Britain
by Anglia [illegible] Press
[illegible] West End, [illegible]
Cambridgeshire

ISBN 0 900380 23 3

FOR BERYL

CONTENTS

An Eminent American Warns of Envelopment

THE Chairman of the Committee for the Present Danger in the United States, Professor Eugene V. Rostow concluded his evidence to the US Senate Budget Committee on 1 March, 1978 with the following words:

"The real problem of the Administration's budget proposals with regard to NATO runs deeper than the assumptions it makes about tanks, anti-tank weapons and the number and types of planes and artillery pieces available. Those proposals are addressed to the Central Front in Germany. Many experts believe that the Soviets will strike towards Hamburg one day, and present us with difficult problems indeed. That may, of course happen.

"But I regard the risks of a strategy of envelopment as much greater — a strategy that would utilize Mediterranean positions and opportunities, or Norway, or Iceland, or Africa, as a way to cut the lifeline between Europe and the United States, and thus gain a position of dominance in the entire area of Europe, Africa, and the Middle East — the classic heartland which has long been the central theme of strategic thought. To deal with risks of that magnitude, a much broader policy is required than an adequate defence of the Central Front: a strategy which is based upon a much more active diplomacy, more naval and air power, and above all a much wider field of vision."

FOREWORD

by The Rt. Hon. Julian Amery, M.P.

Former Minister of State for Foreign and Commonweath Affairs

THE Soviets have achieved at least nuclear parity with the US and marked conventional superiority over both NATO and China. They have also shown a capability of intervening with their Cuban allies, not just in guerilla, but in major conventional, operations elsewhere, e.g. the Ogaden. They have thus achieved the "two and one half" capability which had been the standard set for themselves by the US. A standard now sadly reduced by the US to "one and one half" — i.e. a major war in Europe or in Asia but not in both.

This massive change in the military balance of power between the super powers brings the danger of a world war much closer than it has been at any time since 1945.

The imperialist character of the Soviet regime is not in doubt, but "the Bear" is a cautious creature. The risk of nuclear war involves a fearful gamble. You know where the journey starts but not where it ends. The signs are, for the time being at any rate, that the Soviets have opted for an indirect strategy.

This indirect strategy consists in cutting off the West and Japan from free access to the essential raw materials on which their economies and social structures depend. The means of doing so are two fold. They are, first to develop sufficient naval power to threaten sea communications between the US and its friends across the Atlantic and across the Pacific; second, to obtain physical control of the sources of raw material supply by putting pro-Soviet forces in control of them.

The most important source of raw materials is the oil-bearing Gulf. Without access to it, Japan and the West would face an all but mortal crisis. Access to the oil, other than by pipeline, depends upon the freedom of passage through the Straits of Hormuz.

Afghanistan, now turned into virtually another Central Asian Soviet republic like Uzbekistan and Tadzhikstan, is only some 300 miles to the north east of the Straits. Soviet controlled South Yemen is also only some 500 miles to the south west of the Straits. The pincers are closing on what is perhaps the world's most vital waterway.

Across the Indian Ocean, the Straits of Malacca, previously guarded by the British presence in Singapore and Malaysia, are now unguarded. They are Japan's jugular vein.

West of the Straits of Hormuz the entrance to the Red Sea — the Bab el Mandeb — is already under Soviet control from Aden and Massawa. If the Soviets are allowed to consolidate their position in the Horn of Africa, passage through the Red Sea to the Mediterranean will be by their leave. The only other route from the Gulf to Europe and the one already essential to larger tankers is round Central and Southern Africa by the Cape of Good Hope.

The second most important source of raw materials in the world is Central and Southern Africa, providing gold, diamonds, platinum, uranium, chrome, cobalt, nickel, copper as well as many other minerals used in the making of steel and other technological processes. The Soviets have established virtually a colonial regime in Angola and a protectorate over Mozambique. From these two countries, they are poised to extend their influence over Zambia and Zaire's copper-rich province of Shaba. Meanwhile they have already begun guerilla operations to the south against South-West Africa and Rhodesia. The guerilla forces involved, are trained, equipped, indoctrinated and financed by the Soviets with East German and Cuban help.

Rhodesia and South-West Africa are both significant mineral producers but their chief importance is that they guard the approaches to South Africa, the biggest mineral treasure house in the world and the guardian of the Cape. The outcome of the struggle for Rhodesia and South-West Africa could thus determine the fate of the industrial West and Japan as surely as the struggle for the control of the Straits of Hormuz.

General Sir Walter Walker has just concluded two visits to Southern Africa. He does not claim to be an African expert but he is an undoubted expert on both guerilla warfare and Soviet grand strategy. General Walker commanded Gurkha troops in the Malayan emergency where the Communist guerillas were soundly defeated. Later he was Director of Operations in the "confrontation" with Indonesia in Borneo. This was a major guerilla campaign mounted by the Soekharno Government against Britain and its fellow members of the Commonwealth. Its defeat by General Walker confirmed how useful a military presence can be for the defence of the status quo. Had the guerillas won, there is little doubt that Singapore and Malaya would have fallen to President Soekharno and his Communist allies. As it was, the failure of the Indonesian operations led to Soekharno's overthrow by his generals. The Indonesian Communists suffered the grim fate which they had doubtless reserved for their adversaries.

These experiences make General Walker admirably qualified to judge the capabilities of the Rhodesian and South African armed forces and of the SWAPO and Patriotic Front guerillas who confront them. His experience as Deputy Chief-of-Staff Allied Forces, Central Europe and as Commander-in-Chief of NATO's Northern Flank have also enabled him to see the local military and political problems of Southern Africa in the context of Soviet world strategy, by land, sea and air.

His book is primarily concerned with the military aspects of the Southern Africa problem. But Soviet strategy — a compound of gunboat diplomacy, guerilla war, propaganda and disinformation — cannot be separated from policy. Much of the book is thus naturally devoted to the political as well as to the military issues involved.

I strongly recommend this penetrating report of what General Walker has seen and the conclusions he has formed to all concerned about the onward march of Soviet Imperialism in Africa and the threat which it poses to the survival of the West.

Julian Amery

112 Eaton Square,
London, S.W.1.
July, 1978.

His book is primarily concerned with the military aspects of the Southern Africa problem. But [illegible] complicated of summit diplomacy [illegible] information cannot be separated [illegible] the book is thus naturally devoted to the political as well as the military issues involved.

I strongly recommend this penetrating report of what General Walker has seen and the conclusions he has formed to all concerned about the [illegible] of Soviet interference in Africa and the threat which it poses to the survival of the West.

Julian Amery

112 Eaton Square,
London, S.W.1.
July, 1978.

PREFACE

THE subject matter of this study is global in its aspect, and I try to warn Western public opinion of the ever-growing Soviet worldwide threat. Strategically the Horn of Africa, Southern Africa and the Cape Route are every bit as important to the Soviets as is the Central Front, and NATO's northern and southern flanks in Europe. The Soviet Union has a global strategy, the West has not. NATO's present southern boundary ends at the Tropic of Cancer. A new charter is required and a new outward looking strategy. I will explain how this should be evolved.

Unless drastic steps are taken in time by the West, the Soviet Union will be able to achieve her aim of world domination without firing a shot, merely by the threat of her ever-increasing massive military might, combined with gunboat diplomacy and the technique of revolutionary war by proxy forces — using mercenary hatchetmen from Cuba or Warsaw Pact states and Communist-indoctrinated, trained and armed terrorist forces to do their dirty work for them. Unless we wake up in time, the West will be "nibbled to death in conditions of nuclear stalemate."

The Soviet Union intends to absorb the whole of Southern Africa including its great mineral wealth; to dominate the Cape sea route, the Red Sea, the Persian Gulf and the Indian Ocean, and to bring NATO to its knees without firing a shot. This is why Southern Africa is so important to the Soviet Union. Moscow is prepared to take great risks in Africa because detente is dead in that continent.

For the past decade and more, the United States has made a serious strategic miscalculation in failing to appreciate that Africa is a theatre of power. Moscow, on the other hand, tumbled to this long ago. Now, after less than 18 months in office and without any previous personal experience of the complexities of African problems, Washington is producing slick, over-simplified solutions which are merely playing straight into the Soviet Union's hands and furthering the Kremlin's designs. The world may have to pay dearly for the incredible stupidity of the United States' dangerous policies.

Instead of supporting the countries that are actively opposed to Moscow's expansionist designs, the US is cravenly competing for the favour of the Soviet Union's puppet regimes in the hope that they can be wooed away from the fatal Kremlin bear-hug.

The United States is being just as hostile to South Africa and Rhodesia as is the Soviet Union. Indeed, President Carter's sidekick, Mr. Andrew Young, is doing much of the Soviet's dirty work for them. There are several reasons for America's hostility. First, her guilt about the treatment of her own negroes in the past, as well as in the present. Second, Carter's reliance on the negro vote in America. Third, America's traditional anti-colonialism. Fourth, her dislike of Mr. Vorster and Mr. Smith. Fifth, the salutary lesson she learned in Vietnam. Sixth, her secret war against South Africa which is described in chapter 23.

The veneer of altruism with which Britain's Labour Government shields its attitudes to Southern Africa is becoming increasingly transparent.

The embarrassing speed with which they recognised the not yet victorious Communist-backed Popular Movement for the Liberation of Angola (MPLA) as the "legitimate" government in Angola, and their equally embarrassing refusal to endorse the internal settlement in Rhodesia, far from being inconsistent, have one sinister characteristic in common. Both decisions support Marxist factions who have the financial and military backing of both the Soviet Union and Cuba, whose expansionist intentions in Africa have for some time been undeniable.

The Communist bondage which awaits those poor Africans (black and white) who still have the good fortune to remain free offers precious little in the way of democracy or human rights.

In Rhodesia, a victory for the so-called Patriotic Front would be a major political and strategic defeat for the West. It would enable the Communists to complete the encirclement of South Africa and prepare for the final assault on our only potential ally in Southern Africa, and the capture of its mineral wealth and bases vital to our sea communications.

With the Horn lost beyond recovery to the Soviet Union, Rhodesia becomes the West's last bastion in Africa, and if we fail to defend it, we shall have lost the present stage of the Third World War and made it almost impossible for us to win the next.

For the past 11 years or so, our politicians and news media by expounding views on Rhodesia based upon ignorance, have been seeking to influence the affairs of a country about which they are so patently lacking in knowledge. They simply did not go and see for themselves.

No wonder the British public is deeply confused about Rhodesia and the Government's attitude to that country and people. Those who write and speak about Rhodesia must visit the country. There is no excuse for not doing so in these days of sophisticated communication and travel.

The picture of South Africa that is painted by the lamentable international mass media, reinforced by statements by the know-alls in London, Washington and Moscow, is that of a country on the brink of a mass eruption, with the government desperately trying to stem the tide of discontent.

The reality which hit me in the face could not have been more different. Compared to the violence and crime in the USA and in Europe — particularly in strife-torn Italy — and the varying degrees of open warfare, guerilla warfare, civil war, insurrection, or civil unrest, in such areas as the Middle East, Africa, India, Pakistan, South-East Asia and elsewhere — including Northern Ireland, which is part and parcel of Britain — the reality I found is a country that is almost unreal in the contemporary world in respect of peace and law and order.

Of course, South Africa is not utopia. It has a racial composition which is unique in the world: 16 million blacks, two million mixed blood or coloured, some one million Indian and some five million people of European descent. Institutionalised discrimination is being eliminated and a multitude of injustices are being swept away almost daily — without fanfare. The threat of Communism and violence is ever present, but because Prime Minister Vorster is taking pre-emptive action to meet the threat, it pales almost into insignificance when compared to the situation anywhere else in Africa. Consider the situation in Italy, for example, which is approaching a civil war as civil disorders, violence, kidnappings and murders increase and the Communist Party gets closer to power.

Naturally, fulfilment in South Africa still falls short of intention and the gap between reality and aspiration remains wide. But a multi-racial people is on the move, and the only thing that could bring the momentum to a halt would be the ganging-up of foreigners against South Africa, designed to disrupt the economy and to encourage a terrorism that would not be spontaneous but organised and manipulated from outside. There is not a shadow of doubt that it is violent revolution that a large part of the world dearly wants to happen to South Africa. It is precisely this that Prime Minister Vorster is absolutely determine to prevent.

General Sir Walter Walker
Charlton All Saints
Salisbury
Wiltshire
May 1978

CHAPTER 1

Visits to Southern Africa

WITHIN the past six months I have paid two visits to Southern Africa, the first in October 1977, and the second in April-May this year. On both visits my programmes were so comprehensive and the travelling facilities by road and air made so readily available that I met more key personalities and saw more of Rhodesia, South-West Africa and South Africa, and their peoples, than many visitors could hope to achieve in a lifetime. Also, in my case, I was treated as a privileged guest and, therefore, no secrets were withheld from me, no doors closed, no security restrictions imposed — military or otherwise — and, above all, no strings were attached to either visit. Accordingly, I am writing this book entirely of my own volition.

On my first visit to South Africa I visited Johannesburg, Pretoria, Durban, East London, Cape Town, the Naval Base at Simonstown and the Underground Communication and Surveillance Centre at Silvermine, near Simonstown.

I had long interviews with Prime Minister Vorster, with Mr. P. W. Botha, the Minister of Defence, the Deputy Minister of Information, the Chairman and the Heads of all the Departments of the South African Broadcasting Corporation, the Rector of the Rand Afrikaans University, the Director of the Institute of Plural Studies, University of Pretoria, the Director of the Foreign Affairs Association, the Deputy Chairman and Board of the Anglo-American Corporation, the Shadow Minister for Defence of the then-Opposition — the Progressive Federal Party, the Secretary General (black) of the Committee for Fairness in Sport, the Secretary General of the Islamic Council of South Africa, and Development Head of the Indian University of Durban, the Friends of Rhodesia who are providing so much voluntary aid to Rhodesia, in the form of ambulances, medical supplies, horses, etc., Professor Christian Barnard and a large group of officers of South Africa's Citizen Forces.

At Combined Defence Headquarters in Pretoria, I faced a panel of Senior Army, Navy and Air Force Officers and Civilian staff and was questioned on the tactics and techniques for border, rural and urban anti-terrorist and anti-guerilla operations employed in the 12 year Malayan Emergency when I raised and commanded the jungle warfare school; commanded an infantry battalion, and then became commander of a brigade group. More precisely I was cross examined on the Borneo Campaign against Indonesian Confrontation when I was Director of Operations for three years. The following day I faced a simlar panel at the Bureau for State Security.

On my second visit to South Africa, I visited many Coloured and African Townships, including Soweto and have given an account of this in Chapter 13.

In May 1978, I paid a private all day visit to Exercise Quicksilver, the biggest Army and Air Force Exercise to be held in Southern Africa since 1973. My impression of this conventional mobile warfare exercise, which was up to NATO standards, are given in Chapter 22. I also addressed the National Defence College, Pretoria.

I had long meetings with the Minister of Defence, Mr. P. W. Botha, the Chief of Defence, General Magnus Malan, the Department of Foreign Affairs, Mr. Neil van Heerden, the Minister of Justice, Mr. J. Kruger, the Minister of Information and Plural Relations and Development, Dr. Connie Mulder and the Head of the Arms Corporation. I also met the Minister of Foreign Affairs, Mr. P. K. Botha. I dined and lunched with Members of Parliament of all parties and members of the business community.

On my first visit to South West Africa (SWA), I had a long meeting with Judge Steyn, the Administrator General, and with the then retiring Commissioner General in Owamboland. I also met Mr. Dirk Mudge who had just formed his new multi-racial party, which broke the power monopoly held for nearly three decades by the white Nationalist Party. I visited the operational area on the Angolan border and saw and talked with South African soldiers actually in operations and also visited the various Headquarters from South West Command to brigade, battalion and company headquarters.

On my second visit to SWA in May 1978, I had meetings with the Administrator General, Judge Steyn, Advocate Mouton, one of Mr. Mudge's right hand men, members of the Black Community, Windhoek, the Town Council Walvis Bay, the Town Council Swakopmund, and members of ex-Servicemen's Associations — Army and Air Force. I carried out a reconnaissance of Walvis Bay which is described in Chapter 24. I visited the uranium mine at Rössing, not far from Walvis Bay, which is the world's largest uranium mine — one of at least five uranium strikes in the area — and which went into full production this year. Britain's nuclear power programme is dependent on its output. It has already been infiltrated by SWAPO agents posing as ordinary members of the work force. I visited Black and Coloured Townships at Windhoek, Walvis Bay and Rössing Uranium Mine. I inspected the training of a recently raised Coloured battalion and I again visited the operational area near the Angolan border, this time to be briefed on the recent pre-emptive strike into Angola, to see the SWAPO "prisoners of war", the wounded and the captured Soviet weapons. An account of this pre-emptive strike is given in Chapter 25.

My first visit to Rhodesia in October last year was not pre-planned. It came out of the blue while I was in South Africa Lieutenant General Peter Walls, Commander Combined Operations, took me completely into his confidence, gave me a personal, private and privileged briefing behind locked doors and then arranged a working lunch with his combined staff in Salisbury. I then flew with him and his Army and Air Force Commanders to Umtali, on the Mozambique border, where I was given another briefing by the local Brigade Commander and his combined civil and military staff. That night we all sat down to a full, frank, working dinner and the next day visited, by helicopter, infantry and artillery positions some distance away overlooking the border with Mozambique.

I had a meeting with Prime Minister Ian Smith, with Mr. P. K. van der Byl, his Minister for Foregin Affairs, with all the Service Chiefs, the Police, Intelligence and Special Branch, and met a number of retired British Army Officers and others who had settled in Rhodesia after the Second World War.

During my second visit to Rhodesia in April-May of this year, I had meetings with Prime Minister Ian Smith, Bishop Muzorewa, Rev. Sithole, Chief Chirau, Mr. P. K. van der Byl, Mr. Cronje, co-Minister of Manpower, Service Chiefs, the Head of CIO, Counter Intelligence Organisation, Mr. Cambitzis, Chairman Industrial Development Corporation and Mr. Pope-Simmonds, Registrar General.

I visited ten Black and Coloured Townships and spent one day and a night with farmers in a vulnerable area 150 miles North of Salisbury. This visit is described later in the book.

I visited Combined Operations Headquarters in Salisbury where I received a secret briefing and had a discussion with the National Joint Operations Command (JOC), led by the Deputy Commander Combined Operations, Air Marshal Mclaren. I paid a visit to the police armoury to see a cross section of captured Soviet weapons.

I spent two days with the Commander of the Army, Lieutenant General Hickman, flying to the operational areas, seeing and talking to the troops on the ground and being briefed at the various JOCs and sub-JOCs. We were flown in a civil aircraft by a farmer who belonged to the Air Wing of the Police Reserve. A map of the five operational areas is shown on page 60.

I spent one day and a night with Major General MacIntyre who flew me to Kariba to visit the power station; accompany a boat patrol on Kariba lake; visit gun and mortar positions; talk to the soldiers and be briefed by the JOC of the operational area.

I visited the School of Infantry where the emphasis is on modern conventional warfare against a first class enemy, rather than on guerilla-type warfare. The standard of equipment and training and the methods of training were quite exceptional — well above NATO standards.

I spent one day with the Air Force and was shown their newly developed and locally manufactured weaponry. All I am prepared to say is that it is highly sophisticated and extremely lethal and I would not care to be at the receiving end of it.

I inspected a Protected Village (PV) in a Tribal Trust Land and watched the training of the all-Black highly efficient garrison. There are now more than two hundred PVs.

I was in Rhodesia as a visitor and was grateful for the opportunity to listen and learn. It was not my business to offer advice nor state my views. Indeed, I was not in a position to do so because their security forces have developed tactics and techniques far superior to anything I have encountered hitherto. As far as I was concerned, I was an ordinary civilian and the Internal Agreement had, in my view, legalised the previous so-called "illegality".

The other country I visited for several days last October was Transkei. I had a whole afternoon with the Cabinet, followed by a private meeting with Prime Minister Matanzima. It is a sad state of affairs when a father — Britain — disowns its son, the Transkei. Yet we recognise the independence of the Marxist-dominated dictatorships of Angola and Mozambique, and we lavish millions of pounds on Mozambique which spends the money on equipping and training terrorists to fight our own kith and kin in Rhodesia. Meanwhile the inhabitants of Mozambique are starving; the children are not being educated; medical facilities are not available and the jails are full of political prisoners.

There is an American Embassy in Maputo, the capital of Mozambique, but the US Administration refuses to recognise Transkei which is more independent, democratic, and practises human rights at a far higher level than Mozambique and many other states in Africa.

What were my impressions of Prime Ministers Smith and Vorster?

I found Prime Minister Ian Smith relaxed, cheerful, buoyant, radiating confidence and every inch an outstanding leader. He looked lean, fit and as fresh as a daisy. He stands out as being in a class of his own and it was easy to see how, for twelve years, such an astute and intelligent man has made a monkey of British

Ministers — including four Prime Ministers.

The spirit he has injected in his countrymen is like that which existed in Britain at the time of Dunkirk. I was uplifted by the calmness, cheerfulness and courage of everyone, and the faith and trust they have in their leader. They are, in my view, the best and bravest people in the world.

The effect of the attempts by the world's media to denigrate Mr. Ian Smith, is like pouring water on a duck's back.

Of course, there are a number of exceptions among the media. For instance, it was refreshing to see how one of Britain's mass circulation Sunday newspapers rallied to his side on 12 February. "By its charter, the BBC," said the **Sunday Express,** "has the duty to be politically neutral. Does anyone ever hold it to account?

"Notice whenever Rhodesia or South Africa is discussed, the same dead-beat Left-wing journalists are trundled to the microphone.

"The other day one spoke punctiliously of 'Bishop' Muzorewa, the 'Rev.' Sithole, and even 'Mr.' Mugabe, but spat out his venom against the Rhodesian Prime Minister as plain 'Smith.'

"Notice too how the BBC newsreaders still describe Mr. Smith as the leader of the Rhodesia 'regime'.

"Who do they think has been running the country for the past 12 years — Ken Dodd?"

It was not so refreshing to read a few days earlier on 20 January that **The Times** of London had given a very misleading, though eye-catching, title to an article on Rhodesia. I felt compelled to put the record straight. Accordingly, I wrote a letter to the editor who was good enough to publish it ten days later. This is what I wrote:

"As one who has recently visited Rhodesia as a tourist and managed to twist the arm of the powers-that-be into allowing me to proceed into the main operational area without any restrictions whatsoever, may I say that your headline 'As the war intensifies, Rhodesia staggers to the brink of collapse' published on 20 January, could not be further from the truth.

"In my professional judgment, based on more than 20 years practical experience, from lieutenant to general, of counter-insurgency and guerilla-type operations, there is no doubt that Rhodesia now have the most professional and battleworthy army in the world today for this particular type of warfare. Their army cannot be defeated in the field either by terrorists or even by a much more sophisticated enemy.

"Not one inch of territory has been given up and not one permanent terrorist base established within Rhodesia. The casualties inflicted on Rhodesians, black or white, are far less than we suffered during our 12-year Malayan Emergency, while the casualties inflicted on the terrorists are many times greater.

"The Rhodesian security forces, 85 per cent of whom are black, are in complete control, their morale is sky high and the terrorists are petrified of meeting them in pitched battle. Here is a breed of men, the like of which has not been seen for many a long age. It made one feel almost ashamed to be British in these squalid and shameful times in which we live. As for Dr. Owen and his travelling circus they are held in utter contempt".

I was pleasantly surprised to find how polite and relaxed Prime Minister Vorster was and how genuinely pleased he was to see one. Within a very few minutes, I realised I was in the presence of a powerful man and exceptional leader who, like Mr. Ian Smith, radiates confidence and secures immediate respect. He spoke with great clarity and firmness and explained his policies logically, convincingly and fairly. He is perfectly aware of all the criticisms levelled at him; where he is vulnerable; what improvements are required and how he intends to plan the way ahead.

He knows that South Africa is the strongest military power in Africa, and, therefore, the only real bastion left against the Soviet Union's relentless encroachment by land from the North and also encirclement by sea. I pray that he also knows where his real front line lies.

No one is going to push him around. Mr. Vorster is open to criticism and reasoned argument and I personally did not find him either dogmatic, overbearing or intimidating. As the object of the exercise was for me to glean information, I remembered the words of the late King Feisal, who said — "God gave men two ears and one tongue so that we could listen twice as much as we talk". Oh, that this quotation could be hung round the neck of every television chat show entertainer.

Woe betide professional entertainers of the media who are foolish enough to subject Mr. Vorster to hostile questioning in their usual manner of counsel for the prosecution, seeking nothing but the weak points in their victim's argument. Mr. Vorster has no need to weave and duck to avoid being trapped into an indiscretion, for he knows his business backwards. Unfortunately the television screen gives an immense forum to today's artful interviewers whose only distinction is that few of them have ever had to carry heavy responsibility.

Mr. Vorster has said that the black migrant workers from the homelands would have more control over their own affairs in South Africa than foreign workers now had in Western Europe. He explained how they would be able to elect municipal councils to run the townships; run their own schools and also share responsibility for law and order. This stands in sharp contrast to most other states of the African continent where 20 now have one-party regimes and another 19 have military dictatorships.

I came away convinced that Britain, the United States and the West would be well advised to cease to dictate to South Africa what form evolutionary changes should take; when they should be made, or warn of punitive action if their advice is not taken. It is even more important that we should guard against double standards, such as when goodwill missions to crude dictatorships are made the occasion for threats of economic boycotts against South Africa. Such expediency will only lead to defiance and is bound to set the clock back.

one-party regimes and another 17 have military dictatorships.

I remain convinced that Britain, the United States and the West would be well advised to cease to dictate to South Africa what form developmental changes should take, when they should be made, or warn of punitive action if their advice is not taken. It is even more important that we should guard against double standards, such as when goodwill missions to crude dictatorships are made the occasion for threats of economic boycotts against South Africa. Such expediency will only lead to defiance and is bound to set the clock back.

CHAPTER 2

The Soviet Union Intends to Absorb the Whole of Southern Africa

THE first thing to get clear is that the Soviet Union, whether by blackmail, revolutionary war by proxy or by brute force, intends to absorb the whole of Southern Africa, and thus deprive the West of vital minerals and control of Europe's lifeline round the Cape. Southern Africa holds key bases of fundamental strategic importance to the control of the sea lanes and trade routes in the South Atlantic and Indian Oceans. The possession of these bases would give the Soviet Union overwhelming superiority in global strategy.

When reviewing Mr. Ian Greig's authoritative study **The Communist Challenge to Africa**[1], the Observer Foreign News Service stated:

"The conclusions Greig reaches are quite dramatic . . . Greig hopes the West will realise the 'enormity' of the military and economic disaster that faces it if Soviet policies succeed: 'Not only would virtually all hope of protecting the Cape route from menace have long since disappeared, and sources of vital raw materials be under constant threat, but in time of war, the West's opponents would be able to cut the world in two'."

What the West suffered as a result of the Arab cutback in oil supplies is a fraction of what would happen if the Cape route were to be blockaded. What is at stake now is not only the whole future of Western Europe, but civilisation itself, the Western way of life and whether or not our children and grandchildren are to lead their lives as free men and women.

---

1. **The Communist Challenge to Africa.** By Ian Greig. Foreign Affairs Pub. Co. 1977.

CHAPTER 3

The Free World Would Do Well to Listen to the Voice of NATO

WHEN the South African Government decides to clamp down on indigenous organisations, in what is seen in Pretoria as a bid to end racial unrest, the shockwaves are felt around the world. But while such action may well lead to a deterioration in diplomatic relations with Western nations, military strategists at NATO Headquarters in Brussels are not allowing emotions to outweigh realism.

Last year's North Atlantic Assembly of Parliamentarians of 15 nations went considerably further than previous years in calling attention to the growing Soviet naval threat in the south Atlantic and Indian Oceans. At that meeting, a paper was approved which underlined the dependence of NATO member states on a substantial range of energy supplies and raw materials from the developing countries. It expressed grave concern over the ease with which the transportation of such supplies could be interfered with. See the map of the Cape Route on page 129.

In particular, the report stressed the importance of Southern Africa's mineral wealth to the West and the sea lines of communications in the Atlantic and Indian Oceans which carry oil from the Middle East. The report stated that the Soviet Union has little need of Southern Africa's minerals for its own use as it is largely self-sufficient. However, should the Soviets or their client states secure, even temporary, control over Southern Africa's resources, the Soviet Union would then possess 74 per cent of the world's gold production and 68 per cent of its reserves. With South African gold sealed off, the Soviet Union would be left as by far the biggest gold producer. This would have crippling implications for world trade and finance, and could be used to hasten the long-promised collapse of capitalism throughout the world.

The Soviet Union, which already produces more chrome than South Africa, would have 67 per cent of the world's production, and it is known that 75 per cent of the world's chrome ore deposits are in South Africa. Chrome is a metal without substitute and is already in critically short supply in the United States.

Chrome, like platinum, manganese, titanium, vanadium, nickel and other key minerals are all essential for the production of modern weapons. The percentage of other key mineral resources that would fall into the hands of the Soviets are equally startling. The USSR would possess 94 per cent of the world's platinum production and 99 per cent of the world's reserves; 62 per cent of its manganese ore and 93 per cent of its reserves.

Other vital percentages would be 97 per cent of the world's vanadium, 50 per cent of its fluorspar, 46 per cent of its iron ore, 35 per cent of its asbestos, 21 per cent of its titanium, 17 per cent of its nickel, zinc and lead and, above all, 30 per cent of the world's uranium.

It is little wonder that senior NATO parliamentarians are demanding that Western policy-makers should recognise the crucial strategic position of Southern Africa with regard to Western supply routes. The defence of the oil routes in particular presents a staggering problem because of Europe's ever increasing fuel requirements. Every day there are 200 tankers of Western nations at sea in the Indian Ocean engaged in the transporting of oil from the Persian Gulf. Furthermore, the evidence of recent Soviet naval exercises suggests that the Russians are now preparing for anti-convoy actions, and, therefore, themselves envisage a longer war well below the nuclear threshold. Soviet aircraft are well poised to support their naval deployments to the South Atlantic and to the Indian Ocean where they permanently maintain a squadron.

Pressure on South Africa is likely to increase in the months ahead. But as it does so, government officials will do well to listen to the voice of NATO.

A few days after my return from South Africa, it was stimulating to read in Britain's **Daily Express** newspaper how Mr. John Ellison, Foreign Editor, is just as much alert as NATO is to the fact that South Africa's monopoly of the world's most vital mineral resources is so complete that strategists reel at the thought of it being denied to the West.

In amplification of the NATO paper, the following are the points that warrant special attention in Mr. John Ellison's trenchant report.

Most frightening of all the key minerals is uranium. There is no doubt Vorster sees it as his ultimate deterrent. Plans are well advanced to turn South Africa into the world's second biggest uranium producer behind the United States by the early 1980s.

This would mean not only that Mr. Vorster would be self-sufficient in nuclear bombs and cheap nuclear energy, but would also become a cherished supplier of a string of nations whose nuclear ambitions are at present stymied by President Carter.

One strategist says: "Israel is one obvious client State, and more important, so also is Iran. There is little doubt that the Shah would like a bomb of his own and equally little doubt that he is intensely concerned with the unimpeded passage of his oil round the Cape. Brazil might be a third in the same league."

No wonder the Third World's fellow travellers are forcing the pace on sanctions. What better vista for them than a West deprived, on the one hand, of one of its most valuable markets, and, on the other, of the very minerals on which it depends today for its economic independence.

No wonder the Soviet Union is urging on the case for sanctions in New York. For the first faces to be wreathed in smiles if South Africa is isolated from the West will be the faces around Mr. Brezhnev's table in the Kremlin.

For the rest of us, the message must be clear. Like her or loathe her, South Africa is an indispensable part of the West — just as Northern Ireland, for all the nightmares, remains an integral province of Britain.

Nothing can be achieved by ostracising her — except the gratification of our enemies.

CHAPTER 4

The King-pin behind the Scenes in Southern Africa

THE real crime of which both South Africans and Rhodesians are guilty of is standing in the way of Soviet ambitions to absorb the whole of Southern Africa.

The Soviet Union is intent on wrecking the chance of a peaceful negotiated settlement in Rhodesia and of an orderly transfer of power, for Rhodesia is merely the first obstacle on the Kremlin's path to South Africa.

The king-pin behind the grave problems besetting the three countries, South Africa, South-West Africa and Rhodesia has his office in Lusaka, capital of Zambia. When he took office just over a year ago, he was told that the sub-continent must be cleared of Whites within five years of his appointment. That man is Dr. V. G. Solodovnikov, the Russian Ambassador to Zambia, one of the leading experts in the Soviet Union of African affairs and one of the KGB's senior officers. He was in London in 1975 for the Annual General Meeting of the Anti-Apartheid Movement. He is a former Director of the Africa Institute of the USSR Academy of Sciences and one of his publications **The Political Parties of Africa,** is not only the basis for Soviet designs in Africa, but has also been described as "a primer for subversion".

The aim of posting such a senior man to this modest appointment is to co-ordinate terrorist activity based on Zambia, Mozambique, Angola and Tanzania. He is directly involved in the terrorist campaign of the so-called Patriotic Front against Rhodesia. With an apparent role of promoting Soviet influence by conventional economic and diplomatic means, he is, in fact, persuading Kaunda to enter the Soviet camp and manipulating changes in the strategy and tactics of the so-called Patriotic Front.

What are my overall impressions and conclusions from my fact finding missions?

CHAPTER 5

No Faith in Britain's Labour Government

THE Rhodesians and South Africans realise it is no good relying on Britain's Labour Government to play a useful role as middleman, for the simple reason that the whites despise and distrust it, and doubt its good faith. It is deplorable that, under the present exhausted, bankrupt and discredited government, Britain should have almost abandoned any role in world affairs because of our loss of weight as a military-political force.

Britain's Marxist manipulated and trade union dominated government sees nothing degrading in living on borrowed protection as well as on borrowed money and borrowed time.

The British Labour government, long affected by Moscow's influence, is either completely blind to what is happening behind the scenes in Africa or just quietly running along with the Soviets as ideological allies or co-belligerents. The Foreign Secretary, Dr. Owen, stated six years ago in his political testament:[1]

"It is not too fanciful to imagine a situation occurring in other parts of the world — for instance in South Africa — where a Russian deterrent presence could be used to ensure that South Africa did not invade an African country which was harbouring and encouraging guerilla action."

I was told that what repels even those whites who are disposed in his favour is his seeming chilling indifference to the achievements and interests of the whites, both in Rhodesia and South Africa, his indifference to the loyal and spontaneous response of these two countries in coming to the aid of Britain in our hour of need in two World Wars — as volunteers not as conscripts — and his indifference to the fate of Britain's kith and kin.

The Rhodesians are convinced that Dr. Owen's aim is the overthrow of Mr. Ian Smith who has dared to stand up and defy the efforts of the Western world to sacrifice his country. They are also convinced that as far as Dr. Owen is concerned, provided the symbol of British Imperialism is destroyed, it matters not who governs the country, provided only that he is black. If a bloodbath ensues, the blame can be laid on the shoulders of the "imperialist rebels".

---

1. **The Politics of Defence.** By Dr. David Owen. Jonathan Cape, 1972.

Mr. Winston Churchill, MP, was correct in saying that the relationship between the Callaghan Government and the masters in the Kremlin is characterised by the subservient, unctuous remarks of Dr. Owen in Moscow in November 1977, when he shamelessly declared to his hosts that "Britain's interests are exactly the same as the Soviet Union's" in regard to Rhodesia. What a humiliating spectacle for the people of a once great country!

That eminent British journalist who has his own column called 'Way of the World' in the London **Daily Telegraph** and writes under the name of Peter Simple, had these harsh words to say about Dr. Owen on 20 January 1978, under the heading 'Let Brezhnev Tremble'.

"Dr. David ('Outstandingly Able') Owen is reported to have made in the House of Commons some remarks of almost unparalleled inanity. The Soviet Union he said in a debate on the war in the Horn of Africa is under no illusion that if they wish to create some new-found form of imperialism it will be resisted.

"The Soviet Union has no need to create some new-found form of imperialism. It has been practising the old form of imperialism (that is, occupation of other people's territory by violence or otherwise) with extreme brutality ever since it came into existence, taking over in due course the former empire of the Tsars in the Ukraine, in the Caucasus, in Central Asia and in Siberia.

"Since then it has occupied seven previously independent European countries and parts of two others (plus part of Japan). It has occupied, if only by proxy, several African territories including the latest country to come under its imperial sway: the ancient Christian Empire of Ethiopia.

"Nor, I grieve to say, has it been resisted, except by guerillas and by a South African expeditionary force in Angola which, for reasons we may suspect but do not know, had to be withdrawn when it was in sight of victory.

"There is only one exception to the rule. The only organised military force which is at present resisting Soviet imperialism is the Rhodesian Army. And Dr. Owen's way of helping this resistance to Soviet imperialism is to try and stop it, using any underhand methods he can find.

"Soviet imperialism has not been resisted in the past. Is there any reason to think that it will be resisted in the future, except, perhaps when resistance has become hopeless. Not much."

Lord Carrington, Leader of the Opposition Conservative Peers, said that for Dr. Owen to say publicly in Moscow that the British and Soviet Government's intentions over Rhodesia's problems were the same was to call into question his credibility as Foreign Secretary.

Dr. Owen wants a success on his track record before the next General Election, just as President Carter needs some kind of success any time, any place, anyhow.

Former Labour Government Foreign Secretary, Lord George Brown, accused Dr. Owen of giving comfort to the Soviets by "organising the destruction of the present white-dominated regime and security forces in order to install the guerilla forces of Mugabe and Nkomo backed by the Russians and their allies". There can be no question of the Rhodesian security forces being disbanded and/or replaced by terrorists. This would be tantamount to proposing that the Brigade of Guards should be replaced by the IRA in Britain.

The newspapers that once praised Dr. Owen so glowingly are now deriding him as "a fathead" and a petulant bureaucrat who "can only sulk and pout". In the House of Commons, he is now jeered at for what some members consider his naïveté. Dr. Owen's critics maintain that he has brought it on himself. His brusque, often arrogant manner — "I suffer fools rather badly", he readily admits — has alienated erstwhile friends and his overriding interest in "the nitty-gritty of administration" as one friend put it, has upset many career civil servants in the somewhat hidebound Foreign Office.

The setbacks that Dr. Owen suffered in his Southern Africa shuttle diplomacy — which occupied much of his first twelve months in office — did the most to whittle away his wonder boy image. His apology ("grovelling, humiliating and shameful," a Labour M.P. called it) to the Saudis after the Foreign Office had condemned their public execution of a Saudi princess and the beheading of her lover stirred up more ire.

Within minutes of Dr. Owen's apology to the Saudi royal family, 15 MP's signed a House of Commons motion branding the Foreign Secretary's action as "totally incompatible with his defence of human rights". "It all goes to show the extent to which he lacks the depth, breadth of vision and maturity that the job requires", said shadow Foreign Secretary Mr. John Davies, MP.

Labour Party Left-wingers like Mr. Dennis Skinner, a member of the Party's left-wing Tribune group, charge that Dr. Owen has been "outflanked and outmanoeuvred by Ian Smith at every turn." Conservatives complain that Dr. Owen's reluctance to support Mr. Smith's Internal Settlement — along with what one Tory MP has called his "blatant advocacy of the Patriotic Front" — only serves to increase the difficulties of a peaceful resolution to the Rhodesian conflict.

Even more disturbing is the evidence of manipulation by Dr. Owen's Foreign Office of British public opinion against Western interests in Southern Africa. See Appendix 4 "Is the Foreign Office

Orchestrating the Media?" on page 243.

In a commentary from London in early March after Dr. Owen's sudden return to London at the time of one of Mr. Andrew Young's outbursts, the **New York Times** suggested that Dr. Owen's political career "after fast ascent, now seems in peril." It quoted Mr. Winston Churchill, MP, a junior Opposition spokesman on defence, as saying of the Foreign Secretary: "He's arrogant and he's ignorant. You could forgive the arrogance if he wasn't so wrong-headed about everything. It seems to me he's become Andy Young's poodle".

The paper's London correspondent, said that talks at random with a dozen MPs from all three major parties "found that even those who respected Dr. Owen's intelligence and supported his policies resented his manner".

" 'David has a tendency to lecture everyone' ", the correspondent quoted one MP who he described as "a Labour moderate of Dr. Owen's own generation. He acts as if he is the first person ever to think a moral thought or analyse a complex situation."

The commentary declared that much of the criticism — even from Cabinet colleagues — stems from Dr. Owen's manner. "His detractors consider him aloof, arrogant and self-righteous.

"But he is also criticised on substantive grounds — particularly for his efforts, in partnership with Mr. Young, to foster a Rhodesian settlement that includes all major nationalist groups."

In the **Wall Street Journal**, an editorial drew attention to the dashing figure which Mr. Joshua Nkomo, the Rhodesian leading a Communist-supported army of bush guerillas, has been cutting at the United Nations.

"He has been sporting expensive suits, what seem to be diamond cufflinks and a Rolex watch said to cost £3,000," the editorial added. "It's a touch difficult to be persuaded of the overwhelming superiority of his moral case."

Is it not time that we were saved from the display, each Armistice Sunday, of the hypocrisy which allows the Foreign Minister of the British Government to lay a wreath on the Cenotaph "to the Rhodesians who died in the two World Wars" for our cause, whilst Britain is doing its utmost to disrupt and destroy the country from which they came and shattering the peaceful existence of the relatives they left behind?

When listening to the radio broadcast of the Cenotaph service on Remembrance Sunday last year, one noted with no surprise, but much sadness, the pointed omission of the Rhodesian and South African dead of 1914-18 and 1939-45 among those listed who had fought for our common ideals. On the contrary, many of those countries mentioned were not even in existence in 1939, much less in 1914. Let the countless war graves of South African and Rhodesian volunteers (not a man a conscript), scattered around the world's bloodiest battlefields, bear witness to our debt to those nations.

On the front page of many British national newspapers published on 12 July 1976, was a photograph of a Lancaster bomber flying past Nelson's column in Trafalgar Square, London. One of the captions underneath the photograph read as follows:

"Legends of the past united as the RAF's **last** flying Lancaster bomber cruises above Nelson's Column during a nostalgic flight over London yesterday. It swooped low over Horse Guards as part of the Royal Tournament Parade 500 feet below".

The irony of this event was that the Lancaster bomber flying over Trafalgar Square carried the code letters of No. 44 **(Rhodesia)** Squadron.

CHAPTER 6

A Visit to Rhodesia, October 1977

MY first visit to Rhodesia was unexpected. I received a very warm welcome from General Peter Walls who treated me as a brother officer from whom no secrets were withheld. Peter Walls was operating not all that far from me during the Malayan Emergency when, at the age of 24, he was a Major in the Rhodesian SAS, fighting a Communist insurgency in the form of tough, well-trained Chinese Communist terrorists. Therefore, he knows the form and has had many years of unrivalled operational experience to refine, improve and introduce up-to-date operational techniques, to deal with counter-insurgency and guerilla type warfare to suit the type of enemy he is fighting and the type of country in which he is fighting. He is prepared for any eventuality, including contingency plans to defend his country against a more sophisticated and more highly trained type of enemy equipped with tanks and modern aircraft.

Peter Walls is a real professional, a true and inspiring leader, a man of decision and action who radiates confidence. He is not only respected and held in high esteem by his officers and men, but is also extremely popular and well-liked. He would be second to none as Chief of Defence in any country and no-one I know would have any hope of taking him for a ride.

He is respected as being scrupulously fair, even by many black nationals.

Rhodesia's whites are vehemently opposed to dismantling the Rhodesian Army, Air Force and Police. Dr. Owen's deplorable cease-fire plan, however, called for a merger of Walls' forces with Communist-indoctrinated brutal terrorists who owe their allegiance to the Black Marxist nationalists, Mr. Robert Mugabe and Mr. Joshua Nkomo. It is significant that the latter, after his meeting with Lord Carver, the British Commissioner Designate, left straight for Moscow.

Peter Walls has said "With the political developments taking place there is an atmosphere, a changing scenario in which, if a chap in my position speaks out and takes a definite stance or states a preferance for a policy, it removes his flexibility. While you are fighting, you fight hard going right to the cease-fire stage. But I am not against any negotiated settlement or any political development. I claim to be non-political which I reckon I am".

THE MAJOR TRIBAL GROUPINGS IN RHODESIA WITH APPROXIMATE PERCENTAGE OF AFRICAN POPULATION

NDEBELE ORIENTATED TRIBES

	Tribe	Percentage	No. of Chiefs
1	Ndebele	14%	44
2	Kalanga	5%	3

SHONA ORIENTATED TRIBES

	Tribe	Percentage	No. of Chiefs
3	Rozwi.	9%	20
4	Korekore	12%	20
5	Zezuru	18%	22
6	Manyika	13%	9
7	Karanga	22%	35
8	Ndau	3%	11

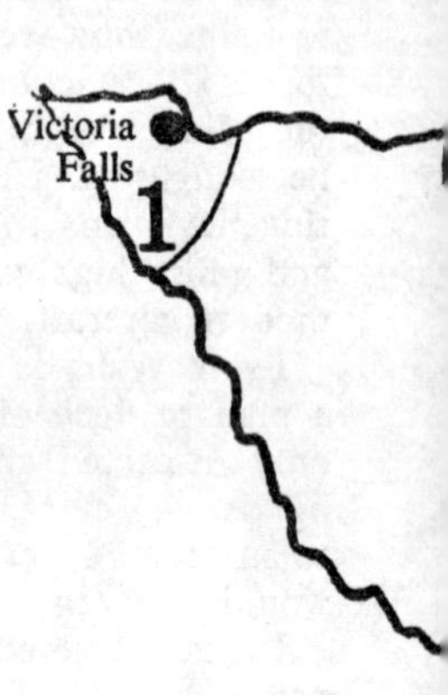

OTHERS

	Tribe	Percentage	No. of Chiefs
9	Tonga	2%	27
10	Venda	1%	6
11	Shangaan	1%	5

NOTE

1. The three above divisions are based on historical fact. They do not necessarily mean that a modern African from the KALANGA group, for example, automatically considers himself to be NDEBELE orientated in matters of politics, sport or any other aspect of organized life.

2. Some of the above groups have further sub-groups. The NDEBELE, for example, have 12 such sub-groups, the ZEZURU have 8, and the KARANGA have 15.

3. The SHONA language group has approximately 65 sub-groupings.

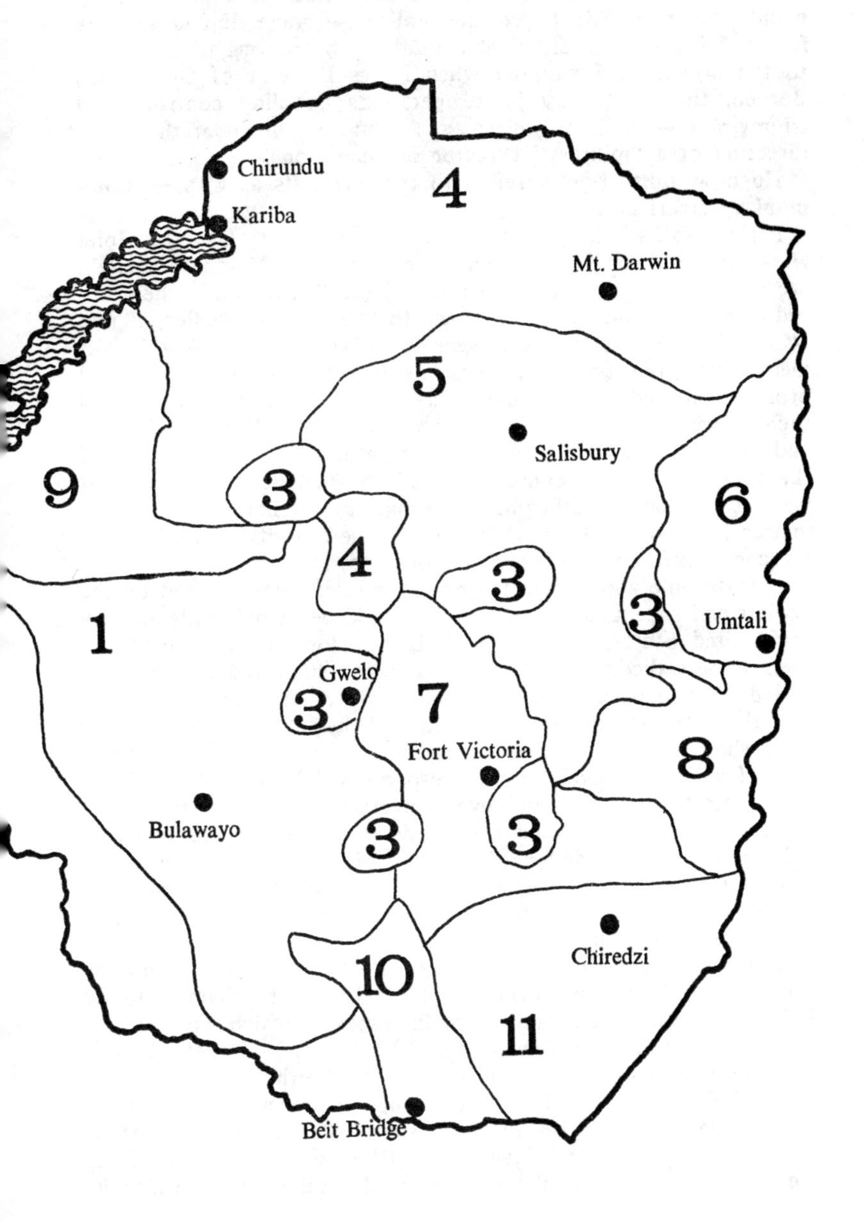
Chirundu
4
Kariba
Mt. Darwin
5
Salisbury
9
3
6
4
3
3
Umtali
1
Gwelo
3
7
Fort Victoria
8
Bulawayo
3
3
Chiredzi
10
11
Beit Bridge

Earlier last year, Prime Minister Ian Smith appointed him from Army Commander to the country's first Chief of a unified command — Army, Air Force and Police — some 45,000 security forces. I found his method of conducting operations to be similar to the procedure I adopted when I was Director of Operations, Borneo, that is to say joint operations entailing control by a triumvirate — civilian, policeman, military — all under the single direction of a "military" Director of Operations.

He now, quite rightly refers to the terrorists as CTs — **Communist** Terrorists.

Peter Wall's Army Commander, Lieutenant General John Hickman, and Air Force Commander, Air Vice Marshall Mussell, are equally professional, and so are all the Brigade and other subordinate commanders, right down to the private soldier. I met NCOs, Rhodesia domiciled, wearing British Second World War medals and the British General Service Medal. Such hardened professional soldiers have unrivalled operational experience behind them. Every able-bodied man does two years' National Service and is then called up every other month, that is six months of the year. I heard no complaints, only a steel determination that no matter what the difficulties; no matter how hard the road; no matter how apparently great the odds, the security of their country comes first and their civilian jobs second.

A loathsome and savage foe howls at their gates, backed by the Soviets and succoured by those who should be their friends, namely the United States, together with Britain for whom so many of their fathers died. Instead, they are being subjected to sustained and deliberate diplomatic and economic strangulation.

If the battle should wax fiercer, and if the forces arrayed against them should become immeasurably stronger, there can be no question of surrender, every inch of ground will be fought for. They will contest every hill and every river; every village and every town; every crossroad and every bridge. Inevitably and unavoidably, the land will suffer. Indescribeable chaos and irreparable destruction will follow. The farmers will destroy every head of cattle and implement a scorched earth policy unless a just and secure settlement is achieved.

This is a breed of men, the like of which has not been seen for many a long age. It made one feel almost ashamed to be British in these squalid and shameful times in which we live.

In the London **Daily Telegraph** of 19 January, 1978, Peter Simple had this to say in his column Way of the World:

"Will Field Marshal Lord Carver be remembered as the most remarkable of all British Field-Marshals? This man described as 'British Commissioner-Designate in Rhodesia' has returned to England after what he calls 'very successful' talks with the Marxist

Machel, described as President of Mozambique.

"He says he has 'cleared up a number of misunderstandings' and that there is a 'wide measure of agreement' between them, presumably on how to prevent the people who actually live in Rhodesia, whether white or black, from deciding for themselves how their country should be governed.

"Lord Carver, as he buzzes hornet-like about the periphery of that much put-upon country, cannot of course be compared in his power for mischief with the prodigious prestidigitator Dr. Kissinger, who not so long ago was flapping his leathern bat's wings in the same region.

"Yet in every photograph of him which appears in the Press the Field Marshal looks more strange and even sinister."

Lord Carver must have found, like others before him, that there is nothing like meeting with Prime Minister Mr. Ian Smith for restoring a sense of reality. The reality was that there was a long way to go before a ceasefire became practical politics.

Lord Carver must also have found considerable scepticism among Rhodesia's military commanders when he held talks with them on the possibility of arranging a ceasefire between the Rhodesian security forces and the CTs. No doubt he learnt that there was not going to be a ceasefire until there is agreement on the handover of power and a new constitution for Rhodesia.

This is not because, being military men, the Rhodesian military leaders have a built-in abhorrence to a waterproof ceasefire. But the Rhodesian forces have already been involved in one abortive attempt at a ceasefire which is an experience they do not intend to see repeated.

This occurred at the end of 1974, when South Africa, intent on establishing detente with black states to the north, tried to get both sides in the war to stop fighting. The South African police, who were then assisting the Rhodesian security forces, were recalled to base camps and the Rhodesian troops were ordered to stop offensive patrolling.

The ceasefire lasted just over a month. By January 1975, according to Rhodesian military sources, there had been so many infringements by the CTs that the Rhodesian Army found it necessary to return to the offensive.

It took the Rhodesian security forces a year to recover from this brief interlude. They lost a lot of territory psychologically because while they were standing still, the terrorists were going around the country politicising every kraal they came to.

It was only at the end of 1975, after the introduction of the protected villages scheme in tribal areas, that the Rhodesian forces were able to regain the initiative.

The situation has changed radically since then. The whole of the country's 2,000 mile border is now potentially hostile except for the 150 mile strip adjoining South Africa in the south. Contacts between the guerillas and security forces have become a daily occurrence.

During the first ten months of last year, the security forces had killed more than 2,450 CTs. The number of security forces personnel killed during the same period was more than 180, a big increase over previous years, which reflects the growing intensity of the war.

No one I met made any attempt to disguise the fact that the war had intensified, but the security forces were confident that by the end of this year they would still be able to fight the war if necessary, and still be calling the tune.

The Rhodesians point to several facts in their favour. First, and most important, is the quality of their own troops, who in five years of fighting have become what is probably the finest counter-insurgency force in the world.

The Rhodesian Army's controversial raids across the border into neighbouring countries — now termed "self defensive pre-emptive strikes" — have also forced the guerillas to move their bases farther away from the operational areas thus stretching their supply and communication lines. At the same time, persistent harassment has prevented the guerillas from setting up permanent bases inside Rhodesia.

The object of the pre-emptive strikes and attacks deep into Mozambique and Zambia were to deal crippling blows against the armed CTs who were in their defended camps poised ready to launch heavy attacks into Rhodesia. Offensive action is the very essence of successful military operations against guerilla and terrorist forces which are able to operate from a "safe" sanctuary. In the case of Mozambique, the attack coincided with the outbreak of the rainy season when movement and concealment is made that much easier for the CTs.

It was, and is, essential to stop these terrorists attacks from being launched, for in the main the target of the CTs is the massacre of innocent black civilians, including women and children. If it is not the responsibility of the Rhodesian security forces to protect the civilian population against murderous attacks by the CTs then, pray, whose responsibility is it?

Mr. Mugabe has made it plain that his organisation is not in the least interested in peace or having settlement talks. His intention is to set up a Communist regime in Rhodesia, and he has said such a system can only be imposed on Rhodesia by force. The cross border operations into Mozambique show that Mr. Ian Smith has no intention of allowing this to happen.

If women and children are allowed to reside in or near high

priority military targets they are bound to suffer. The responsibility lies entirely on the Marxist governments concerned. Some of those referred to as "women and children" have been trained as terrorists and are every bit as cruel and barbaric as their male counterparts, just as are those in the PLO.

The Zambian-based ZAPU leader Mr. Joshua Nkomo, only had himself to blame for the pre-emptive strike in early March against his terrorist bases across the Zambian border, for he had only very recently threatened a new offensive.

Mr. Ian Smith realised only too well that there were bound to be hostile reactions from the United States, Britain, the United Nations, the OAU and the Third World, etc. But Rhodesia finds itself beleaguered almost without friends and is not prepared to be attacked by Cuban trained and Russian armed Communist terrorists with impunity.

Mr. Ian Smith has no alternative but to resort to a form of offensive self-protection because the United States and Britain have so far refused to accept an internal settlement that will lead to majority rule. British and United States inaction can only encourage the so-called Patriotic Front and their political allies, and is, therefore, bound to increase the need and the risk of self-protective strikes.

In June of last year, 1977, I felt compelled to write to the Editor of the London **Times** because of a succession of letters published by that newspaper in which the authors had condemned a recent Rhodesian raid into Mozambique. I wrote as follows:—

"It ill becomes any of us in this country to adopt a holier-than-thou attitude to the recent Rhodesian raid into Mozambique. It is no longer a secret that during the three year Indonesian confrontation against Malaysian Borneo I, as Director of Operations, was authorised by the then **Labour** Government to conduct cross-border operations several miles deep into Indonesian Borneo. Indeed, a cordon sanitaire was eventually established and virtually all contacts with our enemy took place on his side of the border.

"Offensive action is the only solution to guerilla or terrorist operations. A policy of containment is the passport to defeat".

In this letter, I was not referring to the hot pursuit of hostile forces across the Indonesian border, but with day-to-day cross-border operations. Mr. Tom Pocock, the author of my biography[1] revealed this nearly five years ago. He described how we not only dominated the border, but how it became quite usual for a forward battalion to have only one quarter of its strength on our side

---

1. **Fighting General: The Public and Private Campaigns of General Sir Walter Walker.** By Tom Pocock. Collins, 1973.

of the border and the remainder inside, and well inside, Indonesian territory.

From recent events it is apparent that the Rhodesian Army, as well as the South African Army on the Angola border, are but emulating our admirable example.

How many retaliatory raids — and on a far greater scale — have the Israeli forces launched into neighbouring territories with no more than a token rebuke from the American State Department?

Had the Rhodesians done as Israel has done, Rhodesia would by now be in occupation of Mozambique, Zambia and other neighbouring territories, whose inhabitants would certainly be far better off than they are at present.

The sheer professionalism, high morale, self-confidence, physique and stamina of the Rhodesian Security Forces has to be seen to be believed. Their means of inter-communication in the field are probably the best in the world and enable the security forces to react immediately to any incident. The CTs are petrified of meeting the Rhodesian soldiers in the field and avoid contact whenever possible. Hit and run is the CTs tactic, plus attacks against soft targets, intimidation, bestial brutality and barbarism usually against unarmed black Africans.

Having seen the terrain and the type of operations involved, one must immediately ask oneself the question: where on earth is an **impartial,** highly trained and properly acclimatised United Nations Force to be found which would be capable of conducting prolonged operations in the bush and the difficult topography particularly where navigation is concerned? Road bound mobile patrols and static Observation Posts (OPs) would be worse than useless. The same problem would apply in the operational area in South-West Africa (Namibia) along the Angolan border.

For their mobility, the Rhodesian Forces, like the South African Forces, depend on the helicopter, light aircraft and mine-proof troop carrying vehicles and armoured cars. It would be a serious matter if South Africa were to give in to outside pressures and become so timid and jittery as to stop the flow of oil and essential equipment to Rhodesia. As a result of the United Nations embargo, one can but hope that South Africa realises more than ever before that their military border must now extend as far north as Mozambique and Zambia, and that on no account must they withdraw their troops from the Angolan border.

I got the impression that South Africa's large Citizen Forces would certainly not be prepared to see Rhodesia go under and that South Africa would ensure that the Rhodesian economy did not collapse.

What was particularly striking was the good humour, cheerful efficiency and strong comradeship between Rhodesian Officers and their men. The young Air Force machine gunner in the helicopter in which I flew along a certain valley, knowing that the passengers would consist of about 14 stars worth of military brass (one full General, two Lieutenant Generals, one Air Marshal and one Brigadier), had stencilled the following inscription on the back of his steel helmet:

"Yeah though I fly through the valley of death,

"I shall fear no evil,

"For I am the meanest son of a bitch in the valley".

Whatever the morale of the ordinary civilian in Salisbury may be, there was no doubt that the morale of the farmers on the border was as high as that of the soldier. A few days before I arrived at Umtali, on the Mozambique border, 18 out of 18 CTs had been killed by a "stick" of Security Forces — a stick being the passenger load of a small helicopter.

Rhodesia has reached the stage where, more and more, the Army is showing the way. The Army has become the spearhead of the nation and the population as a whole have put their trust in the Army. When the soldiers are out in the Operational Area, they sit down with the villagers; get to know them; talk to them and discuss their problems with them. This is part and parcel of the Army's hearts and minds campaign.

It is also true to say that the people are growing weary of the terrorists' politics. Many of them are sick to death of their lies and deceit. What future is there for a country and its people when a terrorist leader states openly that, if he wins, he will put the African leaders in the country on trial and then execute them by a firing squad?

Obviously the Army was wondering what was going to happen on the political front. They fully realised that their Government was striving for a settlement on terms that would best suit all the peoples of the country. But what they have been promised by the Commander of the Army, Lieutenant General John Hickman, is that there must always be an Army, a formally disciplined, highly trained, professional Army that owes its total allegiance to the state.

Rhodesia's future is dependent on the Army's stabilizing interest and so the Army will remain intact. As General Hickman said this publicly on 21 October, 1977, I am surprised that such a firm pronouncement was not absorbed by Dr. Owen, and his henchman, Lord Carver. It might have saved an unnecessary journey and considerable loss of face.

The Rhodesian Army is not influenced by party politics and never will be. The people see this for themselves and admire it for its firmness, fairness, justness and its operational efficiency and successes.

The fact that the Rhodesian Army's immediate enemies happen to be the black terrorist armies of Karl Marx from Mozambique; that most of the CTs have probably never heard of Marx; and have perhaps only the haziest idea of what they are supposed to be fighting for, is neither here nor there. The Rhodesians, I imagine, would much prefer to be fighting their **real** enemies, who are mostly white and out of reach. The Rhodesians **do** know what **they** are fighting for. They know they are fighting for the fine and potentially even finer country they have made for themselves, whether they are white or black; and they know they have the **only** fully organised military force in the world which is **now** in action against the forces of International Communism. That is to say, they have the only organised military force in the world which is fighting and dying for the West, or in plainer terms, your freedom and mine.

Leaving aside the military picture, Rhodesia is now self-sufficient in food for four times the size of its population of six million. They would be capable of feeding the whole of Africa south of the Sahara if the necessary finance was forthcoming. They use only ten percent of their water capacity, and the very high grade coal at the Wankie coal mines south of Victoria Falls would be capable of producing oil, just as oil is now produced by South Africa from its coal.

Two Rhodesian Africans were sent to Italy and France on an official visit. They returned earlier than expected because they found that the standard of living of the peasants there was far lower than their own in Rhodesia.

I was horrified to be informed by South Africa's Deputy Minister of Information that when he visited Britain in July last year, some Conservative MPs told him that they believed in backing the winner, and in their opinion, the safe bets were Mr. Nkomo and Mr. Mugabe.

Are they so naive and ill-informed that they do not realise that this would inevitably result in a Marxist revoluntionary regime?

I do not believe for a moment that their view represents the feelings of the millions of people who up to now have voted Conservative or worked for that party. A referendum would show that an overwhelming majority support Mr. Ian Smith, just as they have great sympathy for the white South Africans as they face the relentless hostility of nearly all the governments of the world.

We, in the West, have quite enough problems of our own which we seem incapable of solving, and it is high time we got off South Africa's back. The United States, for instance, is certainly no exception, and have nothing to crow about when they have 25 million people living below the poverty line, of whom six million are blacks.

CHAPTER 7

Red Shadow Over Rhodesia

AFTER my first visit to Rhodesia, my appreciation of the situation was tersely summed up in four words by the **London Daily Telegraph** in the title they gave to a letter that I dictated from Pretoria on 19 October, 1977. The title of the letter was 'Red Shadow over Rhodesia'. Nothing that has happened since this letter was published on 24 October has made me change my appreciation of the situation in any way. This is what I wrote:—

"Rhodesia is now standing alone, branded as an illegal regime by the Russians, and the West and the United Nations, about one-third of whose members have come to power through bloody revolution. Rhodesia has become a bone in today's international power politics.

"These Powers have decreed tiny Rhodesia as a threat to world peace and so her stable government which has done more to elevate the black man than any in African history is to be turned over to phony liberators who we are asked to believe will restore human rights and dignity as in the Marxist-dominated Angola, Mozambique, Uganda, Cambodia, etc.

"The real issue in Rhodesia is this: Will the black government be truly elected from Rhodesia's 6,500,000 blacks and whites, most of whom are pro-Western moderates, or will a settlement be forced on Rhodesia by the British, the United States, the Russians and the Marxist front-line countries and the United Nations which will ultimately put Communist terrorist leaders into power?

"If the latter were to take place, then a bloody civil war would erupt in Rhodesia. Millions of innocent blacks would die and if the whites were ultimately forced to leave, Rhodesia would fall into the hands of the Russians just as has happened in Angola and Mozambique.

"The Rhodesian pot is boiling. The characters in the cast are jockeying for positions and the outcome is in doubt. Meanwhile, the British and Americans have proposed a new set of initiatives far more radical that Dr. Kissinger's initiatives and are busy rallying support for these proposals among the black African States, the Patriotic Front and the United Nations. The new Anglo-American proposals would involve a United Nations police action in Rhodesia and set a dangerous precedent for United Nations troops to overthrow other pro-Western, anti-Communist governments.

"The Rhodesian security forces, made up of no less than 82 per cent black Rhodesians all of whom are volunteers, is the finest counter-insurgency force in the world today. In addition, the Selous Scouts are striking fear into the hearts of the terrorists. The best trackers and jungle fighters in the world, they can live in the bush for months at a time and are taking a heavy toll of terrorist infiltrators.

"Aside from invasion, i.e. the United Nations police force, the Rhodesian Army cannot be defeated in the field. This is precisely why the Russians, why the United Nations, the Patriotic Front and the new proposals put forward by Dr. David Owen and Mr. Andrew Young, are all demanding the dismantling of the Rhodesian Army for this is the only way the Communists can possibly take the country."

CHAPTER 8

The Solution to Rhodesia is Internal not External

HAVING now observed the Rhodesia scene at first hand twice within the past six months — including at grass roots level — the following are the factors that stand out in sharp relief.

On 24 November 1977, Prime Minister Ian Smith announced that discussions were to open with the three black Rhodesians Nationalist leaders for an internal settlement, incorporating the principle of majority rule based on universal adult sufferage.

This removed the last major obstacle to drawing up a constitution that provided for elections and the institution of a majority rule government with the participation of the three black leaders inside Rhodesia who already commanded the support of about 70 to 80% of the black population.

Mr. Smith had already agreed to majority rule in September 1976 when he gave his assent to the Kissinger Package.

To have accepted the Anglo-American proposals would have been to seal the doom of all white and most black Rhodesians, just as the South Vietnamese acceptance of the Kissinger Peace Plan was the last nail in their coffin. So, Mr. Smith decided to negotiate an internal settlement with his moderate blacks to bring about black majority rule in a multi-racial government with political and security safeguards that would protect all minorities.

The integrity of Britain and America is at stake. They demanded majority rule and a peaceful settlement. Mr. Ian Smith acceded to this and he, together with the three internal leaders, representing 70 to 80% of the people of Rhodesia, reached an internal settlement leading to black majority government.

What matters now is that the new Zimbabwe should become the sort of country in which Europeans with their skills and training would be welcome to stay.

Mr. Nkomo and Mr. Mugabe represent the external minority in the form of Soviet-guided and Soviet-supported force and terrorism.

Their so-called Patriotic Front exists in name only. It is merely a paper link between the faction-ridden Mr. Robert Mugabe's ZANU and Mr. Joshua Nkomo's ZAPU. The five so-called "Front Line" Presidents created it as a device to hoodwink the West that there was a bond of unity between these two hostile movements. In fact, they have no common policy, no common strategy, no unified military command, no co-ordinated political committee, and no joint administration.

Although Mr. Nkomo and Mr. Mugabe are seen together at such events as the United Nations debate on Rhodesia, they neither like nor trust each other.

Mr. Mugabe has ridiculed Mr. Nkomo as an old fashioned African demagogue whose links with the Soviets are based solely on the need for money, arms and supplies and calls him "a fatter capitalist than any in New York".

For his part Mr. Nkomo has jeered at Mr. Mugabe as "an upstart who thinks he can win Zimbabwe with a Marxist's text-book". Each has suspected the other of plotting against him.

Repeated attempts to unify the two military forces have failed, often bloodily.

Neither Mr. Nkomo nor Mr. Mugabe enjoy much popular support in Rhodesia, and in a genuinely free election — free from terrorist intimidation they would probably poll together less than 25% of the total vote. Since they could not hope to be elected, their modus operandi has been to try and seize power through "the barrel of a gun".

Their strength lies in their fallacious international image as the "liberators of an enslaved black people" and their support from the Black African Marxist States, the Soviets, the Cubans, the UN, OAU, Mr. Andrew Young and Dr. Owen.

To many it must seem incredulous that Western statesmen should regard the wily fox, Mr. Joshua Nkomo, as a moderate when, as long ago as 1961, he made the threat:

"I will not rest until the rivers of Zimbabwe run red with the blood of every white man, woman and child, and every African who supports them".

Is Mr. Nkomo a Moscow puppet despite his background of a Christian lay preacher? While Mr. Nkomo is, indeed, Moscow's favoured candidate, nevertheless, he is at heart a political opportunist rather than a dedicated Marxist. Mr. Nkomo gives lip service to the unity of the Patriotic Front and makes threatening noises against the whites because he hopes — with the help of the West — to emerge on top of the heap if Rhodesia were forced to capitulate to the Patriotic Front by external pressures. Rhodesia, of course, will never capitulate to any Patriotic Front military action.

Mr. Nkomo's support now is largely tribal and comes from the Matabele who number only about one-sixth of the population. The support from the Shonas is minimal and this is evidenced by the poor crowds he himself used to draw, and the numbers his deputies within the country can rally today in Mashonaland. Thus he does not have the trust of the Shonas though he has papered his executive with a few Shona faces.

Did Mr. Nkomo, knowing that the West wanted him as Rhodesia's first President, torpedo the US/UK initiative because he insisted on effective power before elections, knowing perfectly well that he would never receive the necessary votes?

Mr. Nkomo and his sponsor President Kaunda, have tried to get the West to agree that Mr. Nkomo should be the first President. Mr. Nkomo and the Patriotic Front have been using tactics similar to SWAPO in South West Africa by asking that the country should be handed over to them and they would run elections after a "pacifying" period. This gave both the Patrioctic Front and SWAPO away; they know they could never achieve power through the ballot box as they simply do not have the electoral support to see them home in free and fair elections.

Thus, either they have to employ all the weapons of intimidation, vote-fixing and so on, to win the day, or knowing the impotence of the Western Powers, hope to achieve power through military victory.

Mr. Nkomo's ambition is to become President of the new Zimbabwe and he feels deeply about his present position, for he is the only African leader of the Commonwealth of the fifties and early sixties who has not yet reached the top. He feels a deep sense of betrayal at being thwarted after long years spent in detention and exile. This accounts for his near-hysterical outbursts. Therefore, it is essential to try very hard to get Mr. Nkomo involved, if only to deny him an excuse for not taking part in free and fair elections.

Another factor to be considered is that Mr. Nkomo is the natural leader of the Matabele, and although they number only one-sixth of the African population, they were without a really credible voice at the Salisbury talks and this must be remedied. Therefore, the way should be kept open for reconciliation, particularly between Mr. Nkomo and the Salisbury leaders.

The Executive Council has maintained throughout that Mr. Nkomo should return to participate in the Transitional Government and take his rightful place as the original nationalist leader so that he can participate in free elections. It has to be recognised that Mr. Nkomo enjoys a special status with black Africa, Britain and the United States. His return would obviously help in gaining international recognition at the earliest time.

At the end of May 1978, Mr. John Vorster, the South African Prime Minister, urged Britain and the United States to try to persuade Mr. Nkomo to join the internal settlement in Rhodesia, "if you have any influence with him at all".

He said black and white Rhodesian leaders had told him that

they were prepared to work with Mr. Nkomo and to accommodate him in the interim government and the Council of Ministers if he returned in peace and abjured violence.

But all along, Mr. Nkomo has so far scorned the idea that he would return except on his own terms. He has also dismissed with contempt the Salisbury agreement in March that set up the interim government. "You must not associate my name with that treasonous and faked agreement" he said.

His difficulty is that, in any election, he would emerge as a minority leader. Support for his Zimbabwe African People's Union is confined mainly to south-west Rhodesia. Guerilla war offers him a prospect of gaining power.

If Mr. Nkomo cannot be persuaded to return, neither he nor Mr. Mugabe will settle for anything less than the outright leadership of Rhodesia. They cannot agree to share leadership of their terrorist organisations so there would not be the remotest possibility of their agreeing to share control of the country, given the opportunity.

It follows that the only manner of fulfilling their ambitions is by force, i.e. the use of the gun not only to gain control but to maintain control. It will be necessary to kill all political opponents, and to use an army to keep one of these minority leaders in power. No valid popular elections would do that.

Accordingly it is illogical to continue to withhold support for the present political settlement within Rhodesia in the hope that Mr. Mugabe and Mr. Nkomo will agree to return to Rhodesia and take part in elections. It is entirely in the terrorist's interests that sanctions are maintained against Rhodesia in the hope that by sheer weight of Soviet arms they will start to break up Rhodesia; to make it a country unfit for people to live in; to destroy its businesses and its farms; in short, to reduce it to the parlous state existing today in Mozambique, Zambia and Angola where food is short, employment a mere figure of speech, political rights non-existent and violence the order of the day.

Mr. Nkomo is not alone in having to think of his political future. Dr. Owen is the Foreign Secretary of a Labour Government whose members feel a particular animosity towards Mr. Ian Smith. There are some who regard Mr. Smith as a traitor and although they may not wish to see him hanged, they are determined that he should be publicly humiliated. For a Labour Foreign Secretary to endorse publicly an historic achievement by Mr. Ian Smith who has defied one Tory and three Labour Governments over 12 years, would not only ruin Dr. Owen's chances of being elected to Labour's National Executive Committee, but would also make it that much harder for him to procure a fresh Parliamentary seat were the electors of Devonport to unseat him at the coming General Election.

Another reason why there is a nasty suspicion that Dr. Owen has done his level best to denigrate, obstruct and scupper the Salisbury negotiations is his over-riding fear of doing anything that might upset the terrorist leaders, the mainly Marxist "Front Line Presidents", the Organisation of African Unity, the Afro-Asians and Third World in general — and, of course, Mr. Andrew Young.

The so-called "Front Line Presidents", Kaunda of Zambia, Khama of Botswana, Nyerere of Tanzania, Machel of Mozambique and Neto of Angola, are all dictators, (the last two Soviet puppets), and all five support Mr. Mugabe and Mr. Nkomo.

Prime Minister Ian Smith's decision to negotiate with the three black Rhodesian nationalist leaders who operate legally within the country produced, of course, a fearsome outcry from the Front Line Presidents, Mr. Mugabe and Mr. Nkomo and their supporters in the Organisation of African States.

The British Foreign Office tried on 9 January to discourage hopes that the Salisbury talks on a Rhodesia Settlement would end in success.

A statement was issued saying that the Foreign Office had "noted" reports of the Salisbury negotiations, and added: "We would not expect any settlement to be acceptable to international opinion unless it is substantially in accord with our (Anglo-American) proposals.

"Moreover, any settlement which fails to involve all the parties concerned, as envisaged in the Anglo-American proposals, is unlikely to gain international acceptance".

It is significant that the statement stopped short of actually condemning the Salisbury talks. But it made it crystal clear that even if they were to end in agreement close to the principles of the Anglo-American plan they would not get Britain's blessing unless the Front Line leaders, who have the guerillas behind them, were brought into the act.

The statement also betrayed some nervousness that the Salisbury talks had moved faster than the Foreign Office expected. Dr. Owen was evidently trying to slow them down to give him time to work on Mr. Nkomo and Mr. Mugabe.

In a leading article of 10 January, entitled 'Dr. Owen's Spoiling Act', the London Daily Telegraph hit the nail right on the head:

"Yesterday's statement by the Foreign Office on Rhodesia represents an attempt by Dr. Owen to put a spoke in the internal settlement talks which Mr. Smith is having in Salisbury. Dr. Owen perceives that these talks, if they succeed, would pull the rug from under his own proposals in the White Paper of last September, with their absurd suggestion that the guerilla forces should take over law and order after independence. The Foreign Secretary is therefore trying to breathe new life into the moribund 'Anglo-American plan', which has been rejected by all concerned. To this end, Lord Carver was despatched to Maputo to seek an audience of President Machel of Mozambique. This he achieved, and yesterday went on for a meeting with Mr. Botha, the South African Foreign Minister. Dr. Owen has also requested, for the second time, a meeting with the two 'Patriotic Front' leaders, Mr. Nkomo and Mr. Mugabe.

"Why is Dr. Owen apparently so desperately anxious to keep on pushing the 'Patriotic Front' guerillas and terrorists to the front of the picture, and to keep Mr. Smith and the internal black leaders, Bishop Muzorewa and Mr. Sithole, out of it? Lord Carver gave away what is obviously Dr. Owen's thinking when he referred in Pretoria to the current Salisbury talks as 'a principle obstacle'. Is it simply that Dr. Owen cannot bear the thought of Mr. Smith who is obviously in earnest this time, reaching an internationally acceptable settlement without the stamp of Dr. Owen's approval? It looks very much like it".

I was informed by a very reliable source that it was clear that Owen and Carver not only expected the local settlement attempts to fail, but were eager for this to happen, so that they could claim that only the Anglo-American proposals outlined in their White Paper had a chance of success.

The future of the Security Forces is a tricky problem, but not insurmountable. While the local Black leaders have to espouse the idea of allowing some ex-terrorists to join the future forces, they do so with an eye to their future electoral support, knowing in their hearts that in senior political positions in any new government, they would need non-political, effective and stable forces every bit as much as the present government.

This did not prevent Dr. Owen and Lord Carver trying to resuscitate the White Paper proposals, as well as promoting the meeting at Malta with Mr. Nkomo and Mr. Mugabe on 30 January. The latter two had become more amenable to the talks, only because they feared that the Salisbury talks would succeed. Neither of them took kindly to the idea that Lord Carver might become Resident Commissioner with dictatorial powers during any transition period. The internal Black leaders did not want this either as Lord Carver and others affronted them during visits to Salisbury in mid-1977, when Lord Carver showed clearly that it was British policy to lean heavily towards the Patriotic Front. The locals felt that while the Patriotic Front might have a grand total of 20,000 terrorist recruits, the internal Black leaders could command the loyalty and support of perhaps 5½ million Africans.

My source stated that Dr. Owen was certainly doing the Kremlin's work for them. He asked: "What further knavish tricks will the Owen-Carver circus devise as they plan to destroy our decent, prosperous country which has done no harm to anybody and was at peace until our enemies from without intervened?"

The pressures on Dr. Owen arise from Britain's policy towards sub-Saharan Africa. As the London **Daily Telegraph** so aptly put it on 9 March, it goes like this: "At all costs we must avoid action which might cause offence to black African countries with whom we trade and upon whom (Nigerian oil is one example) we are in some degree dependent. Principles, when it comes to Rhodesia, are all very well, but we live precariously and beggars can't be choosers. Above all we must avoid attitudes which the Third World might construe as racist. So we must steer clear of decisions which could involve us in a confrontation at the UN and the furious condemnation which would accompany it. Furthermore, though America's experience of the subject is elementary, and her opinions at the top are palpably divided, we must avoid getting out of step with the President's men".

The next and, in some ways, most alarming consideration weighing on Dr. Owen is that Britain's foreign policy vis-a-vis Africa (and other places) today has no back-up power at all that we could deploy. "It is toothless", says the **Daily Telegraph.** "Suppose, for example guerilla war fostered by outsiders, and their Soviet and possibly Cuban allies, threatened to overthrow the new Rhodesian regime. Majority rule conceded, that regime could and probably would demand of us material support. Our armed forces would be ruled out; not so arms and essential material of which Rhodesia is short. And what response might be expected from the Labour Government to such a request? It would have, under prevailing pressures, to reject it — though it could be counted on to condemn South Africa, as at the time of the Angola invasion, when Mr. Vorster provided Rhodesia with what we had refused to send.

"Not even the most sanguine supporter of Rhodesia's internal settlement could rule out a harder war against Rhodesia. Rather than risk the embarrassment of then deserting a regime which we had publicly endorsed, Dr. Owen and his Government deem it more prudent to withhold endorsement — at least until they can be surer which way and how far the Patriotic Front's cats will jump".

What we are witnessing now is a policy of unconditional appeasement, in spite of the fact that what is even more at stake than the future of Rhodesia's citizens, is the whole future of Africa in a band stretching from the Horn across to Angola. This is the target for the most determined Soviet thrust since the annexation of East and Central Europe.

Rhodesia's neighbours — the very ones that Dr. Owen is seeking to placate — have already fallen under Soviet influence.

Rhodesia may well be small but she has strong resolve and effective armed forces. With a genuine majority government commanding support from white and black, she would be a very effective barrier against Soviet expansionism.

Yet this chance too will be thrown away if the internal agreement fails.

In an effort to avoid jettisoning the Anglo-American Communist compromised plans, Mr. Andrew Young, President Carter's principal globe trotter produced on 8 March, yet another outspoken gaffe in an already overlong trail of indiscreet off-the-cuff terse remarks on tense issues.

In answer to an American reporter's question about what seemed to be Britain's increasingly favourable official comments on the Salisbury Agreement, this "unguided missile" replied: "What are they (the British) going to do — run out and leave us with 30 years of trouble the way they did in 1948?"

The historical reference to "1948" and "30 years of trouble" were to the ending by Britain of its mandate in Palestine despite the fact that no agreement had been reached on how the territory should be shared between its Jewish and Arab populations. In effect, therefore Young's insult inferred that Britain might dump the Rhodesian problem in the United Nations lap.

This Black non-conformist minister turned politician thrives on controversey and being outspoken and has blazed a trail of provocative gaffes.

Once described by President Carter as being a "great national treasure", Mr. Young, who is 46, has enraged many of Washington's allies.

At different times he has accused Britain of "inventing racism" and being "chicken on race".

He has also said that the Swedes, and former Presidents Gerald Ford and Richard Nixon were racists.

In December 1977, he insisted that the Cuban presence in Africa posed "no real threat" to American interests and it was a mistake to react.

He has described the guerilla forces operating in Rhodesia as "well-educated, restrained and patient individuals".

On the other hand, he has called the South African Government "illegitimate" and said it practices "Stalinism".

He has also accused colleagues in the State Department of trying to undermine him and of leaking derogatory material about him to newspapers.

The counter to the loud-mouthed Andrew Young's fraudulent assertion that an internal settlement will lead only to greater violence is, of course, that it requires only the majority to be well armed and well equipped for the minority to be deterred from taking the offensive.

This is unacceptable to Britain and America, for America is prepared to pay a high price for the Negro vote back home, even to the extent of sacrificing Rhodesia, South West Africa and South Africa.

Britain should, of course, have the moral courage to do what it knows is right. As Lord Home stated on 3 April : "Provided that the new Constitution is consistent with the Six Principles, which it is virtually certain to be, Parliament should pass an Act to confer legality on Zimbabwe in its relations with the British Crown, and treat her thereafter as a State independent in her own right."

On 26 April, the Archbishop of Canterbury, Dr. Donald Coggan, gave surprise backing to the Rhodesian internal settlement. In a debate in the House of Lords, the Anglican church leader, said the settlement which the British Government has refused to endorse should be welcomed as a first step towards establishing a multi-racial democratic Rhodesia.

Dr. Coggan rarely asserts his ancient right to speak in the House of Lords and then not usually on contentious political issues.

Two of the Executive Council, Bishop Abel Muzorewa and the Reverend Ndabaningi Sithole, are churchmen belonging to the United Methodist Church in Rhodesia.

Dr. Coggan told the House of Lords that the internal settlement proposals for an interim government should be implemented as soon as possible.

But he said, he feared terrorism would almost certainly continue under the new system — "although, one prays, on a smaller and steadily diminishing scale".

On 26 April, the former US President, Mr. Gerald Ford, accused President Carter of supporting the wrong side over Rhodesia.

Mr. Ford said he strongly supported the Salisbury Agreement.

It was the first time an American political figure of Mr. Ford's stature had lent his support to the internal settlement.

Mr. Ford said the Transitional Government set up under the internal agreement would lead Rhodesia to democratic rule, and he could not understand why the US was not supporting it.

"They (the Transitional Government) have, in effect, provided for open and free elections — which is what we want in this country.

"Now, there are two black leaders who are . . . supported indirectly by the Russians and potentially the Cubans, who want to move in and take over Rhodesia," Mr. Ford said.

"And I don't comprehend why this Administration is supporting those that want to prevail by warfare when they've got a chance to support those that have a transition in a peaceful way."

At the end of May 1978, Mr. Vorster made it clear that his Government was not prepared to support Anglo-American efforts to urge Mr. Ian Smith, the Rhodesian Prime Minister, and his interim leaders to join an all-party peace conference.

"On behalf of southern Africa," he said "I appeal to the British and American Governments: Why do you not co-operate with those Rhodesians who want peace? Why do you not abandon your own schemes which these people say are not viable?

"Why do you not build on the foundations these people have laid? Why do you not lift sanctions against Rhodesia to the benefit of black and white Rhodesians.

"As the leader of the most developed state in Africa, I have the right to plead for Africa's continued existence. We are the most developed nation on the continent and also the nation which had the courage as small as we are to stand up four square against the Marxists.

"In the interests of the Free World and in the interests of the anti-Marxist world, I make this call on Mr. Callaghan and President Carter. Africa does not need any more politicking. Africa today, as a result of too much politicking is getting poorer".

The recent mission to Pretoria by Mr. Cyrus Vance, the American Secretary of State and Dr. David Owen, the Foreign Secretary, appears to have been totally abortive.

Mrs. Margaret Thatcher should now state loud and clear that the policy of a Tory Government would be not only to lift sanctions immediately, but to gird Rhodesia with money and arms for their self-defence, and to cut off any form of assistance to the shipwreck states of Zambia and Mozambique as long as they continue to provide sanctuary to terrorists.

Unless Rhodesia is supported in this way, the Soviets and their Cuban mercenaries emboldened by their easy victory over the Somalis in the Ogaden, and the recent tragic events in Zaire, are bound to intervene increasingly in Rhodesia and South-West Africa. The omens are there for all to see.

Meanwhile Rhodesia's Transitional Government is confident that a ceasefire can be achieved. The Executive Council claims to have information that the terrorist forces support the accord and that if co-operation could be achieved between the security forces and terrorist commanders under the supervision of the Transitional Government, the terrorist war could be ended.

To have reimposed sanctions on Rhodesia after Smith has proved strong enough to withstand them for 12 years, is proof enough that the British Government is attempting to transfer power, not peacefully to a black majority, but forcibly to a violent minority.

The last voting in favour of continued sanctions was 119 to 25 which is a good indication that the Conservative Party is fearful of antagonising the African States, particularly Nigeria which supplies Britain with so much of its oil. Presumably, Conservative MPs also feel that if sanctions were ended, Mr. Smith would feel he had been vindicated and had the support of the British public. Well, hasn't he? A referendum would soon show how solidly the British public is behind Mr. Smith.

In fact, economically, sanctions have benefitted Rhodesia in many ways by making the country remarkably self-sufficient and by creating a strong national spirit.

If sanctions are lifted and the present political agreement encouraged and fostered, the terrorists' cause would wither. The Rhodesians are militarily in control but their economy is suffering. Given the economic and political boost that recognition would bring, the rank and file terrorist would be sufficiently disheartened to return to the fold. Not only that, but the future of Angola, Mozambique and Zambia would immeasurably improve if they were rid of alien terrorists' camps and were able to open their borders and resume normal trading with a country which is naturally a powerful and beneficial trading partner.

CHAPTER 9

United Nations

BRITAIN lost the battle against the UN's gag on Bishop Abel Muzorewa being able to present to the Security Council the moderate Black Rhodesian viewpoint on the internal settlement in Rhodesia.

While the 15 member council agreed without dissent to hear Mr. Joshua Nkomo and Mr. Robert Mugabe, the co-leaders of the Communist-supplied Patriotic Front guerilla movement, the 49 nation African bloc in the United Nations forced a difficult vote on Bishop Muzorewa's right to speak to the council.

As one of three Black nationalists who signed the agreement with Mr. Ian Smith for Black majority rule in Rhodesia by 31 December, the Bishop is now regarded as an integral part of a regime the United Nations has repeatedly branded as illegal.

Although he has been invited in the past to participate in deliberations as the leader of a major Black nationalist movement in Rhodesia, his new formal relationship with the Smith Government now casts him in the role of political leper in UN eyes.

At a caucus, the African bloc, which asked for the Security Council debate on the Salisbury agreement, agreed to work to prevent his appearance before the council.

The three African and three Communist countries on the Security Council opposed the bishop's participation in the debate. Since it is a procedural decision, the veto power held by the five permanent members of the council could not be exercised.

The council heard a particularly sinister interpretation of the internal agreement from Mr. Nkomo and Mr. Mugabe.

They saw it as part of a plot hatched by South Africa and White Rhodesians to establish "a belt of puppet regimes across Southern Africa the chief purpose of which is to make the world safe for apartheid". Mr. Nkomo said the agreement could lead to a "conflagration not only in Africa but in the whole world".

The double standards which are adopted by the UN have lost this organisation any semblance of respect. There is a constant barrage of words and application of sanctions against Rhodesia and South Africa and yet countries like the Soviet Union and the Eastern bloc generally and a number of African countries can oppress and imprison people with hardly a protest.

The West is being pushed around by the new and unrepresentative majority in the cockpit of the UN. This element consists mostly of small, insignificant, developing countries which indulge in anti-colonial postures at the behest of their Soviet tutors.

The activities of the United Nations now fluctuate between a Broadway farce and a Punch-and-Judy show. Its only reason for its existence is to help keep the peace. But in the clutches of the Third World/Soviet bloc, the UN is doing precisely the opposite. It is blatantly encouraging what it euphemistically calls "armed liberation struggles". This in plain language means the use of the gun as the sole weapon for resolving disputes.

The situation was succinctly described in the leading article of the London **Sunday Express** on 12 March:

"In the Security Council of the United Nations, the apostles of hate and violence strut arrogantly across the stage, after having won a major propaganda victory against the Rhodesian peace deal.

"Mr. Robert Mugabe, who wants to bring Mr. Smith down by bloodshed, is given an ecstatic reception. His equally fanatical colleague, the expensively suited, jewel flashing Mr. Joshua Nkomo is treated with the deference due to an Egyptian Pharaoh.

"Meanwhile Bishop Abel Muzorewa, that essentially decent man who seeks progress through the ballot box rather than through the bullet, is publicly snubbed. The Security Council refuses to allow him to speak.

"Could anything illustrate more clearly the moral bankruptcy of the UN?

"All the Security Council has achieved is encouragement for the gunmen and the bombers. Their behaviour will surely encourage more indiscriminate slaughter, more ruined lives, more orphans and widows and cripples.

"The time has come for Britain to stop running after such a discredited crew, in a hopeless effort to win international agreement on Rhodesia.

"Ian Smith and the African moderates have come up with the best chance of a settlement since UDI. We should back them to the hilt".

CHAPTER 10

Terrorist Atrocities

ON 5 December, 1976, a group of Mr. Mugabe terrorists entered a village in North-Eastern Rhodesia, North of Mt. Darwin, and demanded at gun point that Mr. Chikombe Mazvidza, a Black Christian, give them food. When he refused, they tied him up and in front of his wife and children; cut off his nose, two ears; lips and chin (their next desecration is not printable). Mr. Mazvidza lived.

On 5 December, 1976, a member of the Mr. Nkomo terrorist organisation, ZAPU, denouncing his victims as "enemies of the people" executed Bishop Adolph Schmitt, Father Possenti, Weggarten and Sister Maria Frances, all Catholic Missionaries. Sister Ermenfried survived to tell the horror story.

On 19 September, 1976, a group of Mr. Mugabe terrorists from Mozambique slaughtered 27 defenceless Black African workers on a tea estate in the Honde valley in front of their wives and children. After machine gunning their victims, they systematically bayoneted each of them.

On Sunday, 6 February, 1977, a group of Mr. Mugabe terrorists machine gunned to death three Roman Catholic Priests and four nuns at the St. Paul's Mission, Musami. One more priest and one nun witnessed the massacre and miraculously escaped to report the atrocity.

All of the above were devoting their lives to helping Rhodesian Blacks.

On 15 July, 1977, Mr. Mugabe terrorists entered a remote village, took the village headman, Mr. John Chiruva, his nine wives and 13 of his 36 children, crowded them into a small grass hut, and set the hut on fire, burning the 23 helpless blacks to death. six of the children were under six years of age. The terrorists left a note at the scene of the massacre saying "Zimbabwe will come through the barrel of a gun".

On 6 August, terrorists placed a bomb in a crowded Woolworths' store in the centre of Salisbury which exploded killing eight blacks, three whites and injuring 76 more. The Mugabe terrorists organisation took credit for the bombing.

Little Natasha Glenny was just six months old when she was murdered in September, 1977.

Black CTs who attacked the remote border homestead in Rhodesia where she lived dragged her from her nanny's arms, threw her across the verandah and bayoneted her three times in the back. Then they held her tiny body at the end of their rifles like some prize trophy. Decent people could not find a name for creatures who would commit such an act of bestial horror.

Surely no patriotic Briton who read the leading article in London's **Sunday Express** on 2 October, 1977, could but agree wholeheartedly with the stinging rebuke administered to Dr. Owen in these condemnatory terms:

"Until now Dr. David Owen, Her Majesty's Principal Secretary of State for Foreign Affairs, has dignified the terrorists as 'freedom fighters'.

"Indeed, he has concentrated his bile on the Rhodesian security forces who, on occasion, have roughed up a few suspects, thundering that the culprits would be 'rooted out' of the country's new army.

"What will he do about the men who killed little Natasha? Has he any words of anger about them, any plans to hunt them down and punish them? Or are they still freedom fighters to whom we would entrust, without any safeguard, the lives of thousands of helpless men, women and children of British stock?

"Let Dr. Owen tell us."

The above atrocities are just a few of the thousands of terrorist atrocities that are being perpetrated by the Patriotic Front against Rhodesian blacks, white missionaries and occasionally Rhodesian whites. It is not surprising that the Soviets, the UN and the front line Presidents support these terrorists, but it is a bit disturbing that they are also supported by Dr. Owen, Mr. Young, the US State Department, and that they receive much of their funding from large Church organisations such as the World Council of Churches in the US and Western Europe.

CHAPTER 11

A Second Visit to Rhodesia April-May 1978

ONCE again I found Mr. Ian Smith warm and friendly and completely relaxed. He has a very incisive mind and must have an ice cold brain to have achieved what he has against tremendous odds and against both outside and inside pressures. Here is a man with leadership, dogged determination and an iron nerve. He seems to thrive under pressure and will go down in history as a shrewd and clever negotiator without equal — a world statesman.

For a long time, the West has been led to expect the political extinction of Mr. Ian Smith, whereas, he has proved himself to be one of the great survivors of politics and has remained firmly in the driving seat. He has every reason to be proud of the exemplary leadership and ingenuity of the commanders of the armed forces and police at all levels and the pronounced fighting qualities and morale of those under them. There is no doubt that this high respect is reciprocated.

Having won support from the South African Government for the internal agreement, he announced on 26 May that he would step down as Prime Minister by the end of the year and had no intention of standing in the proposed general election. "By then my task will have been completed and I will have done all I can to reassure the people of Rhodesia", he said.

I found that the armed forces had a particularly healthy regard and liking for Mr. P. K. van der Byl, the present joint Minister of Foreign Affairs in the Rhodesian Transitional Government. This stems from the time when he was Minister of Defence and Foreign Affairs. Having been an officer — in the British Army — he knows how to speak to soldiers and how to get the best out of them. They like his forthright manner, his powers of expression and his mastery of his subject. All soldiers appreciate a man who has the courage of his convictions — moral force is to physical as four to one.

While I was in South Africa, **The Star's** Africa News Service reported that the American Secretary of State, Mr. Vance, was said to have told the Rhodesian Transitional Government that the US would not imperil its political and economic interests in Africa — particularly in Nigeria — for the sake of a Rhodesian settlement.

This was disclosed on 9 May by Mr. van der Byl who stated that Mr. Vance had said "it was more important to the United States that the Nigerian dictator was satisfied with political developments in Southern Africa than that a truly democratic process be brought about in Rhodesia with the consent of the majority of the population".

"He made it plain that the American administration would not go along with anything which failed to receive the approval of the Nigerians because of their dependence on Nigeria for imported oil.

"They would not imperil their political and economic interests in the continent for the sake of a Rhodesian settlement even if it fulfilled all the original prerequisites".

Answering questions, Mr. van der Byl said Mr. Smith would never be party to any devious conduct or bluff or mislead the black leaders and black compatriots with whom he had made the settlement "and with the results of which, we would have to live for the rest of our lives".

The London **Times** newspaper reported on 28 May that Mr. van der Byl said in an interview published that day that the Kolwezi massacres could be a blessing in disguise for those who have been speaking out about the dangers of Soviet penetration in Africa.

The intervention of French and Belgian troops in the Zaire fighting indicated that the West was waking up to the realities of Soviet aggression, he told the Salisbury **Sunday Mail** in an interview, much of which was devoted to criticising Mr. Andrew Young, the United States representative at the United Nations.

Mr. van der Byl said: "President Carter has admitted now that this was a Cuban and Russian enterprise. So much for Mr. Andrew Young's talk about the Cubans being a stabilizing influence in Africa.

"But it is a pity that this sort of ritualistic sacrifice has to be made, and these miseries inflicted, before anyone wakes up to what we in this country have been warning for years."

Mr. van der Byl praised the French Government's approach to African affairs, saying its policy was vastly superior to that of any other Western nation.

"They have an understanding of the reality of the situation", he said. "But, more important, they have the courage of their convictions, to go in and do something positive when necessary. One cannot express too highly one's admiration of the performances they have put up".

He added that if the West had generally acted in the same way in the Horn of Africa "it could well be that central and southern

Africa would not now be confronted with a dominating Soviet presence".

The London **Times** Salisbury Correspondent wrote that in the interview Mr. van der Byl described Mr. Young as a man out of touch with the realities in Africa.

Mr. Young, he said, had referred to the Patriotic Front as being in many ways non-violent. Mr. van der Byl declared: "It is difficult to believe that anyone in their right senses could claim the Patriotic Front was non-violent, particularly when you look back over its record of brutal murder, pillage and every crime possible to inflict on human beings — white and particularly black".

Mr. van der Byl said it was appalling that somebody holding such an important position as Mr. Young should be so ignorant or, even worse, to be so determined to twist the truth.

Mr. Young had committed some incredible indiscretions and said some rather ridiculous things from time to time "but there has never been anything quite so vicious as this".

I have already referred to the thousands of terrorist atrocities perpetrated by the CTs of the Patriotic Front. On 1 June a letter was published in the London **Daily Telegraph** from a Dr. B. L. Williams, Surgeon Emeritus, Portsmouth Group of Hospitals, Hayling Island, Hampshire. The title given to this letter was 'The Lurking Fear in Rhodesia'. It sums up precisely my own sentiments after having travelled throughout the length and breadth of Rhodesia and seen so much and met so many people:—

"Events in Kolwezi move me to write to you concerning my experiences in Rhodesia, from which country I have recently returned after working there as a surgeon in a large hospital devoted entirely to the treatment of Africans.

"Although familiar with the results of violence (I served as a surgeon in the Royal Army Medical Corps in operational areas throughout most of the last war, and for much of my professional life in a hospital which dealt in civilian trauma) I was appalled by the nature and extent of the deliberately inflicted injuries that I saw.

"I have brought back with me memories of men and women shattered by high-velocity bullets which the Russians, as is their custom, had generously provided for other people to fire. In particular, I will not forget a little girl of fourteen, shot through the rectum and vagina.

"I recall too men with their noses, lips or ears cut off as part of terrorist policy. The results of landmines indiscriminately sown were devastating, and the principal victims were members of the civilian population. It was abundantly clear that intimidation and torture were very much part of the African scene, and that wanton cruelty was never far from the surface.

"In spite of what goes on in the frontier areas and the tribal trust lands, the towns remain orderly and peaceful, protected as they are by the Rhodesian Army. This army, whose help we were happy to accept in Hitler's War, maintains its tradition, and remains an efficient and disciplined force. Eighty-two per cent of its soldiers are black, all of whom are volunteers.

"Perhaps it would not be out of place to point out that so far this little country, whose whites enjoy a high standard of living by European standards, and whose blacks enjoy a similarly high standard by African standards, has managed not only to fight a war, but to cope with sanctions and inflation as well, ever since 1965.

"This is a feat which could not have been achieved without responsible government. Rhodesia is now engaged in building 'with the inevitability of gradualness' a truly multi-racial society in which the blacks, will, in the fullness of time, have a majority say in ruling a nation which has a sophisticated modern economy, built up from virtually nothing in some 80 years. Is it not time that we started to give them a little help instead of hobnobbing with Russian-aided revolutionaries who, if they succeeded in their avowed objective of conquering the Rhodesian army, would set about destroying the country (and finally themselves) in a holocaust in comparison with which the horrors of Kolwezi would be just a curtain raiser?

"Let us call a halt to all this political humbug and have the courage to recognise that the battles these gallant people are fighting are not only theirs, but in the long run ours as well!"

I was told in Rhodesia that Dr. Owen had been more reasonable at his April meeting with Mr. Ian Smith than he had been at their first meeting. On the latter occasion I was told by someone who was present that Dr. Owen "was brash and had given an appalling display of ill manners, rudeness, arrogance, impertinence and impudence. The temptation to seize him by the throat had been hard to resist".

Also severely criticised by civilians and military alike was the first appearance of Field Marshal Lord Carver wearing uniform. This went down extremely badly and was regarded as a tactless display by a British Field Marshal arriving to negotiate with people who had to be reminded that they were outranked in status and seniority. One General put it to me like this: "By his attitude and fantastic proposals for our Army anyone would think that he was dealing with a bunch of colonial hangovers suffering from heatstroke. He did not seem to realise that we were all trained at Sandhurst and the British Army Staff College, Camberley".

It was at the end of April that what should have been no more than a storm in a teacup developed into a crisis of confidence, threatening the entire internal settlement agreement.

The man in the middle, Mr. Byron Hove, the sacked co-Minister of Justice and of Law and Order, left Salisbury by air for England amid mounting confusion and mystery over his dismissal by the Executive Council. This 38 year old black lawyer, who had been residing in England for the past eleven years, was dismissed for his refusal to withdraw or apologise for any of his controversial statements on the police, judiciary and civil service during his term of office lasting less than three weeks. Bishop Abel Muzorewa said that neither he nor any United National African Council (UNAC) Minister was present when the decision to sack Mr. Hove was taken.

Chief Chirau, April's Chairman, said that all four members had been present at all the meetings of the Council and no decisions had been taken other than at formal meetings.

The Reverend Sithole confirmed that Bishop Muzorewa was present at the Executive Council meeting and the decision to sack Mr. Hove was unanimous.

UNAC provincial and branch organisations in many parts of the country demanded reinstatement of Mr. Hove or alternatively that the party should pull out of the Transitional Government.

Bishop Muzorewa announced that the decision on future participation in the Transitional Government and other UNAC action would depend on his consultations "with the people". He warned that the withdrawal of the UNAC from the Government would cause it to "crumble". The implementation of the Salisbury Agreement would be impossible, he said.

When Mr. Sithole was asked what he thought if the UNAC decided to pull out of the Transition Government, he said: "It would not affect the agreement at all because the agreement is for the people and not for individuals".

One man, particularly one who had only recently returned to to Rhodesia from England after an absence of eleven years, could not possibly be allowed to wreck what had been achieved so far. If this sort of thing was to be allowed to pass how could the really big issues be tackled?

Reports were circulating in Salisbury that Mr. Hove was alleged to have stated some time ago in England that those who had held Ministerial rank in Rhodesia and senior positions in the armed forces should be arraigned before a Nuremberg type trial.

Bishop Muzorewa has a large following but his main weakness as a political leader is that he is erratic, unpredictable and indecisive. This inability to make decisions does not augur well for the future, but one can but hope that the power and responsibility of high office will bring maturity with it.

The Reverend Sithole is much more positive and is an able,

astute and firm politician. My official meeting with him was postponed so in the end I had an evening meeting with him in his private residence. We talked alone in his sitting room and the discussion was informal, relaxed, frank and friendly. He listened attentively to my explanation of Soviet Union's plan for African domination and the order in which the dominoes had fallen and would continue to fall unless the meticulous planning and steady advance of Moscow's Africa crusade by land and sea was halted. Protestations, I said, were useless. What was lacking was a Western strategy. I expounded my views on what this strategy should be.

Mr. Sithole certainly did not adopt an attitude of see-no-evil and hear-no-evil in connection with the Soviet Union. But he was confident that Rhodesia's internal settlement would go ahead as planned, that the interim government would hold firm and that the Patriotic Front would wither away if the internal agreement succeeded. He referred to his newly-published book **In Defence of the Rhodesian Constitutional Agreement** in which he explains the true nature of the agreement and the circumstances from which it was born. He said he was convinced that it would become evident to all who read his short work that, measured against objective criteria, the agreement could not be faulted.

He was optimistic that the sensitive measures already being taken to achieve a cease-fire would succeed. He asked me if I had met any guerillas during my extensive tour of the operational areas. I said, No, whereupon he asked me to follow him outside. We went out into the darkness by the front of the house and then round to the back to a separate small building which he said was his office. Inside were three men, two dressed in blue denims and the other in an open shirt and trousers. Stacked along one wall were piles of parcels addressed to London, America and Europe. Mr. Sithole explained that these were copies of his book which were being sent by air the next day for distribution to every Member of Parliament in Britain and every Senator in the USA, plus certain politicians in Western Europe, etc.

We then returned to the house. Mr. Sithole said: "You have just seen two of the guerillas who are conducting negotiations on my behalf."

We continued our discussion for some time and when four guests arrived for dinner I was introduced and then hastened to make my departure. But Mr. Sithole asked me to sit down and finish our conversation. When I looked at my watch and saw I had been there forty minutes, and by this time had caught the smell of cooking, I rose and took my leave. Mr. Sithole insisted on accompanying me to the gate which was unlocked by the sentry on duty and he saw me to my car. It would be difficult to experience a better display of courtesy and nice manners. This does not mean to say, however, that I did not recognise in him a tough streak and every indication of being a highly intelligent, articulate and wily politician.

Chief Chirau is sound, reliable and dignified and although not a professional politician is gaining in stature in this respect. A Meshona tribal chieftan with tribal lineage of chiefs dating back 800 years, Chief Chirau is president of the Council of Chiefs. This Council consists of 254 tribal chiefs, both Meshona and Metabele. He is also leader of ZUPO (Zimbabwe United Peoples' Organisation). He is staunchly anti-communist, anti-terrorist and in favour of moderate black rule with protection of all minority rights. Because he was a former Cabinet Minister in the White Government he was called a "white sell-out" by his enemies and given the cold shoulder by Britain and the United States. This is why he is not well known outside Rhodesia, and because of his moderation is bitterly opposed by the Soviets, the UN, the Front Line Presidents and the so-called Patriotic Front.

A certain amount of infighting can be expected among the political leadership, both inside and out, and it is pertinent to quote a few facts. In the event of an election, the following tribal divisions may play a part:—

		Percentage of total population
NKOMO: Kalanga 5% + Ndebele 14%	=	19%
SITHOLE: Ndau 3% + Manyika 13%	=	16%
MUZOREWA: Manyika 13% + Muzezure 18% + Mkorekore 12%	=	43%
MUGABE: Muzezuru 18%	=	18%
CHIRAU: Muzezuru 18%	=	18%
TONGOGARA: Karanga 22% (Chief of Staff to Mugabe and committed Marxist)	=	22%

It will be seen that the Karanga have the clearest majority and whilst Muzorewa can be said to carry the most weight, he has to share his following with Mugabe, Sithole and Chirau, all of whom will make considerable inroads.

The tribal groupings with the above approximate percentage of African population is shown in the map on pages 24-25.

Everywhere I went in Rhodesia I found an acute awareness of the sinister aims and growing appetite of the Soviet Union and a steel determination to ensure that Rhodesia does not suffer the same fate as Angola, Mozambique and the Horn of Africa. No-one had a good word to say about America, Britain or the Western powers for their futile attempts to bargain with Marxists, instead of lending full support to free and fair elections and giving aid to the one group which offers the only hope of a viable and demo-

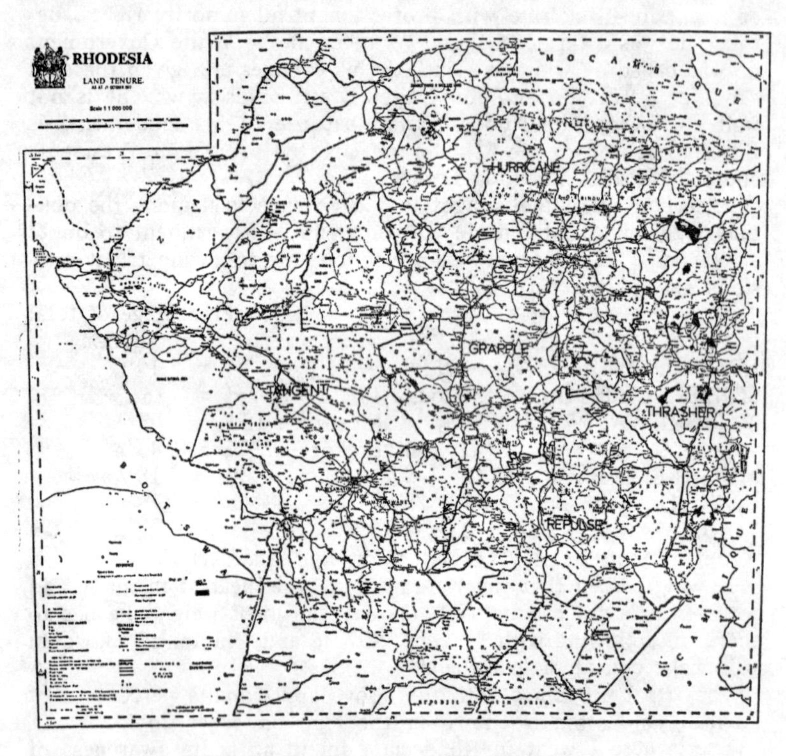

The Operational Areas in Rhodesia

cratic black-ruled state. This means the lifting of economic and other sanctions now and not after the elections. Britain imposed sanctions; Britain can drop them. The lifting of sanctions would start the economic ball rolling again, together with jobs, food and education. What a weapon that would be against the so-called Patriotic Front and its Marxist ideologues. The Internal Agreement would then succeed and the whites could live securely under a black government.

What is the situation in the military field?

The external threat consists of:

First, ZPRA (Zimbabwe People's Revolutionary Army) which is the military wing of ZAPU (Zimbabwe African Peoples Union) and its members owe their loyalty to Mr. Joshua Nkomo.

Second, ZANLA (Zimbabwe African National Liberation Army) which is the military wing of ZANU (Zimbabwe African National Union) and its members owe their loyalty to Mr. Robert Mugabe.

The strength of Mr. Nkomo's ZPRA on 1 May 1978 was as follows:—

Trained terrorists available for immediate deployment ...	6,000
Recently completed training in Angola and returned to Zambia	2,000
Under training in Zambia, Angola and Cuba	7,000

One of the main training camps for Rhodesian terrorists is based in South-East Angola, under the control of both Soviet and Cuban instructors. This camp not only contains Rhodesian terrorists, but also nationals from Zaire and South-West Africa, for use against those particular countries.

Since January 1978, a further 10,300 "followers" have been flown from Botswana to Zambia. Women and children are included in this figure, but the exact breakdown of males is not known.

The strength of Mr. Mugabe's ZANLA on 1 May 1978 was:

Trained terrorists available for immedite deployment ...	2,000
Under training at Nachingwea in Tanzania	5,000
Undergoing training in camps throughout Mozambique ...	5,000

In addition to these figures, there are indications that there are at least 30,000 Rhodesian Africans living in refugee camps within Mozambique who fall within the known non-combatant category.

The assessment I was given was that on 1 May 1978 there were approximately 6,406 terrorists representing **both** factions currently operating in Rhodesia.

Documents recovered in external operations, both in Zambia and Mozambique, confirm that both factions intend to grab as much territory as possible.

On 1 May, the situation was that Mr. Mugabe's ZANLA were pushing west as far as they could possibly go with Mr. Nkomo's ZPRA reacting by trying to move as far east as possible. The intention of both factions is to ensure the maximum number of tribal trust lands are, and, thereby the inhabitants, under their influence and not the opposing factions. This is as a prelude to any election in Rhodesia. Both ZANLA and ZPRA groups have been given instructions to eliminate the opposing factions if they encounter them. Contacts between these groups have taken place in the Maranda and Belingwe Tribal Trust Lands (TTLs) and the threat of contact is apparent throughout the centre line of Rhodesia.

What is being set up here is a forerunner to civil war unless the Rhodesian Security Forces (SF) are able to counter the threat. The Rhodesian SF consider that they are now in the strongest position they have ever been. They had, in November 1977, over 100 black Rhodesians volunteering for duty with the Security Forces **per day.** They cannot handle this number. However, they have increased the size of their Security Forces considerably mainly by the recruitment of black Rhodesians. What is particularly striking is the high percentage of black participation in their Security Forces, all of whom are volunteers:—

Army		
Territorial and Reserves	—	no blacks
Regular (other ranks)	—	78% to 80% Black
	—	20% to 22% White
(Officers)	—	Small percentage of blacks but increasing.
Police		
Regular	—	80% black
		20% white
Reserve	—	31% black
		69% white
Air Force		
Regular	—	25% black
	—	75% white
Territorial and reserves	—	no blacks
Guard Force	—	87% black
		13% white

All whites, Asians and coloured people up to 49 years of age are liable for call-up whereas no Africans are called up for national service. Mr. Gibson Magaramombe, black Co-Minister of Manpower and Social Affairs in the Council of Ministers, has called for Africans to do national service. He said that by creating a strong army the country could build racial harmony.

It will be seen from the following composition that the Rhodesian Army is a hard-hitting force to be reckoned with, containing more parachute trained regular soldiers than in the whole of the British Army:—

1. The all white Rhodesian Light Infantry Regiment (1 RLI)

which consists of 850 regular soldiers. They are all parachute trained and organised on a Commando basis.

2. The all white SAS Regiment which consists of three squadrons of regular soldiers, the squadrons being the same size as the British SAS Regiment. All, of course, are parachute trained.
3. One all white Armoured Car Regiment which consists of one squadron of regular soldiers and the other squadrons of Territorial and National Service soldiers. All the regulars are parachute trained.
4. One all white Artillery Regiment, consisting of one battery of regular soldiers — parachute trained — and three batteries of Territorial and National Service soldiers.
5. Two battalions of the Rhodesian African Rifles (RAR), each battalion consisting of 1,100 White and Black regular soldiers, all of whom are parachute trained.
6. Six Independent Companies, each of a strength of 130 of whom 90 are African regular soldiers and 40 are White National Service soldiers
7. Eight all Black Battalions of the Rhodesian Regiment each consisting of four companies, with an element of White leadership and specialists.
8. The Selous Scouts consisting of White and Black Regulars (parachute trained) and Territorials, of battalion strength.
9. The Grey Scouts which is a battalion of mounted infantry manned by White and Black regular and Territorial soldiers.
10. Two Rhodesian Defence Regiments, composed of Coloured and Asian Territorial soldiers and employed on guard duties and convoy escorts.
11. One Psychological Warfare Unit consisting of Regular and Territorial Officers (two of whom are Black) and 200 Black soldiers.
12. The Services Corps which combines the logistical back-up.
13. The Guard Force of 3,500 Black soldiers deployed in more than 200 Protected Villages (PV).

If the "Owen Circus" had taken the trouble to visit this army, as I did, and seen for themselves its composition, capability, equipment and esprit de corps, and the fact that it is as highly trained for conventional warfare as it is for guerilla warfare, they would not have put forward such a half-baked solution for the virtual disbandment of its hard core.

By comparison, the terrorists are riff-raff, and at present intent on banditry, the odd ambush, attacking soft targets, laying mines, rocket attacks, intimidation and committing atrocities. A more aggressive type of terrorist would have long ago constantly sabotaged the main railway line and ambushed rail traffic. They are

Photograph captured at the ZANLA High Command HQ at Chimoio in November 1977 showing female terrorists receiving military instruction.

Photograph captured at the ZANLA High Command HQ at Chimoio in November 1977 showing female terrorists receiving military instruction.

frightened stiff of the Security Forces and avoid all contact, except of a hit and run nature.

When the Security Forces succeed in forcing a contact, either by ambush or otherwise, their technique is to bring to bear an immediate response in order to inflict the maximum casualties before the terrorists can split up and escape. This immediate response takes the form of a series of fire forces held at short readiness to move, consisting of two armed helicopters, two troop carrying helicopters and a Dakota aircraft with a load of parachutists. If the situation demands, a second lift can then be deployed.

In addition to their various techniques, of which the above is only one, and their external pre-emptive strikes, Rhodesia has put into operation a number of other strategies and tactics which will pay dividends during 1978, which I do not propose dealing with. Suffice it to say that they are confident that they can defeat terrorism provided they see the establishment of a moderate black majority rule government and provided international support is afforded to this black government.

A cordon sanitaire, consisting of a double belt of mines and booby traps, has now been completed along a considerable length of the operational border, and its development is continuing apace. It is succeeding in its objective and is inflicting a satisfactory percentage of casualties on the CTs, particularly at night.

It will be seen from the map on pages 24-25 that Rhodesia has a 3,000 km border. Of that border, only 225 km can be considered friendly. This is the border with the Republic of South Africa (RSA) which runs along the Limpopo river. In this area, runs the strategic lifeline of Rhodesia, namely, the road and rail link through Beit Bridge to the RSA. Rhodesia has always had extremely good relations with the RSA and these relationships continue.

Rhodesia has an 800 km border with Botswana. Botswana's attitude has altered in recent years from that of a neutral African state to an increasingly militant posture against Rhodesia as Seretse Khama gets drawn into the alliance of "Front Line States". However, Botswana in itself is powerless to act against Rhodesia in view of its own grave economic situation and the pitifully small Security Force it maintains. It is allied both ethnically and politically to Mr. Joshua Nkomo's ZAPU organization and gives support to that organisation. It allows ZAPU terrorists to pass recruits into Botswana from where they are air transported into Zambia for terrorist training. Botswana has not prevented small sabotage and recruiting cells from operating from Francistown into Rhodesia.

Through Botswana passes what used to be Rhodesia's only rail link. This railway line is Rhodesia Railways owned and operated and is of great economic importance to Botswana. There are moves afoot for Botswana to take over this railway line and Rhodesia obviously is planning accordingly. That railway line no longer has the strategic importance it did although of course it is still of importance to Rhodesia for imports and exports. It is of interest to note that a considerable quantity of Zaire's copper exports and mining imports travel on this railway line through Bulawayo and up through Victoria Falls on to the Zambian rail network to Zaire. Botswana has recently constructed a road link, with Canadian and American assistance, which runs up Rhodesia's South-Western border to Kazungula on the Zambesi where a ferry is operated into Zambia.

Rhodesia has a 700 km border with Zambia. This border runs along the Zambesi river from Kazungula through Lake Kariba to Kanyemba. Zambia achieved its independence in October 1964 and since that date has been the main sanctuary for terrorists operating against Rhodesia. Prior to the fall of the Portuguese in Mozambique, Zambia supported all terrorist organizations operating against Rhodesia. In recent years, it has given most of its support to the ZPRA faction under Mr. Joshua Nkomo. There are a number of terrorist training camps and bases within Zambia which are given logistic support by the Zambian Army. In Lusaka are sited the Liberation Headquarters of not only ZAPU but also SWAPO and SAANC. In recent months the Zambian Army has become increasingly more militant in its attitude towards the Rhodesian Security Forces and has created a number of incidents along the border at border posts such as Kazungula, Victoria Falls, Kariba, Chirundu and Kanyemba. These incidents involve the Zambian Army firing across the river at Rhodesian positions. Rhodesia knows that these incidents serve a number of purposes:

a. To distract attention from Zambia's own grave economic situation by trying to throw the onus of provocation onto Rhodesia.
b. To raise the morale of the Zambian Army which is in a very shaky position.
c. To divert the attention of Rhodesia's Security Forces whilst a crossing of terrorists over the Zambesi takes place.

Zambia's economic position worsens daily and it is paradoxical that if she was to open her borders with Rhodesia her economic situation would improve overnight. However, with the stance adopted by President Kaunda, namely, his continued support for the Patriotic Front, this is unlikely to happen in the near future.

Rhodesia has a 1,300 km border with Mozambique. Prior to April 1974, i.e. the coup in Portugal, this border was a friendly border and Rhodesia had very good political, economic and military ties with the Portuguese to the benefit of both countries. Following the fall of the Portuguese Administration and the rise of President Samora Machel, the situation has altered drastically. Mozambique is now Rhodesia's most hostile border and gives tremendous support and sanctuary to the ZANLA faction under the loose leadership of Mr. Robert Mugabe.

The lines of communication are as follows:

a. **North-West.** From Salisbury, Rhodesia has a very good road which leads to Chirundu and 80 miles further to Lusaka. This border was closed by President Kaunda in April 1973, much to the economic detriment of both countries.

b. **North-East.** A road link through Nyamapanda on to Tete and thence into Malawi. This border was closed by President Machel in March 1976 to the particular detriment of Malawi.

c. **East.** From Salisbury, a road and rail link through Umtali on to Beira, previously Rhodesia's main import and export port. This road and rail link was also closed by President Machel in March 1976.

d. **South-East.** A rail link going through Vila Salazar and Malvernia on to Laurenco Marques, now called Maputo. This was a very important rail link but was also closed in March 1976.

e. **South.** The road and rail link across Beit Bridge which has already been described as the strategic lifeline of Rhodesia.

f. **South-West.** The rail link through Botswana. This link is of diminishing importance to Rhodesia.

g. **North-West.** The link with Zambia across the Victoria Falls bridge. The road link has been totally closed since April 1973 but the rail link remains open against Kaunda's wishes to facilitate the movement of Zaire's imports and exports.

The map on page 60 indicates the operational boundaries, namely:-

Op **Hurricane** which was the first of the operational areas opened and encompasses most of Mashonaland.

Op **Thrasher** encompasses most of the eastern districts.

Op **Repulse** — the south-eastern corner of Rhodesia.

Op **Tangent** has a large chunk of real estate with three borders i.e. Zambia, Botswana and the RSA.

Op **Grapple,** which is a semi-active operational area, is sited in the Midlands of Rhodesia.

Op **Splinter** is a small operation designed to control access across Lake Kariba. In the initial phases of the war, terrorists did not have the sophistication to enable them to cross Lake Kariba. Therefore Rhodesia observed a division, when both factions were operating from Zambia, of the Zambian/Rhodesian border. ZPRA operated west of Lake Kariba to Kazungula and ZANLA operated east of Lake Kariba to Kanyemba. However, they now have craft capable of crossing Lake Kariba. It is of interest to note that some of these boats have been supplied by Canada. Accordingly, Rhodesia has had to institute Rhodesia's own "navy" to prevent incursions taking place across the water. This has been a highly successful operation.

The casualty figures from 21 December 1972 to 15 May 1978 given on page 70 show that the Rhodesia SF have been killing at least ten CTs for every one casualty suffered by themselves. African civilians have suffered heavily at the hands of the CTs, the number murdered being about half the number of CTs killed by the Rhodesian SF.

The European farmers have had a tough time. I motored about 150 miles North of Salisbury to spend a day and a night on a farm, and visit two others. A farmer drove me the whole distance and we had no escort. This debunks the exaggerated reports that "it is far too dangerous to move about by road, that the rural areas are largely under the control of guerillas and that there are many snipers in the bushes around the roads".

The farmers are organised into Police Reserve Anti-terrorist units (PATU), each "stick" being of a strength of seven to eight men. One stick is standing by every day and night of the year at half an hour's notice to move in the event of an ambush or a farm being attacked. Six weeks before I arrived a stick had carried out a successful ambush on four CTs and four days before my arrival there had been a follow-up of CTs in the area. The compound of the labour force at the farm where I had lunch was frequently forced to feed CTs.

Each farmhouse is equipped with an Agric (Agricultural) Alert. If attacked the farmer presses a red button which indicates in the local police station the homestead that is being attacked. Each farm is in touch with the local police station by Agric Alarm, as well as with each other. Every morning a situation report is given to the farmers over the Agric Alert. This enables the farmers to be kept in the picture and ensures that the civilian population is kept completely involved in the war. From the morale point of view this has been a tremendous breakthrough. Without the steadfastness and morale of their wives the farmers would have found it difficult to withstand the strain. One cannot speak too highly of their courage. In the area I visited nine white farmers had been killed since December 1972.

There is a continuous stream of hostile propaganda by Radio Zambia directed at the black labour force. Kaunda himself, as President, came on the air and told the boys on the farmsteads to poison their farmer's food and the tractor drivers to put sugar and sand in the tractors.

The price of tobacco that Rhodesian farmers are getting is about half that obtainable in Malawi. This is because of the difficulty the buyers have in Salisbury of selling the tobacco. Notwithstanding, the farmers are determined to carry on and some of them, particularly those who own ranches, have their own aeroplanes and are members of the Police Reserve Air Wing. I was flown for two days by one of these farmers.

Mines on the dirt roads are a constant danger, but the farmer with whom I stayed the night drove me round his farm the following morning on dirt roads without turning a hair.

Most of the roads between farms are now macadam which has succeeded in obviating the danger of mines. The Deputy Commissioner is Chairman of the local Civil Defence (CD) Committee and it is the responsibility of this committee to enforce the fencing of farmer's homesteads, the labour force compounds, the imposition of food control and the cutting of grass verges to avoid ambushes.

I came away feeling proud of the sheer guts of one's kith and kin, their self-reliance, their determination to stick it out to the end, and their high morale. I believe they were as pleased to see me as I was to meet them. It was a great experience and a great honour to be among them even for such a short time.

No one can possibly make a proper assessment of the situation in Rhodesia without visiting the farms, the black townships, the operational areas and travelling extensively throughout the length and breadth of the country. Unfortunately too many visitors never move out of the city limits of Salisbury.

A brief operational history from 21 December 1972 is given in Appendix 2.

Casualty Figures: 21 December 1972, to 15 May 1978

	CT's killed by SF	SF killed in action or murdered by CTs	CIV Africans murdered by CTs	CIV Europeans murdered by CTs
Up to 31 Dec 77	**3,691**	**412**	**1,340**	**133**
Up to 15 May 78	**804**	**146**	**682**	**39**
Grand Total killed in Rhodesia	**4,495**	**558**	**2,022**	**172**

External Operations:

1,200	Tembue/Chimoio attack 23 Nov 1977	) Note: These figures
300	Nyadzonya Camp Aug 1976	) are conservative.
44	Kavalamanja Feb 1978	) Other sources indi-
70	Others	) cate a much higher
		) kill rate.
6,109	Grand Total of CTs killed	

The Security Forces are not being complacent. For instance, they know that teams of Soviet and Cuban advisers have moved into Missao de Boma, South-Eastern Angola, to instruct terrorists in the use of field guns, surface-to-air missiles, "Stalin organ" rocket launchers and other heavy equipment.

The trainees belong to three factions. Mr. Nkomo's ZIPRA, South West Africa's SWAPO and units of the Katangese rebels who recently attacked the Shaba Province of Zaire.

Documents and weapons captured by Rhodesian Forces in their pre-emptive strike on a terrorist base in Zambia in early March showed clearly the Russian and Cuban part in the war against Rhodesia.

The captured documents gave evidence that the Russians are directing guerilla attacks against Rhodesia and that Cubans are involved in their training.

A captured operational order signed by Lt. Col. Kabvita, of the Zambian Regiment, showed that his orders were to protect the guerilla base by "ambushing the enemy". No wonder, therefore, that five Zambian soldiers were killed in the raid.

At least 42 terrorists were killed and a number wounded in what was a "self-defensive" strike to prevent a large-scale invasion of Rhodesia.

The security forces returned with about seven tons of arms, ammunition and equipment, most of it made in Communist countries but including an American-made machine gun and some British-made landmines.

At the end of March, 500 Cuban troops had flown to the Mozambique capital, Maputo, from Ethiopia and Angola to join at least 300 already in the country to train the 10,000 ZANLA terrorists for a new offensive against Rhodesia. The Press and other speculation have produced 250 Russian tanks and 35 Mig 21 jet fighters and scores of Soviet military advisers from Adis Ababa. These figures lack official confirmation in Rhodesia.

At the end of March, Mr. Serge Solokov, the Soviet Union's First Defence Minister arrived in Mozambique, followed by Mr. Peopli, Cuba's Foreign Minister, who arrived from Tanzania.

I could obtain no official confirmation of a report that East Germans have been taught Shona, (the local language) for the past 15 years. If true, this indicates that the territorial designs of the Soviet Union in Africa are no new phenomenon.

The Communist military build-up in Mozambique is, of course, being monitored by South Africa, whose Defence Minister, Mr. Pieter Botha, has criticised Western nations for doing nothing to prevent this from happening. He stated "Our whole defence is directed at our borders." It would be surprising if Russia did not encourage a two-pronged attack on Rhodesia by ZANU forces from Mozambique and ZAPU forces from Zambia, and a third pronged attack on Namibia by SWAPO forces from Angola.

The Soviet Union might be deliberately circulating exaggerated reports of Russian and Cuban military presence and intervention in order to intimidate Rhodesia.

America and Britain — in that order — have also lent themselves to the same deliberate exaggeration and it is this, as much as anything else, that has now placed President Kaunda of Zambia on the horns of a dilemma.

Does he believe the reports and give way to Russian and Cuban pressure?

Or, by threatening to evoke Russian-Cuban help should he blackmail the West into continuing to support the Patriotic Front?

Or, should he take the consequences of an inevitable encroachment by Russia and Cuba?

The man in overall charge of Soviet policy in this part of Africa is the Russian ambassador to Zambia, the Lusaka-based Mr. Vassily Solodovnikov, who master-minds Soviet African strategy. He is exerting an increasing influence over Kaunda and it behoves the West not to underestimate the leverage that the Soviet Union is applying to Kaunda.

The problem is self-generating. Britain and America started off on the wrong foot by supporting the Patriotic Front — in order to please the Front Line Presidents — whereas they should have started in support of the democratic process within Rhodesia. Whether or not they like it, Britain and America will ultimately have to choose between support for the democratic process in Rhodesia, or continued support for the Patriotic Front which means, in effect, playing the Soviet game.

Meanwhile Rhodesia has contingency plans to meet an escalation of the guerilla war to a more conventional level. They would certainly make mincemeat of a Cuban intervention by their seventh rate "asphalt-bound" troops. They have the training and equipment to fight a more conventional type of war against a sophisticated enemy, but this would almost certainly provoke South African reinforcement of Rhodesia. The West would do well to take heed of this warning.

The recent tragic events in Zaire have served to alert white and black Rhodesians alike to the fate that would befall them were they to be "governed" by the Anglo-American backed phony Patriotic Front, and were they to allow their armed forces to be emasculated in the form originally proposed by the Owen/Carver duet. The horrific events of Zaire have stiffened the resolve of Rhodesia not to allow its preparedness and strength to be reduced by one iota. Unlike Britain they put defence and law and order as first priority, regardless of the expense and sacrifices involved. A nation which will not concern itself in the preservation of its free society is no longer worth defending.

Rhodesia knows very well that if a similar situation to Zaire were to break out there, they could hardly expect France to pull Britain's chestnuts out of the fire which Dr. Owen & Co., would have created by their refusal to recognise the honourable internal settlement that has been reached by that courageous country. There would not be the same problem with a Tory Government in power, because they would have the political will to put into operation a contingency plan to send a "fire brigade" task force at the drop of a hat. The object of the exercise would be to move with such speed that the task force would arrive before the fire could break out. The political decision must be taken in time — this is what crisis management is all about. All too often the military have been faced with a situation of "too little too late".

During the years, Rhodesia has had to mount a number of external operations to safeguard the territorial integrity of the country. In August 1976, a raid took place on a ZANLA terrorist base camp in Mozambique. Rhodesia had had information that a major incursion numbering some 900 terrorists was due to be mounted in late August 1976 from Nyadzonya camp. 300 terrorists were killed in this raid which totally destroyed that incursion for 1976. Rhodesian SF suffered no casualties. Papers recovered later from Chimoio show that they, in fact, killed 1,200.

In November 1976 an operation was mounted in the north-eastern area which, although not spectacularly successful as regards the numbers of terrorists killed (only 25 were killed), some 80 tons of war material was captured. Most was destroyed in situ but eight tons of attractive items, namely anti-aircraft weapons, anti-tank guns, mortars and heavy machine guns were brought back into Rhodesia and put on display to the International Press. This operation effectively prevented another planned incursion in the north-eastern area from taking place.

In June 1977, a further raid was launched into Mozambique. Initially a terrorist camp right on the border was attacked in which 33 terrorists were killed. Documents recovered from this camp indicated that the small village of Mapai was the logistical centre for re-supply to the south-eastern operational area. Accordingly, it was attacked and large quantities of war material were destroyed. Again this operation, whilst not spectacularly successful, achieved tremendous results by disrupting their entire re-supply chain for many months.

On 23 November 1977, the SF attacked Chimoio, the main ZANLA High Command Headquarters and also the Provincial HQ for Manica Province. This was a large terrorist complex including the offices of Mr. Mugabe and Mr. Tongogara, the political

Commisar training wing, the women's training wing, the children's training wing, re-education centres and all the training facilities such as rifle ranges, etc. Large quantities of arms and explosives, vehicles, buildings and documents were destroyed and a very high number of terrorists were killed. It was reported that women and children were killed in this raid. Rhodesia does not dispute this but there are photographs of the women and children who were in that camp. They show that they were all undergoing terrorist training and were armed terrorists. Two of these photographs are on pages 64 and 65.

Special Branch Officers who accompanied the raiding party recovered these photographs, as well as many documents, from the office of Mr. Josiah Tongogara. The original coloured photographs had stamped on the back the fact that they were processed in Lausanne, Switzerland, in October 1977. Many hundreds of these photographs were recovered.

On 26 November 1977, that is three days after the Chimoio attack, the Rhodesian SF attacked Tembue terrorist camp. In both these operations, they killed in excess of 1,200 armed terrorists and wounded many more who may subsequently have died. The Rhodesia SF suffered a total of only one soldier killed and eight others injured in both these attacks.

In early March 1978, a pre-emptive strike was launched on a terrorist base in Zambia. This was a self-defensive pre-emptive strike to prevent a large-scale invasion. As described above the captured documents and weapons produced evidence that the Soviets are directing the terrorist attacks against Rhodesia while the Cubans are responsible for training.

CHAPTER 12

South Africa

MOST people I met in South Africa admit there will have to be major changes, but with proper constitutional protection and secure guarantees for law and order and defence. After all, law and order is the first responsibility of any government and defence is, or should be, a national priority, although one would not think so judging by the disgraceful example set by Britain in this respect.

The main disputable point is first, how rapidly change should come about and, more important, what form it should take. Certainly a one man, one vote prescription is an euphemism for Black rule and is something which not only the Whites in South Africa but also the thinking Indian and Coloured people would not accept. Why? Because they have witnessed the massive degeneration into bloodshed, chaos and tyrannical dictatorship that one man, one vote has produced in one African country after another.

The immediate and urgent priority for South Africa is the abolition of what has become known as "petty apartheid", those indignities which daily dehumanise the life of so many people in that otherwise wonderful country and which generate so much unhappiness, bitterness and hatred. Petty apartheid takes many forms: separate entrances at public Post Offices and other government buildings, signposts which indicate separate bathing areas for different races, notices on buildings which allocate separate entrances or lifts for "goods and non-Europeans", the taxis and buses labelled "second class" when they are reserved for Blacks. These and numerous other instances of petty apartheid must be done away with immediately.

A start has been made, for Prime Minister John Vorster has abolished "pass books" for black South Africans, probably the most hated symbol of apartheid, in a move aimed at reducing racial tension. He has also allocated Blacks working in White areas to bring their families to live with them.

Multinational corporations doing business in South Africa, like Fords for example, have already done a great deal to improve the conditions of their Black employees. They have done far more than merely removing apartheid signs on washroom doors and integrating the eating arrangements. They are now giving equal pay for equal work, improved welfare services and training programmes for Black workers and spend a lot of money on things like recreation and so on. There has been no interference from the South African Government which is an encouraging sign that Prime Minister Vorster intends to bring about the changes that are necessary. He has the power, the skill and the standing to do so.

Dr. Barnard is the first to admit that South Africa has a long way to go, but he emphasised to me that the widely held belief that little or no change has, or is, taking place is patently wrong. Considerable progress has been made over the past five years but South Africans themselves are largely to blame for the lack of awareness about this. Most advancement for black people is introduced in far too cautious and low-key a manner for fear of disturbing the sensibilities of the conservative voters in the country and the white trade unions. Instead of taking every opportunity to display as effectively as possible the changes in the right direction that are taking place these matters are given as little publicity as possible.

One of the most serious gaps in South Africa's national defence is the failure to mount a full-scale political and propaganda warfare strategy.

More money is spent each year in America on advertising aspirin than in promoting South Africa.

Certainly an annual budget of $18 million for promotional activities worldwide, including operations within the Republic, looks minute compared with the $350 million spent on Commercial advertising in South Africa each year, or compared with a military budget of more than $2,000 million.

South Africa needs to spend murch more than it does on political warfare, and in particular it needs to spend much more in the US.

South Africa's enemies in the US, including those within the administration, are not supermen.

They have blundered before and will do so again, as many of the premises on which they are basing their arguments and policies are false (as, for instance, the conviction that the internal settlement in Rhodesia does not enjoy majority support).

If they see that their offensive is failing because of South Africa's determined resistance, ultimately the Carter Administration will settle for very much less than one-man, one-vote.

The most dangerous thing South Africa can do in the present crisis, is to believe that by making one concession after another to Western pressure, particularly over Rhodesia and South-West Africa it is gaining time for its own strategic preparations.

South Africa would not be buying time, they would be selling it, for the process of making such concessions would merely lower respect for South Africa worldwide and the West would become increasingly optimistic that it would be able to destroy the Republic without undue expense or inconvenience. They would positively be encouraged to try sanctions.

Racial matters, particularly discriminatory ones, raise strong emotions in today's world and the world communications media thrive on them. It is not surprising, therefore, that South Africa is regularly depicted as the most despicable among nations for their racial policies. Yet South Africa's world contacts show that there is an enormous fund of goodwill available to them if they would heed its **ci de coeur** — "Please help us to help you!"

South Africa can get sympathy, understanding and co-operation if it produces incontrovertible proof that its policies are working and clear evidence that its declared policy of moving away from discrimination is being implemented. It can also get all the material support it needs from financiers, industrialists and trade partners if they can be satisfied about intended measures to ensure racial harmony, justice and stability in South Africa.

During a debate in the European Parliament on 15 November 1977, of which South Africa was the subject, Mr. Uwe Jensen, Danish MP (Danish Progressive Party), having visited South Africa, had this to say:

"Mr. President, firstly I want to point out that I don't sympathize with apartheid and racism — there can be no doubt about the immoral and indefensible aspects of that kind of domestic political disposition — and, therefore, I entirely agree with what Lord Reay has said. However, every country must be free to contemplate and determine their position in accordance with their own presuppositions.

"Therefore I ask: 'Is it the task of the Community to impose political measures against a trading partner?' This is what is being voiced in the enquiry before us. It is a question of principle as to how the Community has imagined that co-ordinating action should be implemented in the foreign policy field. Are the consequences of such action clearly understood by everybody?

"In discussing South Africa one does not talk about colonialism in a normal sense — here it is a matter of a population group which is born and bred in the country it defends. Even if the colour of the skin is different, it consists of Africans.

"It is regrettable that it is not acceptable Western politics to maintain and further worldwide free trade, but that considerations must be taken to the 'right people' with the 'right options' and the 'right' party books.

"The motto for the European Parliament's foreign policy must be: strengthen relations with nations which are friendly towards us and participate in the Free World's work to preserve the greatest possible number of countries against Communist suppression. For what are Moscow's and Cuba's plans other than dangerous new colonial intentions to lead us towards a complete dominance by the Communist system, which has failed so completely in all places where it has been tested?

"Do we have any assurance that the majority of the African States which we support, will live up to our interpretation of democracy? I have great sympathy with all suppressed peoples around the world, I would wish that all countries were good democracies with all the opportunities which this entails, and I wish that everybody had one vote and each one vote counted equally. But, unfortunately, this exists only in a very small part of the world, i.e. the Free World. In South Africa the conditions in many ways are better than in other countries. Though progressing somewhat slowly, developments (in the right directions) are taking place.

"The Community should not interfere in the internal affairs of other countries. We should not condemn and make ourselves the judges because we are not the appointed policemen of the world. On the other hand we ought to enter into a dialogue with all the countries in the world and communicate with them. Most of all, before anybody is entitled to condemn, he should make himself thoroughly acquainted with the problems, and I do not think this is always done.

"It appears that the policies of certain member-States cause controversy within the Community and my advice therefore must be that the Community conducts an open, but neutral foreign policy and avoids a European Socialism which uncritically woos African Communism."

CHAPTER 13

African Residential Areas or Townships

I VISITED 17 African, Coloured and Malay residential areas in Cape Town, Johannesburg (including Soweto), South-West Africa and Rhodesia. In Cape Town, I had an interview at the Coloured Representative Council Chambers, Bellville, with the Chief Whip of the Labour Party of the Coloured Representative Council and Chairman of the Investigating Committee relating to welfare institutions. I had lunch at a Coloured Club with members of the coloured community and found that they were only too well aware of the relentless advance of the Russian-dominated Communist threat coming down from the North, and circumventing them at sea, and equally aware of the internal threat of subversion and violence. There is no doubt in my mind that the Coloured community realise the dangers ahead and that their destiny lies with the Whites. But they would like to move faster, namely with the formation of a multi-racial government without first having to undergo the experience of separate governments — White, Coloured and Indian.

The new enormous Coloured Housing Project at Mitchells Plain, Cape Town, and its plans for development is a remarkable achievement by any standards and should be the first port of call by those who criticise South Africa for lack of progress. This housing project, as well as the 16 African residential areas that I inspected in Johannesburg, South West Africa and Rhodesia, would put to shame the council estates, high block housing complexes, lack of playing fields, shabby terraced houses, slums, ghetto areas and the squalid rubble-strewn back streets of Liverpool, Glasgow, the East End of London etc., and the flimsy houses so many pensioners live in. The same goes for America and Western Europe. As for India, Pakistan, the Far East and the Middle East some of the deplorable conditions there would not be tolerated in South Africa, South-West Africa and Rhodesia.

The townships are served by efficient and cheap public transport including external buses over long distances to the tribal areas. These well developed urban areas include water-borne sewerage, electricity, water, street lighting, refuse removal, shops, supermarkets, banks, schools, public halls, cinemas, clubs, beer gardens, swimming pools, free libraries, modern stadiums and sports grounds catering for all forms of sport, children's playgrounds and tennis courts. The Health department operates infectious diseases hospitals, maternity centres, out-patients clinics and children's day-care centres.

There is a continuing programme of development including home ownership as well as rented accommodation and there are modern well equipped hostels for single men and single girls.

There are no high-block concrete monstrosities as in Britain, but detached bungalow-type buildings, each with its own small garden. The middle-class Africans live in bungalows far superior to many housing estates in England.

Business opportunities in the townships are reserved strictly for Africans and Coloureds and this protection from the competition of large sophisticated White owned concerns has contributed to the emergence of a rapidly growing middle and upper class, some of whom live in suburbs where the average value of a house is £20,000 sterling.

An important source of revenue is derived from the profits on liquor sales within the townships. Municipalities have their own modern breweries which produce a highly nutritious traditional type African beer, and by law the entire profits must be ploughed back into these areas in the form of amenities and subsidies. Further revenue is raised by a levy on employers of Africans in the lower income group. This fund is used for housing and for subsidizing local bus transport, considered to be the cheapest in the world.

In Rhodesia, the policy is that large townships shall be administered entirely by Africans and Coloureds and have their own advisory boards, members of which will be elected by the normal democratic voting procedure. Board meetings will be held monthly and apart from the elected members will be attended by the Director of African Administration and representatives of the City Council. This system will ensure that residents have a definite say in the running of their affairs and will be an invaluable means of two way communication.

In South Africa, I spent a whole morning with Mr. George Thabe who is the Black Chairman of the Community Council of the Vaal Triangle near Johannesburg of 200,000 Africans and covering six townships, all of which I inspected with him. I had lunch with him and his Black colleagues. The South African Government's policy is to grant full autonomy to each black township with the creation of community councils, all elected on non-ethnic lines and with full legislative powers. Within four months of his Council's existence, Mr. George Thabe had taken over his area's capital and expenditure budget.

Mr. Thabe attributes much of his success to Dr. Connie Mulder, Minister of Plural Relations and Administration, who has given great impetus to settling urban Black issues. Now that Mr. Thabe's Council has demonstrated that it can work effectively with legislative powers, other urban Black townships are showing a new interest. This includes nearby Soweto, South Africa's largest black township complex. I had lunch with Dr. Nthato Motlana, the black leader of Soweto's self-appointed Committee of Ten. He and Dr. Connie Mulder had yet to meet when I left South Africa towards the end of May, but having talked to both of them I am convinced that black Africans and White Africans can each exist peacefully as long as each is allowed to demand its rights, and, above all, as long as the nations of the West stop interfering in the internal affairs of a country which in many respects is being run far better than their own. Dr. Mulder is on the move and in his own words: "I'm not trying to build an empire, I am breaking down an empire".

Mr. George Thabe has proclaimed that the most significant aspect of the establishment of the Community Council is its tangible recognition of the existence of the urban Black citizens emerging as a middle class in White areas with their own set of values and desires which are quite different from those of Homeland Blacks. He has stated that the permanence of this group has been recognised and they have now achieved their civic rights. This, he firmly believes, "represents a significant change in Government policy and the outside world should take note of it."

CHAPTER 14

What Right do the Whites in South Africa Have to Decide the Future of South Africa?

THE question generally flung at South Africans is "What right do you Whites in South Africa have to decide the future of South Africa? You are a minority and you are trying to dictate the future of 18 million Africans".

The size of this minority is 4.8 million South African Whites — equivalent to the population of Finland — and they are not colonialists.

What is forgotten is that the White people of South Africa are not merely a conglomeration of individuals, of settlers who went there to get rich quickly and then to retire to their home across the seas. The White people of South Africa are a nation. The Afrikaners are a 2.6 million "White tribe" of Africa, whose Dutch forefathers first landed in Cape Town in 1652. They brought from Europe a culture different from any that existed before in their sub-continent. For more than 300 years they have maintained their life-style against all odds. They have every attribute of nationhood — and the Afrikaner's was, by a long way, the first of Africa's nationalisms.

Their language is the only one of which the very name pays tribute to the continent in which it was conceived and nurtured, and the White Africans are the only people of all the European migrants to the four corners of the earth to establish their own language. History has conferred the right to live in South Africa, not only on White individuals, but on the White nation that has grown up there.

When their ancestors, the pioneers of the White nation of South Africa, planted their civilisation in the shadow of Table Mountain in the middle of the 17th centry, the nearest Black settlements were 860 kilometres away to the north and 1,600 kilometres away to the east, the distance between London and Hamburg and London and Rome respectively. The Whites founded their Mother City at the tip of the African continent when New York was still a small Dutch settlement called New Amsterdam. At one time there were nearly as many White people in the Cape of Good Hope as in Canada. When the British occupied the Cape in the early 19th century, there were twice as many Whites in South

Africa as in Australia, and Cape Town was then a large town that could be compared with Sydney.

This is why the Afrikaners have as much right to live in and express opinions about Africa as any Black Africans, or as any Australian in Australia.

After more than three centuries in South Africa, they have as much right to claim it as their own true home as Canadians have to claim Ontario.

The world conveniently forgets that the Afrikaners, now portrayed as a merciless persecutor of a Black majority, have themselves had to endure a struggle against oppression for 300 years. During the 17th and 18th centuries, while the Cape colony was under the control of the Dutch East India Company, the earlier settlers were denied land rights and subjected to fines for such offences as allowing their cattle to stray.

The British, who seized the colony in 1795, were equally harsh overlords who regarded the Afrikaners as obstinate and treated them as inferiors. In the mid-1830s thousands of settlers fled British rule by migrating into the interior in ox-drawn wagons. The discovery of gold in the Transvaal in 1886 led to an invasion of White English-speaking settlers and eventually to the defeat of the Afrikaners in the hard-fought Boer-War of 1899-1902.

After the Boer War, the Afrikaners, isolated in the heartland, became second class citizens in what they regarded as their own country. Their solution was to take refuge in and inspiration from their churches and societies which knit the community together and they waited for the time when political power would be theirs.

That day came in 1948 when their National Party defeated the United Party founded by Jan Smuts.

CHAPTER 15

Double Standards

THE main lesson of my visits which is indelibly imprinted on my mind is the highly irresponsible, distorted and hostile propaganda constantly disseminated by the world's media, as well as by many politicians of all political leanings, on the true implications of ultimate majority Black rule, about which there is such crass ignorance. Bitter experience elsewhere in Africa has shown that one man, one vote, amounts to one vote, once only, followed by one dictator and a bloodbath.

Western statesmen, politicians, the media and the United Nations are such sanctimonious hypocrites that they conveniently disregard the fact that no such thing as "one man one vote" and "majority rule" exists in Soviet Russia and Red China. Nor does it exist in the one-man dictatorships of Angola, Zambia, Uganda, Malawi, Mozambique and Tanzania. Nor does it exist in Libya, Haiti, Cuba, Vietnam, Laos or Cambodia. It does not exist in Yugoslavia. It certainly does not exist in Poland, Hungary, East Germany, Czechoslovakia, or any of the other captive nations. For that matter it does not exist in Northern Ireland.

At present there **is** a parliamentary government in South Africa and it has a White electorate. Chief Sebe himself, leader of the Ciskei, has stated categorically that to lump all the Black races (Zulus, Xhosas, Tawanas etc.) under the category of "one Black people" is as illogical as to lump England, France, Germany and Russia together as "one people" because they all happen to be white.

These Black nations are **separate** peoples, and wish to remain so. Numerically the Whites are second in the list. As the Zulus and Xhosas are basically rural people, they would not have the faintest idea how to run a country like South Africa. That is why plans are well advanced for them to have their own homelands to govern independently.

The term "South Africa" is now becoming a misnomer, except in a generic sense such as "Europe". There are to be separate names for the Black States, such as Transkei, so perhaps a new name should be found for the areas which are to be White.

The mixture of tribes and races have very little in common because they have different standards, different codes and are at different stages of development. Therefore it makes it quite unrealistic to expect such a plural society to live together in the same geographical area in a free relationship of amity and co-operation. The Afrikaners are vastly the stronger in every way — economically, culturally and militarily. They see no reason or justice why they should accept a subordinate role.

The definition of apartheid is "separateness", meaning that South Africa's 4.8 million whites, 18.6 million blacks, 2.5 million mixed-blood Coloured and 750,000 Asians are to proceed along separate lines of development.

While I personally cannot support apartheid as long as it means racial discrimination, I can see the need for racial differentiation.

For the Blacks, separate development at present means the establishment of nine **independent** Black homelands. The first homeland to be granted its independence, Transkei, celebrated its first anniversary in October last year. In December, a second homeland, Bophuthatswana, officially became independent, and three more are to follow within the next two years.

Again and again one hears the accusation against the South African Government that the Blacks who represent no less than 70 per cent of South Africa's population are being given only 13 per cent of the country for their homelands. What are the true facts?

The Homelands have a relatively high carrying capacity because they are blessed with an average rainfall and climate that are far more favourable than that in the rest of South Africa. The Homelands of the Eastern Cape, Natal and the North-Eastern Transvaal all fall in high rainfall areas. About 75 per cent of the Black Homelands receive in excess of 500 mm of rain a year — while only 35 percent of South Africa as a whole is blessed with such a high rainfall figure. According to a very general climatic classification, 27 per cent of South Africa as a whole has an arid climate — and of this 27 per cent only half a per cent is found in the Black Homelands. It is estimated that Transkei — the first of the Homelands to achieve independence — has the potential to produce more than three million tons of maize, yet in the 1972/73 season the actual production was 0.1 million tons, one-thirtieth of the potential. Bophuthatswana grows only eight per cent of the cash crop products she is capable of producing. In 1970, the average production of maize, the staple food of most of the people living in the Homelands, was 2,300 kg per ha on White farms in the highveld. By comparison the average yield in Bophuthatswana was just over 300 kg per ha, in Lebowa 164 kg and in Venda a mere 64 kg.

These figures make nonsense of the claim that the Black Homelands do not have sufficient land to carry their populations. Those who make the claim conveniently ignore the historical fact that, firstly, the land owned by the White nation in South Africa is land which was legitimately settled by the Whites, and secondly, the traditional Homelands of the Black nations of South Africa include the three independent states of Botswana, Lesotho and Swaziland. Prior to the estabilshment of the Union of South Africa in 1910, this concept of a Greater South Africa was generally acknowledged and the Act of Union passed by the British Parliament stipulated the intention of the British legislators that Botswana, Lesotho and Swaziland should ultimately be incorporated in South Africa. In the event, this was not to be, but, if the historical reality of Greater South Africa is accepted, then the Black nations own about 45 per cent of South Africa and not 13.7 per cent, the figure usually used in political speeches.

Apart from the carrying capacity of the Black Homelands where the potential is outstanding, it is also unscientific in the extreme to aver that size is a decisive factor in respect of the population a country can carry. This is indicated by the case of Botswana, which is about 21 times the size of Lesotho but is having trouble in providing a living for its population which is about half the size of that of Lesotho.

Both Transkei and Bophuthatswana are larger than a European country such as Belgium yet Belgium carries five times the population of Transkei and ten times that of Bophuthatswana.

The proposed new constitution for the three racial groups, Whites, Coloureds, and Asians, entails the creation of three community Assemblies, each of which will have the same functions and powers. At the centre will be the Council of Cabinets, with a membership of six White Ministers, three Coloured Ministers and two Asian Ministers. The State President will be elected for a five-year term by an electoral college.

Boycotts, sanctions the threat of violence and revolution and other isolationist tactics will not bring White South Africa to its knees and will certainly not advance the cause of Black South Africa. The greater the pressures exerted on them, the stronger will their nationalism and national pride grow. If international pressure was designed to moderate the politics of Mr. Vorster and weaken his National Party's hold on South Africa, it will have precisely the opposite effect. Even Opposition leaders have supported Mr. Vorster in speaking out against foreign influence and interference in the country's internal affairs.

The Afrikaners' national survival is at stake and the world would be well advised to realise that South Africans will fight to the last man to retain the identity and all that they have built up over the centuries.

It would be fatal to try and do a "Rhodesia" on South Africa. They will fight for their identity and they mean to retain it. South

Africa can produce the very best in the world and they have the finest academic and business brains on earth.

The French in Algeria, or the Portuguese when they abandoned Angola to its fate, knew that they could return to their country of origin. But the Afrikaners have nowhere to go, because they have no ties to a European motherland. Feeling threatened there is no doubt that they intend to fight tooth and nail for their survival.

My meeting with Professor Chris Barnard was all too short, but a great deal of what he said is included in his book **South Africa: Sharp Dissection,** a copy of which he gave me.

Accordingly, I have taken the poetic licence of quoting liberally from his book, particularly under the section — 'What Right do the Whites in South Africa have to Decide the Future of South Africa?'.

I believe Professor Barnard has been very fair in his well-argued book. He has not hesitated to criticise his country where criticism is merited and he has suggested sensible political reforms. It is a revealing book that merits careful study by us all. Dr. Barnard should go into politics, unlike Dr. Owen who should go back to medicine.

CHAPTER 16

Subversion is rife in South Africa

WHAT Mr. Vorster has done in South Africa in outlawing Black consciousness organisations; banning or restricting a number of Black and White leaders and stopping publication of several newspapers, was forced on him by threats of violence, sedition and subversion, and social unrest.

South Africa is now seriously threatened by the insidious and dangerous subversive form of warfare being waged by the forces of International Communism, and it is in the front line of this Third World War.

Waiting in the wings is the Soviet Union, whose method of Communist advance and expansion is to undermine a nation and capture it from within through revolutionary war by proxy. Its strategists intend to exploit differences between the various races; encourage the differences to widen through propaganda and violent actions, then start to control the various groups — by now fighting each other — and finally take over the group that becomes dominant. South Africa is but a pawn in the Soviet global power struggle. The penalty for failure to meet this challenge — by cringing in the face of Russia's and the West's big stick and slinking away — would be to transform the whole of South Africa into a devastated wasteland, leaving the vacuum to be filled by the Soviets.

Let those states in Africa who are giving launching pads to the Soviet Union's revolutionary war by proxy know, and let the Western world also know, that South Africa has no intention of committing national suicide.

Prime Minister Vorster has declared war to the death against a Marxist revolutionary movement which poses a lethal threat to his country. In doing so, he has cracked down ruthlessly on known and potential subversive individuals, newspapers and organisations — organisations with laudable names which were a smokescreen for their undermining activities. Two later chapters in this book entitled 'The Secret US War Against South Africa' and 'The links of Terror' provide ample justification for Mr. Vorster's crackdown.

If only he had taken the country into his confidence and revealed the brutal nature of the threat, he would have avoided the universal outcry of condemnation. People will support a cause if they are told the truth, however brutal that truth may be.

Events have generally proved him to be right in the past and no doubt they will prove him to be right again.

Disturbances, most of them involving Black students, are becoming endemic in South Africa. To take but one example, on 29 October, there were widespread though sporadic incidents of arson, stone-throwing, petrol bombing and intimidation by masked, marauding gangs of youths. Large numbers of agitators, among them leaders of the recent unrest, were arrested in a second nationwide swoop. Mr. Kruger, Minister of Justice, Police and Prisons, had pamphlets and other information in his possession which proved that subversive elements were busy urging civil disobedience and creating a climate of internal revolution. He had complete knowledge of the political agitators and how they were operating to promote unrest. In addition, his mailbag contained numerous letters from Black people themselves urging him to stop the disruption of life in the African townships.

In September, the Police Minister disclosed that large quantities of arms had been unloaded at the Mozambique port of Nacala for guerillas who were waiting to infiltrate South Africa. Earlier security forces said they had uncovered a massive terrorist plan to invade South Africa and had smashed urban terrorist bases on the Gold Reef and near Durban, seizing caches of Russian arms.

A further urban guerilla warfare group was discovered in Durban in May 1978.

South Africa has dismayed its friends in the West by banning certain newspapers which have been critical of the government. Of course, had the government been Black, there would have been no criticism. The trouble with South Africa is that the ruling tribe is White and on the international stage, Black is beautiful.

The Press has done untold harm to the racial situation in South Africa — and its image abroad — by exploiting the freedom of the Press so blatantly that a confrontation between the government and the Press was inevitable. The Press has had freedom of expression but it has not accepted the responsibility that this implies.

Far from reporting events and news accurately, it had been creating, with the sole purpose of selling its newspapers, issues that concentrated on the sensational. Always on the prowl for bad news, the Press, and the media as a whole, not only in South Africa but throughout the world, has done more harm to race relations than any other pressure group.

In South Africa, the Leftists control many of the major newspapers, therefore much of the news has had a slanted left wing bias, serving up the news deceitfully in the guise of truth. The Press had become a self-appointed opposition movement and law unto itself. It has assumed an opinon-making function out of all proportion to its qualifications or standing in the community.

Newspapers were influencing whole communities of whom they were not even representative. Instead of being purveyors of the news, it is they who were making the news and moulding public opinion, with the result that the public was exposed daily to attempts to influence their thinking on crucial issues. The motto of the news barons in South Africa seemed to be "Indoctrinate the world and the world can be made to go in your directions."

Every English-language newspaper in South Africa, with one solitary exception, has been hostile to the Government. In a Black territory with Black majority rule, no such opposition would be permitted, whether spoken or written.

The World, a newspaper published by the mainly White-owned Argus Group, incurred the wrath of Mr. Kruger for an editorial in which it said:

". . . . it was reasonably happy with the methods of the Soweto students".

Kruger described these methods as "arson, throwing stones, boycotting schools, marching in the streets and intimidating workers" and added, "one does not need a pamphlet to incite against law and order if you have a newspaper to do it for you."

The Chinese knew all about subversion in 500 BC when they said:

"Greatest art is to break the enemies opposition without a fight on the battlefield. The direct art of war is only needed on the battlefield, but a true victory and a lasting one can only be one by indirect and subversive methods and so corrupt all that is good in the enemy country.

"Get the ruling classes mixed in criminal or dishonest deals; undermine their position and good name; bring shame on them in the minds of the citizenry and use the lowest and foulest persons; disturb by all available means the work of Government; spread dishonesty and quarrel among the citizens of the enemy country; push the young against their elders. Destroy with all manner of means the enemies armaments, his supplies and the ordinary orderly functioning of his armies. Abase his traditions and his religious faith. Be generous with offers — with presents so as to be able to buy intelligence and accomplices. Place your secret agents everywhere — do not economise money and promises in this work — you will get great return."

There are forces in South Africa which are using the explosive situation to further their own causes. They have no real concern for the welfare of the Blacks but they are posing as such because this suits their strategy for the overthrow of the government. This happens all over the world, that through chaos, unrest, violence and destruction, these forces are trying to create a revolution.

This is why they are boycotting South Africa, because to remove credit, to discourage investments in South Africa, will remove South Africa's ability to build up its infrastructure — which in turn creates joblessness and violence.

There are so many well-meaning dopes who allow themselves to be sidetracked by leftist pressure groups and the World Council of Churches.

Such things as boycotts create misery for South Africa's Blacks, as they become the first victims. The world is treating South Africa in a most unfair manner because the White community in South Africa is much more concerned about the fate of the non-whites than any of those hypocritical world reformers would have us believe.

Whatever South Africa does is bad in their eyes. I am nevertheless convinced that the future of the non-Whites in a peacefully developing South Africa would be much better guaranteed than if the outside world had its way.

Those who seek to isolate South Africa through boycotts or threaten them with violence and revolution and intend to push South Africa to the brink, must not be surprised if their extremist threat to the very existence of the South African society evokes the ultimate defence as made possible by its **nuclear capacity.** It behoves the world to recognise this and take heed.

The irony of it all is that there is more racial discrimination, more denial of basic human rights and more dictatorship in Black Africa than there has ever been in South Africa or Rhodesia. Only six of the 48 Black and Arab States are democracies; but even there "democracy" has taken on a meaning far removed from the original. For the rest, there is military and civil dictatorship, generally tyrannical, brutal and often totalitarian and intolerant.

CHAPTER 17

Precisely Who is this Man Donald Woods Strutting the World Stage?

MR. Donald James Woods was born in the village of Elliottdale in Transkei on 15 November 1933. The Woods family has lived in the Eastern Cape since early 1820 Settler days. His eldest brother, Mr. Harland Woods, still runs the store at Hobeni in Transkei where the Woods family has been trading since 1916.

Donald, the extrovert of the family, went to Christian Brothers College in Kimberley, where he gained a second-class matric, and then went on to study law at the University of Cape Town.

He was both a good sportsman and active in student politics. He became a Nuffield cricketer and, later, an honorary vice-president of NUSAS.

He joined the **Daily Dispatch** as a junior reporter in 1957. A year later he stood for Parliament as the Union Federal Party candidate for East London North against Mr. Clive van Ryneveld, cricketer and former United Party MP. Mr. Woods gained 728 votes and lost his deposit.

His political hopes dampened, he resigned from **The Dispatch** and went overseas to work as a journalist in Britain, Canada and the US. He once played a piano in a London cocktail bar to earn a living.

In 1960, he returned to **The Dispatch** where, after working as political correspondent, columnist and sub-editor, he was appointed assistant editor in June 1964, and **The Dispatch's** ninth editor in February 1965. He was 31 years old at the time, South Africa's youngest editor.

Mr. Woods is married to the former Wendy Bruce, a professional concert pianist and, before the family's much-publicised dash from South Africa, an enthusiastic member of the Black Sash. They have three sons and two daughters.

As a Cape magazine writer pointed out, his trappings as editor of **The Dispatch** did not exactly conform with the projected Woods image.

It was claimed he was the highest-paid editor in the country. Shortly after his "escape" one British paper disclosed that, together with the fees from syndicated columns in **The Observer** and elsewhere. his annual income was R33,000 a year.

His home was large and luxurious. He bought it for R30,000 in 1970 but, after extensive alterations, sold it to **The Dispatch** for R65,000 a few years later, the transfer going through on 2 June, 1976. He rented it thereafter at R300 a month. His car was a Mercedes 350.

Colleagues say that he was very much the dilettante editor.

All those who have worked with him describe him as "affable, terribly easy-going, always jolly and laughing." There is no doubt, however, that he did enjoy and frequently set out to create controversy.

He also engaged in occasional feuds which could become quite fearsome in their intensity.

One former colleague recalls: "Nothing delighted him more than hassles. For a long time he hounded poor Mr. Hans Abrahan, the former Commissioner-General of Transkei, writing the most virulent editorials about him.

"Sometimes he could be downright childish. Some years ago he had a most tremendous row with a Provincial Councillor. This man had made some remarks in the Cape Provincial Council about the **Daily Dispatch.**

"Donald wrote an editorial challenging him to repeat his statement outside. The PC didn't. Then Donald wrote an editorial saying this PC was a 'bangbroek'. Not only that, but he gave an instruction to all staff that this man should be referred to as 'Bangbroek' in any articles published about him."

Mr. Donald Woods once demanded an apology and R1,000 from a Durban man for allegedly accusing his newspaper of being "communist".

Retired Durban businessman Mr. Noel Jonson said on 26 January how he had written a letter to Mr. Woods at the **Daily Dispatch** about four years ago.

"Concerning multiracialism, I asked him if his newspaper went as far to support multiracial sex. He answered 'yes'.

"At the same time a Natal newspaper published a cartoon showing a booted Russian soldier stepping from Mauritius to South Africa.

"I think it was at a time when Russia was given landing rights in Mauritius or something.

"Well, I changed the cartoon slightly to have the soldier stepping into the country from the South African English Press.

"I had a few of these duplicated and sent them to editors of all the English newspapers.

"Mr. Woods was the only one to react.

"He sent me a letter demanding a registered letter of apology and R1,000 from me for accusing his newspaper of being communist.

"I wrote back to ask what he was getting at and he replied that I should see my lawyer and he would explain it to me.

"Luckily, at the same time, Britain had offered him an all-expenses-paid trip overseas and he forgot about me."

A great many South Africans, particularly English-speakers, still tend to regard Mr. Woods as a moderate and a near-saint. Now one is able to gain a much sharper picture of the man proclaiming himself the "arch-enemy" of the South African Government.

That attitude, of course, is not exactly new. Some years ago Mr. Woods recalled in a private conversation that he had once been asked how he would react if the South African Government should take restrictive action against him. His reply, he said, was that if this happened, he would dedicate his life to closing South Africa off in every country where there is a South African Embassy".

That was a forceful enough response. And all the indications are that there has been an even further hardening in his attitudes since, no matter who suffers.

Speaking to newsmen in Lusaka, on his way to London after the family had skipped out of South Africa, his wife, Mrs. Wendy Woods, said threateningly: "The South African Government has not heard the last of us".

To ram the message home, she said she and her husband proposed "doing all in their power to bring about the downfall of the South African Government."

Simultaneously, Mr. Stanley Uys, writing in London, also had much to say about the forthcoming Woods campaign. While there was a danger that Mr. Woods might prove to be a three-month wonder, he said, he would still in that time succeed in blazing a trail over TV screens, the radio waves, in the columns of newspapers and magazines, in books and in lecture halls."

According to the usually well-informed Mr. Uys, Mr. Woods plans to "campaign internationally for the release of Percy Qoboza," to seek to have the Minister of Justice, Mr. Jimmy Kruger, "declared an international criminal unless he releases all detainees by a certain date", and to do his utmost "to alert the West to the dangers of not applying full pressures on South Africa."

Mr. Woods broke his first lance in this new international onslaught on his home country when he joined forces with the passionately anti-South African human rights organisation Amnesty International, in the launching of its 105-page "special report" on South African political prisoners in London in January this year. AI was reported to be "delighted" with the catch.

Some members of the Fleet Street Press took an apparently carping attitude towards Mr. Woods. They said it would be a graceful gesture on his part if he agreed to turn all the profits of his book on Steve Biko, published in April, over to the dead man's family. His reply, if any, was not published.

Things are likely to prove much brighter for him in the US. Here, it is said, there is "phenomenal interest" in him on the part of the liberal Left, who clearly intended using him up to the hilt in their onslaughts on South Africa.

The fanatically anti-South African Nigerian Ambassador to the UN, Mr. Leslie Harriman, acting in his capacity as chairman of the Special Committee against Apartheid, was quick to invite Mr. Woods to address the UN.

According to UN sources in New York, there was rejoicing in the UN, especially among OAU delegates, that they now had such a powerful assistant in their prolonged but tireless efforts to smash the Republic. Already Mr. Woods has been fawned over by Prime Minister Chief Jonathan in Lesotho, and President Kenneth Kaunda in Zambia. He received the full treatment when he arrived at the world body to address it on the land he so recently left.

Mr. Woods also accepted an invitation to address the extremely active, highly dangerous Congressional Ad Hoc Committee on South Africa. Formed after the death of Steve Biko, the committee comprises 30 US Congressmen, nearly all radicals and all united in their desire to injure South Africa as much as possible.

The tragedy of all this — both for Mr. Woods and for South Africa — is that his campaign comes at what is almost certainly the most critical point in South Africa's history.

Writing in the US journal **The Nation,** in the 12 November, 1977 issue, Dr. Immanuel Wallerstein, listed as a "Distinguished Professor of Sociology at the State University of New York at Binghampton and a former president of the African Studies Association" had this to say:

"In the South African context . . . the US Administration is repeating all the 'preparations' made under Eisenhower and Kennedy for an involvement in Vietnam, particularly the ideology of 'liberal interventionism'.

"The 'aid' programmes are being drafted, the agents being planted all over the place, the pressures felt in Congress and the Foundations and the media to 'co-operate' — all in the name of African majority rule for the 'good' of the African movements, whether they want it or not".

Dr. Wallerstein says the situation being built up in Southern Africa is potentially ten times more dangerous than in Vietnam. In Vietnam, he says, the US administration "did it for political purposes." In South Africa it is for political-economic motives, the "exploitation of Southern Africa's vast mineral wealth."

This then is the appallingly dangerous climate in which Mr.

Woods will be operating — a climate in which South Africa's most dedicated enemies will make every conceivable effort to use him as a tool against his own motherland.

Mr. Woods says he intends aligning himself with the UN thrust for economic sanctions against South Africa.

One wonders if he fully understands the implications of what such a campaign would mean to South African Black workers, or if he has asked himself who would suffer first in such an attack.

Mr. Woods would do well to study these questions very carefully before being caught up irrevocably in the UN maelstrom of hate against South Africa.

On 26 January, Mr. Donald Woods addressed the Anti-Apartheid Committee of the UN.

Although Mr. Woods was banned on 19 October last year under Section 10 of the Internal Security Act, it is important to realise that he is no Communist.

He has never been a member of the Communist Party or any recognised anti-South African body. Politically, he is not even a radical.

On the other hand, he is a very good writer, a good Roman Catholic, who goes to church regularly, a good family man and, in his own way, a man with a deep love of South Africa, even though his political opinoins obviously do not coincide with those of the present Government. He is also good-looking and a born showman.

It is all these facts which made his friends (and he still has many) hold their breath in dread over his UN performance.

Britain's sophisticated BBC-ITV, old hands in propaganda, went to much trouble to present the former East London editor as a "moderate, fair-minded, objective critic of the South African Government — a traditional Cape liberal."

Quite obviously, the BBC wanted to preserve Mr. Woods' credibility. Featured as "moderate, fair-minded and objective," he would prove a potent weapon against South Africa in the circles in which it counted most.

But to join forces with the Afro-Asian militants of the UN Anti-Apartheid Committee is another matter completely. Most Western nations in the UN regard this group as a nuisance and an embarrassment.

It was the AAC which last year arranged the five-day, 60-nation meeting in Lagos aimed at planning Pretoria's annihilation and declaring South Africa an "outlaw" state — outside the protection of international law.

AAC members have never made the slightest secret of the fact that they wish to destroy South Africa by violence. Currently they are campaigning for the Republic's "total isolation, socially, politically, economically, culturally and diplomatically," plus cutting of sports ties of all kinds.

One must, therefore, ask: Is Mr. Woods fully aware of the lengths to which this group and its agents are prepared to go in their efforts to smash South Africa?

As an ordinary South African liberal, is he likely to make much impact on such extremists?

Certainly, they are not interested in "moderate, fair-minded, objective critics of South Africa". They want blood. Someone in the fist-shaking, gun-slinging image of the PLO's Yassar Arafat is more their line.

If Mr. Woods remains even semi-reasonable, they are going to write him off as just another White liberal. But if he provides them with what they want, if he throws all caution to the winds, then he joins the ranks of Miriam Makeba, Michael Scott and similar political widows. His future then will be bleak indeed.

Mr. Woods could find that he has slipped his neck into a noose from which there is no escape — which can be tightened as and when the miltants feel like it. One can only hope that he still has an option.

With the usual drama that seemed to surround everything associated with Mr. Donald Woods, his banning order was served on him at Jan Smuts Airport on 19 October last year, as he was on his way to the US for a command performance before the anti-South African African-American Institute.

By this time, he had, by his involvement in political propaganda and political organisations, forfeited much of his journalistic credibility.

Indeed — and by a remarkable coincidence — **The Friend** in Bloemfontein had announced only hours before the banning order was served that it intended dropping its weekly column written by Mr. Woods.

A statement issued by the paper said: "This decision has been taken regretfully as a result of the closeness of Mr. Woods' personal involvement in a number of running battles with political and other leaders, an involvement which we feel must affect his status as an independent, objective, from-the-sidelines observer of current trends.

"This personal involvement is increasingly becoming more appropriately the subject of straight news reports rather than of a weekly column.

"While we believe that part of a newspaper's function is to provide thought provoking opposing points of view which do not necessarily coincide with those of the newspapers, we feel that Mr. Woods' column in present circumstances lays itself open to the charge that it could be used as a vehicle for personal campaigning."

It was a carefully worded statement, and understandably so. While Mr. Woods himself was always quick with active and caustic comment, he belonged to the fraternity which believes you can hand it out but must not get it back. Over the years he had shown an astonishing predeliction for law suits, even to the point of threatening to sue the Prime Minister himself.

However, by now it was widely known, both in South Africa and overseas, that Mr. Woods was indeed heavily involved in a personal campaign, both for the Black Consciousness Movement and for Black majority rule. This he did, though he was clearly aware of the tremendous dangers inherent in the Black militant movements.

Delivering the 1973 Edgar Brookes lecture at Natal University, he said: "Let us not be naive. We know enough about the Bram Fischer story and of the Rivonia plot and from other straws in the wind to be able to accept the probability that right now there is somewhere in South Africa some ruthless body of men with violent intentions which have nothing to do with liberty and democracy."

Mr. Woods has always insisted, in season and out, that the BCM, like its "father", his friend Steve Biko, was pro-western, an organisation of peace and moderation.

This is not quite the picture of the new Black movements he portrayed in an article appearing in the last quarterly edition of the Anglo-American journal, **Optima,** in 1975.

In this, he quotes an American political analyst, a recent visitor to Transkei. This man, he said, was astonished to discover so many militant young Blacks who took no part in formal homeland politics but who were highly radical, "Either Maoist or Leninist, and whose ideals included Che Guevara and even Idi Amin, 'because he kicked the White man' around in Uganda."

Mr. Woods said the masses in the townships "may not seem to have leaders, but leaders there are who are generally dedicated activists, young, articulate, tough, militant and radical to the point of being convinced doctrinaire socialists.

"They undoubtedly would be members of the PAC-ANC were these bodies not banned. Many of them, if they were not personally banned, were restricted under various security laws or closely watched by the Security Police.

"They follow a hardline and have backed the MPLA movement in Angola and Frelimo in Mozambique.

"They accuse the Matanzimas and Buthelezis of 'entrism' of entering the apartheid process by working within the separate development system and thereby giving it credibility among many Blacks.

"And they seem to be winning increasing support in the ranks of Black support in the ranks of Black youth throughout South Africa in what appears to be the real struggle for Black Power — the radicals against the Homeland leader.

"From time to time their attitudes are discernible in the words of spokesmen of Black movements, including the South African Students Organisation and the Black Peoples' Convention.

"Because they operate unobtrusively and keep a generally low profile, most South Africans have astonishingly little knowledge of these shadowy leaders".

Mr. Woods was then fully aware of the revolutionary threat building up in South Africa, but by now he was firmly dedicated to the ideal of Black majority rule in South Africa. In October 1976, he told a Cape Town journalist that "within five years" South Africa would have a Black Prime Minister and a Black cabinet, except for the Ministers of Police, Defence and Interior.

He apparently still believes in this schedule. On 13 November 1977, Seymour Topping of the **New York Times Magazine** quoted Mr. Woods as predicting that South Africa "will have Black majority rule within four years".

Mr. Woods had no illusions about what this would mean for the Whites. He was well aware that Black nationalist movements have made all possible use of White libreals to gain their ends — and then booted them out; that throughout Africa, with the exception of Kenya and Malawi, there are very few examples of Black nationalists cherishing their White liberal friends once uhuru has been achieved.

In various discussions with BCM officials, he said he often thought of his own role in "the thing" and that it was his feeling "there will probably be no place in South Africa for anyone who is White".

Referring to the National Party, he said: "The important thing is that these bastards must be finished off and what happens afterwards is another problem". He said "if this means he has to end up in California or somewhere, it will be just too bad".

CHAPTER 18

The World Council of Churches

"LOVE thy neighbour". As long ago as 1973 this Christian injunction was given a selective interpretation by the World Council of Churches. In Geneva, the council's committee against racialism approved the expenditure of £40,650 a year on aiding Portguese Army deserters. Already the World Council of Churches had won a reputation for supporting Black African terrorist organisations such as Frelimo — yet it professed to be against racialism.

For a full account of the Marxist penetration of the WCC I recommend Bernard Smith's **The Fraudulent Gospel.**[1]

In August, 1973 a British national newspaper reported that the WCC was attempting to influence Churches in Britain to sell investments in companies with interests in Southern Africa. This, by any religious or philosophical argument, was wholly negative and destructive.

To put anyone beyond the pale is to put them also beyond the reach of all influence for good. Surely this is something that no one claiming to be a man of God could support.

In May 1974, the London **Daily Telegraph** reported that the British Council of Churches had admitted that some British churches were giving financial support to Black guerillas fighting with "liberation movements" in Africa. But the council stressed that the funds were not being channelled through its offices.

Some of the money sent by British churchgoers was going towards fuelling the guerillas' war against the Portuguese Army in Mozambique and Angola.

Already in that year — by May 1974 — the WCC had distributed £24,997 to Frelimo, the Mozambique "liberation movement". And £9,200 had also gone to the People's Movement for the Liberation of Angola (MPLA).

In addition, another £9,200 had been given to the Revolutionary Government of Angola in Exile (GRAE) and £5,600 to the National Union for Total Independence of Angola (UNITA).

Other sums had been given to "liberation movements" fighting

1. **The Fraudulent Gospel: Politics and the World Council of Churches.** By Bernard Smith. Foreign Affairs Pub. Co. 1977.

in Southern Africa, including £12,498 to the South-West African People's Organisation (SWAPO).

On 19 August 1976, the same national newspaper reported that the World Council of Churches in Geneva had just allocated a record £315,000 to "liberation movements" and sympathisers throughout the world. Half went to groups seeking Black majority rule in Southern Africa. The largest payments of £47,000 each were to go to the "Zimbabwe (Rhodesia) Liberation Struggle" and to the South-West African People's Organisation.

Under the title 'Murder Financed by WCC' an editorial of the American **Manchester Union Leader** gave this information on 1 October 1976:—

"The moderator of the Dutch Reformed Church in the Cape Province of South Africa, Dr. J. S. Gericke, provides the following analysis of the terrorism financed by the World Council of Churches, a true account of an incident which occurred in northern Mozambique:

"Freedom fighters crossed the frontier from Tanzania and 'liberated' a Black man's village. Before his 'liberators' riddled him with a Chinese machine gun, they tied him to a tree and made him watch his wife and two teenage daughters being raped and killed. His two sons were nailed to a nearby tree to die . . . the man must have looked across the jungle in the direction of the Geneva headquarters of the WCC to thank it for its aid towards his 'liberation'."

The trouble with these incompetents at the World Council of Churches is that most seem to think they are supporting a civil rights movement similar to that in the United States. They seem to think that these Black savages in Africa are the equivalent of the highly intelligent and developed United States Blacks.

"Obviously, from these observations, they are not.

"As one Black friend of ours said the other day, it is ridiculous to presume that these people, who have just learned to stop eating missionaries, are capable of running a huge industrial society which has been built up over a period of hundreds of years. Yet, in order to gain Black election votes for Ford, Dr. Kissinger is running around Africa encouraging Black aggression against the Whites who have produced these great industrial nations.

"Every Black country supported by the World Council of Churches, once it has been given its independence, has suffered a drop in the standard of living, some almost to the starvation point. In addition to that there is no freedom at all and civil rights have disappeared.

"Readers of the **Union Leader** will remember that some years back we published informative articles by that Black genius, the late Phillippa Schuyler, who was then our correspondent in Africa.

She vividly described the savagery of some of these people.[2]

"The World Council of Churches is a combination of nitwits and some very clever leftist revolutionaries. The latter know exactly what they are doing in sending the good money of unsuspecting US churchgoers to finance murder and destruction in Africa".

If, as is undoubtedly the case, workers for international Marxism have, in the last 50 years, infiltrated every organisation, great and small, which could either impede or serve their purpose, one of their prime targets must obviously be the Churches of every denomination.

Agents of international Marxism enter the organisation they intend to subvert; transform or otherthrow it at a low level, then rise within it, unrecognised for what they are, until they have reached the highest levels and are in a position to exert great and perhaps determining influence.

A priest who entered the Church for this purpose 40 or 50 years ago might now have reached the rank of Archbishop, Bishop, Cardinal or Canon. If one, why not several or many; enough, indeed, to steer the Church along the road from which certain clerics are fervently trying to recall it, the road which can lead only to its downfall?

The Editor of the weekly magazine **To the Point International** had this to say about the WCC in his Editor's Memo of 30 January 1978, under the heading 'The day of the Big lie';

"I notice that the World Council of Churches in its programme to combat racism, has taken it upon itself to controvert the essential teaching of Christianity by equating violence and terrorism with justice. The arguments are terrifyingly plausible: racism is the sin of sins. Southern Africa is the prime example of racism. It is impossible to wipe out racism by the moral and spiritual power of Christianity. Therefore other methods must be sanctioned. No indeed, not only must they be sanctioned, but they must be actively encouraged. 'We do not' says a WCC discussion paper, 'define the Resistance fighters of Occupied Europe who used violence against their Nazi oppressors, as terrorists. Because we accept that their cause was just and their methods disciplined.'

"Now make the comparison with the 'disciplined methods' of today's 'freedom fighters' in Southern Africa. They hack pregnant women to death with panga knives. They slit the throats of babies. They peel the skin off an old man's face and leave him to die in the blazing sun impaled on a barbed wire fence. They plant landmines that rip off civilian arms and legs. They leave bombs in

---

2. **Jungle Saints: Africa's Heroic Catholic Missionaries.** By Philippa Schuyler. 1964.

hotel lobbies or prowl around with AK47 weapons to kill innocent villagers. They cut off lips and gauge out eyes. But, says the WCC paper blandly, as if this kind of thing were perfectly understandable, 'down the ages there have been Christians to whom violence was morally repugnant but who had nevertheless to resort to violence to overcome "a still greater evil". And therefore, on the grounds of exactly such arguments, says the WCC, 'South Africa's Black people today claim our recognition of their struggle as a just rebellion.'

"So-called holy wars of various kinds have been with us for many long centuries. But despite them all, Crusades included, none has any place in Christianity's teachings. Yet here we have a body purporting to represent the Christian churches, promoting atrocities with fanatical zeal, and all in the name of Christ. And if not that, in whose name? The WCC is a large and complex organisation, and not all of its arms are engaged in ideological warfare of this kind. But in recent years it has swung so sharply away from orthodoxy as to merit the title of leader of a worldwide apostasy. Though it claims to speak for Christianity, this itself is part of the Big Lie. If the Black people of South Africa are in danger it is not so much from naked racism as from the deceptive propaganda which the WCC so zealously pumps into their minds."

When I wrote this in March 1978, not one word of formal blessing had so far come from any of our Christian churches for the progress towards a bloodless internal settlement in Rhodesia. This silence is extraordinary. Not only is the settlement a step towards multi-racial tolerance; it is actually being led on the black side by two men of God, Bishop Muzorewa and the Rev. Ndabaningi Sithole.

It was Lenin who said: "We shall find our most fertile field of infiltration of Marxism within the field of religion, because religious people are the most gullible and will accept almost anything if it is couched in religious terminology."

CHAPTER 19

The Links of Terror

FOREIGN correspondents, commentators and others have for many years accused the South African Government of an all out witch hunt on so-called Communist elements within the country. The implication of these many accusations is quite clear — that the South African Government has used the bogy of Communism as a pretext for smothering legitimate dissident political opinion.

The current relationship between the Western and Eastern blocs, as manifested in the relationships of the United States and Western Europe with the Soviet Union, differs completely from the contact situation in Southern Africa. Although there is a great deal of distrust and hostility in the East/West relationship, negotiations do nevertheless take place under the umbrella of detente. In Western Europe, Communist Parties participate actively in the democratic process and Europeans accordingly have a different attitude to Communism than is the case with South Africans.

There is no comfortable umbrella of detente in Southern Africa. The Soviets have moved decisively to exclude any detente from the sub-continent. The consolation of Marxist regimes in Angola and Mozambique means that for Moscow there is no sense in a detente policy in Southern Africa. The intimate support given by Moscow to revolutionary movements in the sub-continent has meant that in most cases the contact situation has revolved around the barrel of a gun, a landmine or the murder of innocent civilians. Foreign observers never take this background situation into account when they judge the position in Southern Africa.

The struggle of the South African Communist Party (SACP) forms part of a global struggle being waged by the Soviet Union for world domination and the SACP is expected to follow directives from Moscow. Ultimate victory in South Africa is not seen as an end in itself; it is viewed as but one important step towards the "final liquidation of capitalism and imperialism", i.e. the United States of America. South Africa is seen merely as a necessary stepping stone in this bridgehead.

Moscow cannot and will not settle for Black nationalism as the ultimate objective in Africa. One has to face the facts and realise that Black nationalism is regarded as merely a brief transitionary period until the real Marxist-Leninist goal is achieved.

Indeed, it would not be going too far to say that the real interests of the Black man in South Africa simply do not come into the picture at all. The "Socialism" that the SACP envisages for South Africa is a Soviet prescribed Marxism in which there is no room whatsoever for genuine African nationalism.

In fanning the flames of unrest in South Africa, the SACP acts as an external manipulator of the situation, under the guidance of Moscow, relying on its liberation front, the African National Congress (ANC) to operate within the country.

The ANC is Moscow's Trojan Horse. It is a front or cover used as a tool to achieve the objectives of the South African Communist Party. This involves the subjugation of the Black national revolution to Marxism-Leninism. The net effect of a successful ANC revolution would be that a White-dominated Soviet-Marxist government would replace the present government.

It is ANC and SACP tactics to portray deliberately a picture of smouldering unrest in South Africa.

Although the world commemorates "Sharpeville Day" as a benchmark of the liberation struggle of the Black man in South Africa, the SACP/ANC actually claims that the Black people had very little to do with the uprising and that the unrest and violence of 1961 were the result of good organization and planning on its part.

The Central Committee of the SACP admitted in July 1971 that: "Leaders of the African National Congress and the Communist Party set themselves to recruit and train fighting cadres which entered the field of action on 16 December 1961, with the opening of a campaign of planted sabotage throughout the country. The process was begun of preparing for armed combat."

The ANC involvement in Soweto in June 1976 was testified to by none other than the General Secretary of the movement, in an interview in Lusaka. He stated that 16 June 1976 was a crucial date in the history of our struggle for liberation. On that day mass demonstrations of youth started in Soweto to bring about a Socialist society in South Africa on the Soviet model.

Certain circles at the United Nations accept without question that South Africa has become a threat to world peace and that it is consequently the duty of the UN to support the "freedom-loving and democratic" peoples in Southern Africa in their struggle for the final liberation of South Africa.

The links between the ANC, SACP and Moscow have been shown quite clearly, but it is also important that Moscow's other connections in Southern Africa be pointed out.

Mr. Oliver Tambo of the ANC has been a regular and much respected guest in Maputo and Luanda in the past year along with delegates from SWAPO, the "liberation movement" fighting in South-West Africa. In order to put the whole picture in perspective it is therefore necessary to refer briefly to SWAPO, Angola and Mozambique.

The SACP supports SWAPO's struggle for political power in South-West Africa. SWAPO is a pro-Moscow liberation movement and the only outcome of its struggle for "freedom" would be a victory for Communism.

The latest developments in Angola indicate quite clearly that the MPLA has moved into the orbit of influence of the Soviet Union. Both the Soviet Union and Angola have testified to the new socialist character of Angola that is in line with Marxism-Leninism.

President Agostinho Neto visited the Soviet Union in October 1976 to sign a 20 year Treaty of Friendship and Co-operation between the Soviet Union and Angola.

Both sides pledged their support for Marxism-Leninism.

Mr. Neto himself stated in no uncertain terms at a reception in the Kremlin: "The Socialist path of development will unite the destinies of the peoples of Angola, Cuba and the Soviet Union despite the difference in their development levels, into the single destiny earmarked for the socialist countries."

In Mozambique President Samora Machel completely shifted his alliance to Moscow in the course of 1976. He visited the Soviet Union in May and before his departure said: ". . . . . the Soviet Union is the first state to which I shall make an official visit . . . We are going to the USSR, the motherland of the great Lenin, since the Soviet Union and other Socialist states are our national allies".

The Third Frelimo congress in Maputo in February 1977 showed that Machel had become totally converted to the cause of Moscow.

What are the conclusions to be drawn from a study of their Links of Terror?

First, the West should not make the mistake of seeing the Communist onslaught on South Africa as a drive aimed at eliminating apartheid. All available evidence shows conclusively that Moscow regards the attack on South Africa as part of a world wide onslaught on the West. The downfall of South Africa would be but an intermediate stage in this onslaught.

Second, Moscow will not tolerate any peace moves or initiatives in Southern Africa that would endanger its foreign policy objectives or its aid to its Communist allies.

Third, the alignment of Communist forces in Southern Africa is quite clear. The SACP is carrying out Moscow's directives and the ANC is being used to carry Communism into South Africa under the banner of a national "liberation movement" playing on Black sentiments.

Fourth, the young Marxist states of Southern Africa — Angola and Mozambique — are being used as springboards to give impetus to the Communist "liberation" of South Africa.

Fifth, the ANC cannot but be accepted as a Communist front organization working in the interests of the Kremlin.

In no way can the ANC be considered as a spokesman of the Black peoples of South Africa. Black nationalism has been brought to the brink of total collapse in Southern Africa, for the language of the Marxist states and of organizations such as the ANC and SWAPO has become the Voice of Radio Moscow.

The "liberation movements" may well be fighting in Southern Africa but it is certainly not for the freedom envisaged in terms of Western democracy. However, typical distortion of words and their meanings by Moscow has enabled Western circles to join freely in the "liberation of Southern Africa" not realising that they are, in fact, supporting Communism and furthering Moscow's drive for global domination.

STEVE BIKO

What is the truth about Steve Biko? I am able to reveal for the first time what his self-avowed aims were, how he intended to achieve them, what support he had, how he saw the White man being brought to his knees, what the sequence of events would be and how sporadic violence would lead to organised violence.

This is revealed in Appendix 3 on pages 237-241. This appendix also includes a reproduction of the leaflet that Biko had in his possession when he was later arrested.

Also in my possession is a pamphlet produced by the South African Students Movement (SASM) dealing with urban guerilla warfare, including patrols, fieldcraft, communications and the handling of arms, mines and bombs.

Other documents I possess are aide memories and letters from the Luzerne and Rome cells of SASM and the Black Consciousness Movement (BCM).

CHAPTER 20

Self-righteous Piety and Hypocrisy

IN looking at the double standards applied by the United Nations and by those who, with self-righteous piety and hypocrisy, condemn South Africa, what does one discover? One finds that racialism and other crimes of which South Africa is accused are not only rampant in small, developing or primitive countries, but the most highly industrialised, the most developed countries, the political heavyweights are certainly no exception.

First, let us look at a small selection of the countries of the Third World. The cases of genocide in the Third World are well-known: the half million black Sudanese who died at the hands of a repressive Arab war machine, those killed in the ethnic war in Nigeria; in Central Africa, the death of about a quarter of a million people in the Watutsi-Bahutu racial pogroms; the 100,000 Nagas and Ahams killed in Burma, another 100,000 — Karens and Shans — slaughtered by the ruling establishment. In Cambodia, perhaps between one and two **million** have been killed. The list is a long one; it covers every continent on earth and extends up to the present day.

Within two years, Angola has become an ever-increasingly Cuban occupied colonial territory with its economy in ruins, the railways disrupted, the roads impassable and the ports virtually paralysed. Civil strife is rampant, with three rival movements, Neto's MPLA, the bearded Jonas Savimbi's UNITA and Holden Roberto's FNLA. The key parts of the rural areas are controlled by UNITA in the southern and southeastern regions of Angola, and by FNLA in the north. All this is happening under the benevolent eye of the world, for the USA and her allies are completely impotent to do anything about it.

The brutal tyrant, Idi Amin, Uganda's dictator, has openly violated every tenet of human rights. Under his rule of terror, arbitrary arrest, brutal torture, random murder, bloodshed and chaos are everyday occurrences. The number of Amin's victims is much greater than the conservative estimate of 100,000 published by the International Commission of Jurists earlier last year. No precise body counts are available, but a recent estimate suggests that since 1971 Amin has probably killed and caused to be killed about 150,000 Africans.

The moral case for boycotting Uganda is easily made. By the end of Amin's first year, the killings had begun in earnest. During the next year, Uganda's chief justice was hauled out of court and decapitated, a former interior minister was abducted and dismembered, and the rector of the university was murdered. The army was brutally purged of several particular ethnic groups. Even in remote areas villagers were assaulted by Amin's henchmen.

Meanwhile, the U.N. and the world have remained silent and permitted this dreadful tyranny to continue and the world press has remained relatively indifferent to the fearful atrocities committed against Black Ugandans. The reason? The tyrant was himself black!

When a few Whites are threatened, it makes news. But the violent deaths of hundreds of thousands of Black Ugandans never make international headlines, while lesser events in other parts of the world are regularly discussed and debated in international forums.

Medical and educational care — once the best in East Africa — are approaching Cambodian levels. For all but the ruling military cadre, life in today's Uganda is mean, brutish, and dangerous.

Only high prices for coffee keep Amin in luxuries and his military cohorts in guns and bullets. Without exports of coffee, Amin would be unable to continue to command the loyalty of his 20,000 military supporters who now deny basic human rights to a once accomplished and proud people, enjoying the rule of law.

Coffee accounts for 87 per cent of Uganda's export earnings.

This creature, Idi Amin, who has eaten human flesh, is admitted to the US and the UN as a respected statesman, but a former US Ambassador to the UN who criticised him is sacked, while two African Rhodesian Senators who have done nothing except try and co-operate with the Rhodesian Whites, are banned. Other European countries did admit them, but they do not have Mr. Andrew Young and a Black vote to consider.

In avoiding effective action against a country like Uganda, President Carter's policy of human rights becomes a fraud: a paper tiger.

The US merely pays lip service to its own human rights policy. Why have Ugandan police helicopter pilots been taking a refresher course at Forth Worth, Texas? Why is the US continuing to import Ugandan coffee for which US companies paid Uganda some $150 million in the first half of last year?

Ethiopia has probably killed over a million of its own citizens. In Cambodia like atrocities have included the murder of millions; the burial of people up to their necks so that their heads could then be cut off by ploughs. In a recent newspaper article, one 21 year old Khmer Rouge was quoted as saying "I enjoyed killing people. I liked it best when their hands were tied behind their backs. I liked watching them twist and turn and roll about in agony. Men and babies were easy, women I didn't like so much unless they were soldiers' women".

Every human right has been violated to the extreme — probably not a single family on the losing side remains intact — their religion, Buddhism, has been outlawed. Their literature has been burned, their schools and universities have been closed, and every imaginable liberty denied to them. In one village 40 desperate people dined off the body of a dead child.

Any individuals showing the slightest possible threat to the leadership are conveniently sent to work on the land, at best. In 1976 a purge began in earnest. Military officers, intellectuals, teachers, students and professional people were dissappearing in their thousands. Four doctors in the provincial capital of Siem Reap were set to work translating French medical text books into Khmer. When they had finished they were sent to work digging ditches (12 hours a day, seven days a week). Seventy thousand monks were forced to forsake their saffron robes to work on the land.

Such unbelievable atrocities are blandly characterised as "the beginning of reconstruction".

There was no outcry in Britain over the arrest of two more newspaper editors in Pakistan, bringing the total to four detained in two weeks at the end of October and the beginning of November 1977. Pakistan, of course, is a member of the Security Council and has bitterly denounced South Africa.

The scenario for the downfall of Prime Minister Ian Smith was worked out in 1975 by the Commonwealth leaders in the indecent contrast between the Conference luxury hotels and the downtown shanty living standards of Kingston, Jamaica.

Kingston is one of the vilest slums in the world with the quarter-million people of the ghetto suffering from a shortage of food and clothing, and living in indescribable conditions of poverty.

Until 8 January 1978, Kingston was one of the most violent and frightening places on earth. For several years, and especially since the bloodshed of the 1976 elections there — when both parties lost some 20 officials in straightforward slaughter — the slum was divided into political 'tribes' and ruled by gunmen on behalf of the politicians. You crossed the borderlines on pain of death. In the first week of January alone, no fewer than 28 people died in shoot-outs.

The two rival top-ranking gunmen, representing the two political parties, declared peace on 8 January, and declared war instead on the politicians. The politicians have used the police as a political arm; countenanced chaos and corruption of the electoral system; failed to provide food, proper sanitation and housing; severely depressed the economy and produced a situation where one third of the workforce is unemployed.

How much of all this is known to those who secrete their venom on South Africa? And Jamaica, let us remember, is a member of the British Commonwealth while South Africa was, in effect, expelled. We should be bowing our heads in shame.

The civilised world learned with disgust of the judicial and public executions in the market place in Jiddah of a 25 year old Saudi Arabian Princess and her lover for conduct contrary to a royal decree and attempting to elope together. The Princess was shot in front of her husband who was then beheaded. Other Saudi Arabian princesses were taken to the market place to watch the gruesome executions in a carnival atmosphere of laughing, chattering, cheering Arabs.

If this barbarity had occurred in South Africa, the revulsion of civilised society would have been recorded by a huge and immediate outcry, particularly from the human rights organisations in Western Europe and the USA. Do they complain about the denial of the vote and civil liberties to women in Saudi Arabia? No, we need oil and the money that goes with it; these will always clog the international machinery on human rights. As for the United Nations, the Organisation for African Unity holds sway in that unprincipled, farcical institution.

In the Isle of Man, a youth is birched for assault and the British Government has to account to an international court. In Saudi Arabia, the horrific habit associated with bloody barbarians one thousand and one years ago is not condemned as an outrange of human rights, for the West knows on which side its bread is buttered. Indignation is contemptibly selective.

Britain does not forget that the Saudis virtually control world oil prices, and with multi-million pound defence contracts at stake, nothing must be allowed to impair relations between London and Riyadh, the capital.

On 21 January 1978, Indonesian students attempted a rally at Jakarta university after the arrest of about 100 of their leaders. They were dispersed by about 1,000 troops in riot gear, supported by armoured cars and a helicopter. The student attacks on restrictions on political activity and the government's failure to take action on several corruption cases had become increasingly pointed over some months, and received wide coverage in the liberal press.

At the same time, the Indonesian government closed eight leading newspapers and arrested dozens of its critics in an attempt to forestall any protest plans, particulary by students to the unopposed re-election of President Suharto for a third five-year term of office.

With the allegiance of the Army generals, Suharto was the only candidate in the March election of a new president by the 920 man Congress of whose members only 39 per cent are elected, while the rest are appointed by the government and the military.

The closing down of the newspapers and the arrests were not condemned by the UN, the West or the Third World, nor given publicity by the majority of the media, in spite of the fact that the International Press Institute sent a message to President Suharto expressing its deep concern at his Government's decision to withdraw the licences of eight daily newspapers.

In its message, the IPI also raised the matter of 24 journalists said to be in detention, many without charge or trial, and asked whether any of them were due for release under the recent amnesty for up to 10,000 political prisoners.

Why is it that those who expend so much energy and resources on human rights overseas decline to campaign on behalf of the many thousands of political prisoners who have been held without trial ever since the abortive Communist rebellion in Indonesia in 1965? This is yet one more glaring example of the double standard and determination of the world to ensure that the searchlight of censure is kept firmly focussed on South Africa.

The International Press Institute has admitted that the most free press in the whole of Africa is in South Africa.

In January 1978, Mr. John Ford, Britain's retiring Ambassador to Indonesia, suggested that marriageable girls be sent to the remote Indonesian prison island of Buru to wed young prisoners there.

Mr. Ford, who had been on a three day visit to the island, said that prisoners who had been held 12 years on the island without trial were in a state of "real deprivation".

The Ambassador said medical supplies on the island were inadequate and homosexuality among the inmates was commonplace. The idea of sending marriageable girls to the island would meet "an urgent need there". Buru Island presently holds some 8,500 political prisoners.

In December 1977, the Indonesian Government released 1,500 prisoners from Buru along with several thousand more from other detention centres.

At the time, government leaders promised that the remaining 20,000 political prisoners held in Indonesia would be set free within the next two years.

In Iran, rampaging crowds estimated in their thousands overwhelmed the police on 18 February and virtually ransacked Tabriz,

Iran's second largest city, in riots which left six people killed and 125 injured.

The rioters according to official reports were led by "Marxist-Muslim" elements. They started 135 fires throughout the city of 600,000 inhabitants, and attacked 73 banks, eight cinemas, four hotels and the Technological Institute. One of the cinemas was burnt as were 28 cars.

The police managed to protect Europeans grouped in the city's two main hotels.

Travellers returning from Tabriz described the situation as chaotic and even insurrectional, recalling violent demonstrations in Qom, south of Teheran, six weeks before during which six people were killed and 60 injured.

Reports said that the trouble had broken out when demonstrators shouting anti-government and pro-Communist slogans marched into the streets; smashing shop windows and stoning cars. Fires burnt in Tabriz for several hours.

In a letter published in the London **Daily Telegraph** on 7 November, a former District Commissioner from Kenya who served throughout the Mau Mau rebellion, felt compelled to express his disgust at the hypocrisy and double standards of the British Government in their dealings in Southern Africa.

He explained that in Kenya, because the problem was a British one, it was considered justifiable to send troops to the Colony to fight the terrorists, to incarcerate political leaders like Jomo Kenyatta on the flimsiest evidence, and to pour money and arms into the country to enable the Government to bring the terrorists "to heel". Detention camps were set up, and detainees held in them numbered some 80,000 at one time.

But South Africa is no longer a British problem, and so, when South Africa comes under terrorist attack, overnight the British Government becomes, as the writer of the letter so rightly describes, very "Pi". Detention without trial is suddenly no longer an acceptable means of combatting terrorism and subversion. (Except curiously enough for a while in Ulster!) The provision of military aid in the form of arms is now absolutely unthinkable — they might be used against the terrorists! In fact it is now the terrorists who receive the financial and other aid from the British Government.

Recently, as the writer reminded us, Britain was represented at the funeral of Steve Biko. Why, he asks, wasn't she also represented at the funerals of Sergeant Mtsintsi and Constable Mrasi who were stoned to death in East London by returning "mourners" from the Biko funeral?

One might also ask why Britain was not represented at the funeral of six month old Natasha Glenny.

More recently still, says the writer, Dr. Owen, referring to the widespread banning and arrests in South Africa, said: "They run counter to our most cherished ideals of personal liberty and free speech." What happened to these cherished ideals when Britain was busy dealing with unrest in India and the Colonies? Mahatma Gandhi, Nkrumah, Hastings Banda and Nyerere, to name but a few, all spent plenty of time in British gaols for so-called political agitation.

These are the double standards that make decent people sick at heart.

Japan is as adept as any other country at indulging in double standards and throwing stones in glass houses. Concealed from the world today is Japan's racial prejudice against her own minority community consisting of an invisible race of no less than three million outcasts, known as the Burakumin. Relegated to degrading jobs in the past, they still come up against prejudice when they seek better jobs or attempt to marry outside their community.

Like India's untouchables, the Burakumin are predominantly employed in menial jobs, considered as degrading centuries ago: street and sewer cleaners, workers in leather factories, butchers and scrap collectors.

Today the Burakumin are also employed as poorly paid daily labourers in the construction industry. Even the few Burakumin who fight their way up to university cannot hope to secure a level of employment commensurate with their standard of education if their background is exposed.

Significantly, a large proportion of Japanese emigrants who are settling in Brazil are Burakumin.

The majority of Japan's outcasts from the main stream of society still live in 6,000 ghettos — both villages and enclaves in urban areas. An estimated 1,500,000 are attempting to conceal their identities after improving their positions in the anonymity of big urban areas.

A typical case is that of Mr. Hideo Watanabe who left his crowded ghetto in Kyodo 24 years ago to establish a new life and identity in Tokyo.

A happily married official in a Yokohama bank today, Mr. Watanabe, 49, is secretly consumed by fear — a prey to blackmailers, prejudice and ruin if his origins are discovered.

This banker changed his address six times before his marriage and has taken other elaborate steps to sever his connection with the ghetto in recent years.

Like another million or so of Japan's unknown minority community of outcasts, Mr. Watanabe has been passing himself off as an ordinary Japanese in the anonymity of urban life for more than two decades. He has successfully concealed his origins from his family, friends and employers since 1954 — and he still lives with the cold threat of exposure in his heart. The social stigma would ruin both his family and his career.

From outward appearances it would be impossible to draw differences between Mr. Watanabe and the average Japanese. They are of the same race, speak the same language and worship the same gods. As a result Burakumin can only be identified if their antecedents are traced back to any one of the existing 6,000 Buraku ghettos.

But, as Mr. Watanabe says: "We are consumed by fear every day. We are scared, terrified that someone will point a finger at us. My son is now 22 years old. He is at university and is not aware of my background. Next year he will look for a job. What happens if his employers check my background. It would destroy my family and my position in the bank."

Japan's prejudices against the Burakumin are founded on class differences which originate in the eighth century. The lower workers were defined as 'hinin' — non-humans — at the time, and the prejudices have been handed down from generation to generation. People who live in the 6,000 ghettos are identified with violence and dirt, and they are ostracized. It is surely a sad reflection on Japan's modern society that such a myth should still persist.

In India, the caste system which is a form of apartheid is still institutionalised even today. Despite offers of a free passage back to India, the Indians in South Africa have refused invitations to return to their homeland.

In the general ganging up against South Africa this is yet another example of a big nation priding itself on its civilised way of life, yet indulging in self-righteous piety and hypocrisy.

South Africa's current internal security measures are not to the liking of Britain and such enlightened countries as Mozambique and Uganda. Had South Africa criticised Britain, or suggested an economic blockade, because the South African Government disapproved of Britain's security measures in Northern Ireland — Britain has been before the European Court of Human Rights, we have imprisoned without trial, people have died in questionable circumstances — we British would have been indignant and rightly so.

To get an idea of what the level of violence in Northern Ireland was up to mid-1976, the equivalent rate for England and Wales with a population of 48,500,000 would have been:

Total number dead	50,176
Number of police dead	2,756
Number of soldiers dead	10,112
Total numbers injured	572,224
Total number of explosions	160,480

Messrs Young and Owen met in London in January on their way to Malta to talk to Rhodesian terrorists whom they insist upon calling "freedom fighters" for Zimbabwe. Messrs Young and Owen insist that the so called Patriotic Front should be involved in any Rhodesian settlement.

At exactly the same time at an IRA roadblock in "British occupied Eire", freedom fighters, whom Messrs Young and Owen insist upon calling terrorists, flaunted a newly acquired American made M60 machine gun which was set up under the noses of the British army who had orders not to interfere. The IRA have links with the CTs in Rhodesia.

Had the incident in Northern Ireland happened in Rhodesia, Messrs Young and Owen would have declared that it was evidence of the way in which the "freedom fighters" were gaining at the expense of the Smith regime, which was clearly losing its grip.

However, as the Irish "freedom fighters" are White and fighting Dr. Owen's own "occupying regime", they will continue to be called terrorists while the Rhodesian terrorists will be called "freedom fighters" because they are Black and fighting a White government which defied a British Socialist regime.

In Africa, a Black man's suffering is only recognised by the press and governments if he suffers at the hands of a White man. If a Black man is killed by another Black, his death is dismissed with a shrug as if his life were of lesser values in this case. A Black man enslaved by another Black is still regarded as free. If Black people are beaten up or tortured by other Blacks, they feel no pain or suffering as far as so-called public opinion is concerned. When such inhumanity is practised on the same Blacks by Whites, however, the whole world is up in arms, with rent-a-crowd demonstrations at Trafalgar Square, and claims at the United Nations that the peace of the entire world is suddenly in jeopardy. Disease and hunger to the point of starvation is ignored when it occurs under Black rule, but how much praise is given to White rulers who prevent such misery? South Africa feeds many countries in Southern Africa outside its borders.

Professor Chris Barnard is the last person to deny the existence of racialism and political intolerance in his country. He has often taken a stand for racial justice and tolerance in South Africa. But as he points out in his book **South Africa: Sharp Dissection.** there must be something radically wrong with what is called world opinion, with the policy-makers in the civilised governments of the West, with the planning and operations of the United Nations, when double standards of such gross dimensions are applied against a single country — South Africa. Since the Second World War there have been two major racial incidents in South Africa: in 1961 when 67 people were killed at Sharpeville, and in 1976 when an estimated 300 lives were lost in township unrest. Yet, in the same period, more than 10 million people have been killed around the world as a result of racial, ethnic and cultural violence and intolerance. In a single country, the Sudan, half a million people have died because of a deliberate policy of genocide. In Cambodia, perhaps four times that number.

Yet, because of the double standards fostered by the United Nations and other instances, there is hardly a ripple of condemnation of those responsible for the deaths of 10 million people, whereas the whole world was in an uproar over the loss of life in South Africa in 1961 and 1976. It must be a very sick society that considers 10 million lives of so little account yet is prepared to expend millions of dollars on propaganda, resolutions and protests when 67 or 300 people are killed.

As the **Daily Post**, a British newspaper, aptly remarked when an African state expelled a group of Asians in 1976: ". . . . we can be sure (they) will not be pilloried in the courts of the world. Oh, had it been South Africa who had been ejected the unfortunate non-White merchants, the tramp of rent-a-crowd would even now be making for Trafalgar Square and Pretoria's embassy in London."

So bad has the political persecution of South Africa by the outside world become that even Prof. Barnard, a surgeon, was subjected to politically pointed questioning after the first heart transplantation. Mr. Malcolm Muggeridge, the eminent British author and broadcaster, had the audacity to ask him on a BBC television show, "Barnard Faces His Critics", whether it was because he had so little respect for human dignity and human life that "we in South Africa were the first to do a heart transplant". Another BBC interviewer, Dr. Gould, asked him: "Dr. Barnard, did you do a heart transplant to improve the image of South Africa overseas?".

There is not sufficient space available to dwell on the situation in the Soviet Union: the persecution of Jews in that country, the labour camps, the denial of intellectual freedom, psychiatric hospitals and the scornful contempt for the basic tenets of common decency and human dignity.

But quite apart from the Soviet persecution of minorities, there is also a great deal of anti-Black feeling in the Soviet Union. It became so bad at the end of 1975 that the African Students' Union asked African ambassadors in Moscow to help put a stop to assaults on black students studying in the Ukrainian cities of Kiev and Lvov. Russians particularly resent blacks dating Slav women, and the assaults stemmed from racial prejudice.

The other super-power, the United States, continues to be plagued by racialism. The violence of the fifties and sixties has subsided, but racialism continues to smoulder under the surface, sometimes erupting, as was seen recently in Boston. "Despite all the progress made through laws and executive orders, racism is still deeply embedded in the American fabric", said Mr. Vernon Jordan, Black executive director of the National Urban League.

Human rights would be a commendable policy for the Carter Administration to pursue if it was based on the premise that America is practising what it preaches. But the plain truth is that the one country that should be conducting an all-out war against crime in its own homeland is the USA itself. How can they possibly justify, for example, the tortures and murders within the Mafia; crime and delinquency costing the country $88.6 billion a year; 77,600 teachers assaulted in US schools in 1976; the July, 1977, New York blackout riots — the 'Night of the Animals' — when Negroes by the hundreds of thousands tore the city apart in an orgy of looting, burnings, robbings and attacks by armed gangs; the violence that erupted in the first week of January 1978, in the strikes by 188,000 American coal miners, with the shooting of a picket in Kentucky, the arrest by the FBI of senior union officials in West Virginia, a riot by more than 500 strikers in Indiana who fired guns and set off dynamite charges resulting in a clash with riot police and state troopers who made 194 arrests. Bombings and individual acts of arson and sabotage spread and flying pickets toured areas where the union is weak, often in groups several hundred strong and armed with guns, pickaxe handles and explosives.

The Communist Party, of course, will have carried out an intensive study of the US coalminers' violence in support of their strike, for it was Lenin who pointed out that violence without an ideological objective was comparatively useless and that the aim of the Communist Party must always be to exploit such situations to create a pre-revolutionary climate.

If tea could spark off the American revolution 200 years ago, what could energy spark off today?

Is it to be wondered at that many countries, for example, Argentina, Brazil and Chile, having seen the state of affairs in the USA and the permissiveness of the American judicial and criminal systems, are resisting the powerful pressures being brought upon them to change their treatment of political agitators, subversives, terrorists and criminals. The Carter Administration, with its clean image, would perform a greater service to its people if it were to use the energies and resources now being expended on human rights overseas on an all-out war against crime in the USA and a programme of penal reform, not to mention the biggest problem of all in America today, namely racism. American society is still plagued by issues of race. Why is the Mafia still so powerful today?

Human rights is the "big stick" of the Carter Administration in determining much of its foreign policy. For example, on human rights, the US is tough on the White rulers of Rhodesia and South Africa, but little is said about Iran, Saudi Arabia and China, because their governments have something America wants and they can answer back.

Selling peanuts is certainly not the best preparation for trying to run the world. That President Carter is eager to learn is not disputed, but the Soviet Union intends to exploit the situation to the full and ensure that the world will have to pay a very heavy price indeed for the education of such a dangerously inexperienced and unpredictable President who cannot distinguish between his real friends and his alleged foes.

Political violence in Italy has reached terrifying proportions. The country is Europe's most explosive society and by January 1978 violence had turned many historic cities almost into battlefields and people were speaking openly of "civil war". A former Prime Minister Moro was murdered by terrorists. By comparison, the Baader Meinhof gang, the Basque separatist movement ETA, and even, perhaps, the provisional IRA, appear almost restrained.

Selected victims of politically-motivated killings included two magistrates, a senior lawyer, the deputy editor of a national newspaper and a prominent neo-Fascist politician. Extremists of both right and left ran wild in the streets — hurling Molotov cocktails, exploding bombs and gunning down their enemies.

Said a senior police official: "It was like two armies . . . on the day of battle". If this scale of violence which is revealed in detail below had occurred in South Africa, there would have been demonstrations of protest throughout the world, an emergency session of the UN Security Council and a demand for the immediate imposition of full economic sanctions.

In Italy, there are no fewer than 115 identifiable extremist political movements, splinter groups and urban guerilla commandos, 94 belonging to the far left and 21 to the neo-Fascist right.

Left-wing extremists pounced on a neighbourhood headquarters of the neo-Fascist **Movimento Sociale Italiano** (MSI) on Rome's outskirts and assassinated two young people. The killers, who included two women, made a clean getaway, but in protest rioting that followed the incident, another young MSI member was shot and killed in a clash with Carabinieri, who had been called in to put down the disturbance.

In revenge, rightist youth rampaged through the district, overturning and burning parked cars, fire-bombing the house of a daily-newspaper editor and ransacking a suburban Communist Party cell headquarters. Guerilla warfare spilled into the streets almost nightly. In the Alberone district near the Appian Way, police had to make repeated baton charges to break up a march of young ultra-leftists who were determined to defy the city's ban against demonstrations. Simultaneously, half a mile away in the Tuscolano district, a contingent of Carabinieri in combat gear had to use five armoured vehicles to end an hour-long shooting spree by young rightists armed with automatic pistols.

More than 100 youths were detained by police and 45 placed under arrest.

After the Italian Interior Ministry and Rome city council had convened emergency meetings nearly 2,000 additional Carabinieri had to be called in from as far as Padua (more than 200 miles away) to reinforce Rome police. Riot police were posted around high schools, the scenes of so much recent youthful rage, and near political party offices. The MSI headquarters attacked by the assassination squad was closed. Roadblocks were set up around the city, and police helicopters clattered over the rooftops.

Widespread leftist-led student protests brought teaching to a standstill, books and scientific instruments destroyed at Milan University; the computer centre at Boccini University, a Milan business school, destroyed by three masked urban guerillas; near the campus of Bologna, a youth rampage in a 20-block commercial district led to a 25-year-old medical student being shot dead and his death triggered off more bloody riots in Rome.

Italy's law and order statistics for 1978 are an appalling revelation: 2,000 terrorist bombings; 11,441 small arms, 937,711 bombs and 15,000 lbs. of explosives seized by the police; 590 arrested for terrorist acts ranging from murder to leg shootings; $55 million worth of damage to factories caused by arson, plus numerous minor bombings of public buildings, goverment offices and political party premises all over the country; reported crimes rose to 2,090,000 of which 8 out of 10 remained unsolved; kidnappings reached a record total of 76 and of these 39 have never been seen alive again.

There is little for the public to respect or emulate in Italy's ruling class scandals that still burst daily from the pages of the newspapers, as the corruption of the past three decades is painfully uncovered.

By comparison with Italy's chronic social and economic problems, the strong upsurge in political violence and the slide to Communism, the conditions prevailing in South Africa are tranquil indeed. Mr. Vorster is one of the few remaining Prime Ministers of the day who implements the principle that defence — from the enemy within as well as from the enemy without — is a national priority. Those who take up arms and challenge the forces of law and order must be dealt with ruthlessly, for they are creating political instability which extremists — acting on the orders of their Kremlin masters — are well placed to exploit.

Neither the United States nor the countries of Western Europe, and certainly not the United Nations, have anything to be proud of where the maintenance of law and order is concerned. In this respect Mr. Vorster has every justification for regarding the civilised countries of the West as sanctimonious hypocrites.

In Britain, the influx of Asians and West Indians is building up to a racially explosive situation. Already hundreds have protested against the immigrants, and there have been street riots on this account.

As Black ghettoes appear in cities such as Liverpool and Manchester and racilism intensifies in schools, factories and on the streets, Rev. David Sheppard, the former cricket captain for England and a bishop prominent in anti-racist circles, warned in a British Council of Churches report that the new generation of British-born Black people is "doomed to exist as outcasts on the fringes of society" and in many ways faces "the greatest experience of alieniation of any generation anywhere."

Despite the incomparably higher number of deaths and the higher level of political repression in many African countries and in a country such as the Soviet Union, and despite the existence of racialism in civilised societies such as those of the United States and Great Britain, South Africa continues to be singled out for vilification.

The reason given is that South Africa, alone in the world, has institutionalised racialism, that discrimination is enshrined in the country's legislation. Prof. Barnard is the first to admit that to a great extent this is true, but, as he so rightly says, it is skating on very thin ice to give this as justification for the shameless double standards practised at the United Nations.

CHAPTER 21

Will Sanctions Really Hurt South Africa?

PRESIDENT Carter and his advisers seem convinced that South Africa's internal conduct of affairs has become a menace to the West by opening the way to war in South Africa and to Soviet and other undesirable incursions. White South Africa is not seen by the US as an ally and bulwark against Communism but rather as a potent, if unwilling, trailblazer for it. This is an extremely dangerous point of view but it is in line with the shocking report that the Carter Administration is waging a secret war against South Africa. I will be revealing details later but suffice it to say now, that the secret war now being waged is to ensure that the end of White rule, and the substitution of Black majority rule, is achieved as speedily as possible — and that when the Blacks take over, the US will have a special and friendly relationship with them, whether they are pro or anti-Marxist.

South Africa is a middle-rank power. Its economic miracle has faded and like other countries it now faces inflation, industrial recession and unemployment. But it is self-sufficient in that it does grow all its own food and is a major supplier of vital minerals to the West.

South Africa possesses — and itself equips — armed forces of great sophistication. The efficiency of its police is of the same standard. Its 41,000 strong army is one of the best trained and best equipped on the continent, with 130,000 reservists who can be mobilised against invasion or insurrection within 48 hours. At present the main gaps in the country's arms production are helicopter technology and warships, including submarines. South Africa has the know-how to join the nuclear club and in my judgement must use its nuclear capability not only as a deterrent but as a bargaining counter. "Might is right" and the only thing the supers powers understand is when they are spoken to from a position of strength.

South Africa could stop the United Nations in its tracks by developing nuclear weapons and announcing its willingness to sell these to other threatened anti-Communist nations such as South Korea and Taiwan. Some foreign observers have claimed that the Republic already has nuclear weapons. This has been repeatedly denied by the South African Government.

If, in fact, the Government does have them, it should say so.

If it does not it should develop them quickly. It has the scientific, technical and raw material resources to do so, and the cost would be moderate.

It is true, as some have argued, that nuclear weapons would have limited military value in the kind of war that South Africa could face. But this overlooks the enormous psychological value and political leverage that their possession would provide.

The atom bomb is a symbol of strength — a symbol that India, a poorer and less threatened nation, came to regard as a necessity.

The world respects strength, and South Africa must have respect if it is to survive. Sir Winston Churchill said, when he announced Britain's decision to develop the atom bomb: "Safety is the sturdy child of terror."

Grim words indeed — and a salutary reminder of how critical the South Africa situation has become. But the message is always there: South Africa can and will survive for they have the will and determination necessary to do so.

Israel has shown that will. South Africa will do no less, for it has the power, the resources and the determination to ensure its survival. Like Israel, it knows that it can lose a war only once.

Unlike the Whites of Algeria, Angola and Mozambique, South Africans cannot be betrayed by a metropolitan government grown weary of war and anxious to cut its losses.

Unlike Rhodesia, South Africa will not depend on any lifelines of oil or ammunition or whatever — ultimately, like the US, it can survive entirely on its own if it is forced to do so.

Its military power is such in relation to any likely enemy that it could not be contested except by one of the two superpowers. Of all the threatened areas in the world today, South Africa strategically has a unique autonomy of action; is best able to defend herself, and is best able to stand alone if necessary.

Those — and its own tough stubborn people — are South Africa's strengths.

South Africa's strategic location makes it indispensable to Western countries whose very survival depends on its mineral riches and the strategic Cape route whose busy sea routes are vulnerable to Soviet submarines. Obviously the South African Navy has an important role to play in helping to defend them.

South Africa's weakness is lack of oil. It has to be imported, 90 per cent from Iran. South Africa has for many years been stock-piling against Domesday. At full consumption the stocks might last 1½-2 years. But by 1981 South Africa aims to produce one quarter of all the oil it needs from domestic coal.

South Africa is a good customer of the US, Britain and other Western states. Therefore sanctions would be bound to boomerang on Britain and the US. A blockade of South Africa would be a blockade against the West. Britain's annual exports to South Africa total £680 million and the Americans export nearly £100 millions. British investments in the republic are thought to be worth £3,000 million. Economic sanctions would therefore have a very severe effect on British jobs and exports. As sanctions against Rhodesia showed, some other industrialized country would evade its obligations to sanctions and fulfil the same export order.

South Africa is, in fact, one of Britain's better export markets — 13th in the list of her major client nations.

Nearly half that business goes to Britain's machinery and electrical industries. If it were ever to disappear, the cost in British jobs is estimated at 80,000 with another 200,000 jobs at stake in ancillary industries.

The prospect is causing dismay in British industry. Mr. Freddie Rump, director of the UK-South African Trade Association, said: "It is an indefensible way to force political change. We don't do it anywhere else — we do all the business we can get with Russia and China.

"And sanctions are never effective — the last time we tried it over arms to South Africa, we simply handed a billion pounds of business to the French."

Most experts agree that sanctions have no appreciable effect for at least three years. The effect of seven years of sanctions against Rhodesia has been to shield the country so effectively from international inflation that the illegal Rhodesian dollar became one of the world's most stable currencies.

In any case, the possibility of a total trade boycott by the West is nothing new to South Africa. Precautions have been taken by the Nationalist Government since it came to power 30 years ago.

One investment expert has said: "There is little doubt that in the event of sanctions, Vorster would nationalise all overseas holdings and grab the profits to continue his industrial investment programme."

That would keep business buoyant for at least three years, which is a long time in world politics. With £5,000 million of British capital invested in South Africa, no one in the City of London wants to speculate on the impact such steps might have on financial markets.

All this, the economists insist, makes a mockery of sanctions.

Furthermore, economic sanctions would cause far more damage to at least 12 Black African states than they would to self-sufficient South Africa itself. South Africa now trades directly with 12 African nations and covertly with a dozen others. Therefore the first to suffer would be the blacks themselves. Without food from South Africa, many Black African states would face famine.

In answer to the question — "What is the implication of world economic pressures on South Africa for the Western economies?" — Henry Ford II recently stated: "Not good. The Western economies depend a lot on the metals that come out of South Africa. In our business, for instance, we need a lot of the more precious metals. When you don't have any other source, this supply is very important. Apart from that, Western economies are not doing well and any form of pressure on a trading partner is not going to help them to recover."

Other questions put to Henry Ford II in January 1978 and his replies were:

Q. Have you experienced pressure to end your operations in South Africa?

A. Well, we do get pressure. From church groups and people here and there. But my personal impression is that the Black leaders in the United States to whom I have spoken think we should stay in South Africa.

We have listened to the various viewpoints, and we think it is to the benefit of everyone — and not least to the benefit of Black South Africans — if we stay and maintain our investment here.

Q. Do you plan to increase your investment in South Africa?

A. We will keep on making investments for retooling and to maintain plant and machinery. We have to keep modern. Otherwise, we have no plans. The profit potential in South Africa is not very great. There are thirteen car manufacturers and twenty truck manufacturers competing in South Africa at present. It is an intense and difficult marketplace.

Q. Do you have faith in the economic future of South Africa?

A. I think the medium term looks bright. Obviously, there are difficult times right now. For instance our industry here is 20 to 22 per cent down and we are not making any money here — but that doesn't mean we move out just because we have a lean period. We are getting our costs into line and waiting for the turnaround."

When President Samora Machel of Mozambique makes inflammatory speeches at international conferences amounting to an incitement to war against South Africa, how many people realize that he is going through the back door to beg money and food from Prime Minister Vorster. When a mining disaster took place in Mozambique, it was South Africa that sent rescuers.

The United Nations Security Council's decision to impose an immediate, total, mandatory and permanent embargo on the sale of arms to South Africa has long been expected and the country is now at least 75 per cent self-sufficient in total armaments, with contingency plans carefully prepared to deal with just such an emergency. Therefore the embargo will not create a defence crisis.

The French Ministry of Defence has made it clear that France will not deliver the two corvettes nearing completion at Lorient and the two Agosta class submarines building at Nantes, consequent upon the UN Security Council's decision to impose a total arms sales ban on the Pretoria Government. France has a wide range of arms contracts with South Africa, and French weapons are also built in South Africa, under licence. It remains to be seen how the details of the total ban are to be enforced.

The Soviets must be laughing all the way to Moscow, for South Africa's requirement for submarines and corvettes is based only on the obligation to patrol and observe Soviet shipping movements around the Cape.

The arms embargo will play straight into the hands of the Kremlin, for South Africa is the only military power that is a barrier to further Soviet penetration. The West's decision to weaken South Africa's military competence will merely help the Politburo's long term strategy to absorb the tip of Africa and isolate it from its Western connections.

In a report published in the **Daily Telegraph** on 5 November, 1977 Mr. Robert Moss presented new evidence that there are some robust governments left that are equally threatened by Soviet expansion and are equally appalled by the apparent failure of nerve among the major Western Powers. Far from feeling obliged to march in step with the organised hypocrisy of the UN, they will hit back and are banding together to ensure their mutual survival.

The unwritten alliance between South Africa and Israel is only one example of the banding together of many countries that form part of the target zone for Soviet expansion but can no longer count, for one reason or another, on unequivocal backing from the NATO powers. The conclusion that many of their leaders appear to be reaching is that some initiative is required to withstand further expansion of the Soviet bloc, but is unlikely to come from a major Western capital in the near future. Therefore, they must find the means of self-defence from elsewhere.

Israel is the strongest military power in the Middle East and therefore the safest bastion against Soviet encroachments.

In January, the Central Intelligence Agency reacted with understandable embarrassment to the mistaken release of one of its secret documents disclosing that it suspected Israel of possessing nuclear weapons as long ago as 1974.

The report, which was released after a request under the Freedom of Information Act from an environmental group, said that the CIA believed "Israel has already produced nuclear weapons". It added: "Our judgment is based on Israeli acquisition of large quantities of uranium, partly by clandestine means, the ambiguous nature of Israeli efforts in the field of uranium enrichment and Israel's large investment in a costly missile system designed to accommodate nuclear warheads."

Nevertheless, the report said, the CIA did not expect the Israelis "to provide confirmation of widespread suspicions of their capability, either by nuclear testing or by threats of use, short of a grave threat to the nation's existence."

The report, dated 1974 and entitled: 'Prospects for future proliferation of nuclear weapons', was among a batch of documents released by the Energy Department. The environmental group which obtained the papers passed a copy to a radio network.

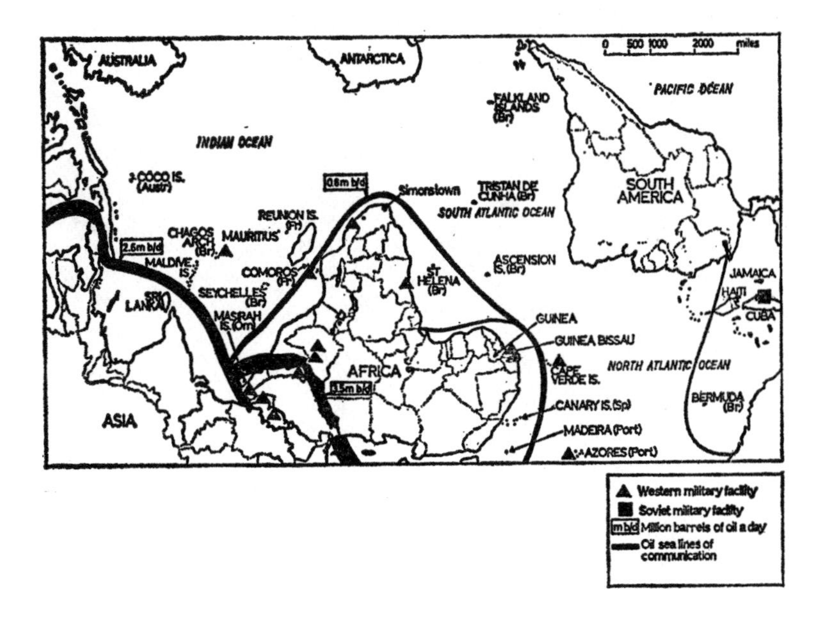

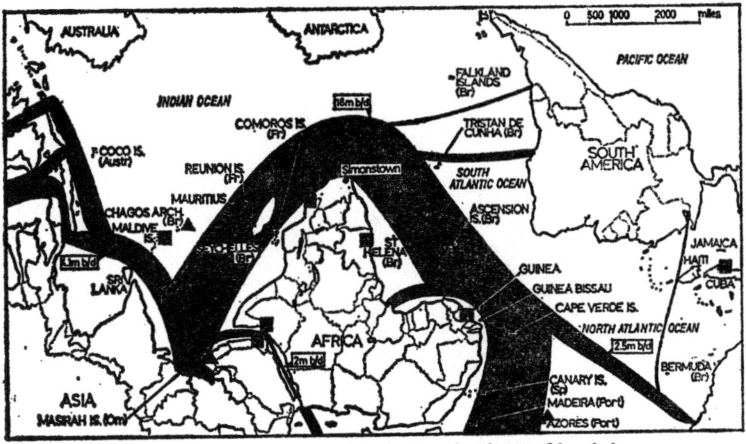

Azimuthal Equidistant Projection centred on Cape Town, South Africa. All distances from the centre of the projection are correct.

These maps are reproduced by permission of the Editor of *Survival*, International Institute for Strategic Studies, 18 Adam Street, London WC2N 6AL, and by permission of the author of an article entitled 'The New Strategic Map', which appeared in VOL. XIX NO. 2, March/April 1977 by Geoffrey Kemp.

These maps are reproduced by permission of the Editor of *Survival*, International Institute for Strategic Studies, 18 Adam Street, London, WC2N 6AL, and by permission of the author of an article entitled 'The New Strategic Map', which appeared in vol. xix, no. 2, March/April 1977 by Geoffrey Kemp.

CHAPTER 22

South Africa's Military Capability

DESPITE the 15-year-old United Nations arms embargo against South Africa, it has been able to build up an impressive military capability. It is far bigger than any of the publicly-available estimates made by military watchdogs such as the London-based International Institute for Strategic Studies (IISS).

The discrepancies between the London Institute and those available from other sources are in some cases vast, as the following table shows:

What is the strength of South Africa's military capability?

	IISS*	Estimated Strength
Combat aircraft	362	650
Helicopters	91	220
Tanks	170	530
Armoured cars	1,600	1,600
Scout cars	230	250
Infantry Fighting Vehicles and Armoured Personnel Carriers	780	1,000
Self-propelled guns	No figures	300
Medium and light artillery	No figures	400

* **The Military Balance** 1977-78, IISS.

From the above table it will be seen that the number of combat aircraft in the South African Air Force is nearly double the figures given by the IISS. The table shows more than twice as many helicopters and three times as many tanks. South Africa has 300 self-propelled guns and 400 medium and light artillery pieces. No figures are given by the IISS.

According to the official statistics of the US Arms Control and and Disarmament Agency, South Africa received £250 million worth of military equipment between 1965 and 1974. The actual figure is nearly three times as great. Between 1963 and 1975 the value of war material imported by South Africa comes to nearly £600 million.

In other words, the UN embargo resolutions, numbers 181 and 182 passed in 1963 because of South Africa's apartheid policy were, in fact, completely ineffective.

Resolution 181 called on all nations "to cease forthwith the sale and shipment of arms and ammunition of all types and military vehicles to South Africa". Britain and France abstained but 182 was adopted unanimously and the ban was extended to "equipment and material needed for the manufacture and maintenance of arms and ammunition in South Africa".

Britain and France reserved the right to supply equipment to South Africa for external defence. Britain announced its total embargo a year later but excluded firm contracts. Subsequently six Canberra bombers, four Wasp helicopters and 16 Buccaneer naval bombers were delivered. France continued to supply arms. The US continued to supply spare parts.

There were three clear loopholes in the embargo — the continuation of existing contracts, the supply of arms for external defence, and the continued supply of weapons components which South Africa did not have the know-how to produce.

South African Navy

The South African Navy provides a small but effective anti-submarine and coastal defence force, consisting of three Daphne-class submarines, one destroyer with two anti-submarine warfare (ASW) helicopters, three ASW frigates each with a helicopter, one escort minesweeper, six coastal minesweepers and two patrol craft. The Navy's total strength of 5,500 includes 1,400 conscripts, while the Citizen Reserve Force is twice the strength with a manpower of 10,500 equipped with one destroyer, two frigates and seven minesweepers.

The South African Navy had always maintained a good liaison with the Royal Navy. However on the abrogation by Britain of the Simonstown Agreement in 1975, this liaison lapsed. The then Chief of the South African Navy stated that since the ending of the Agreement there had been no training in Britain for naval personnel, the supply of most publications and amendments had ceased (the request for Part IV of the Manual of Seamanship had even been refused) and that, in spite of good personal relations with senior officers of the Royal Navy, the South African attachés in London were being ostracised.

A curt signal was received closing the Joint Communications Centre and no thanks offered for many years of co-operation. When the White Ensign was lowered in HMS **Afrikander** there was even trouble over the South African Navy band being present.

Spare parts for the old frigates and for Buccaneer aircraft continued to come through but that was about all. The results were serious for two reasons; firstly, there was a lowering of the efficiency of the South African Navy and, secondly, a lowering of morale and pro-British feeling. Because of the diminution of signal traffic, the Soviet Union soon realised there was a rift between the Royal Navy and South African Navy which considerably decreased the potential of both, particularly as the Royal Navy, as well as NATO, relied on intelligence reports from the South African Navy and Air Force.

The effect of the arms embargo on South Africa's Navy is serious, particularly the cancellation by France of the two corvettes and two submarines. However, no doubt an ingenious solution will be found to counter this temporary setback. The penalty to be paid if alternative sources are not found would be the death of the South African Navy as a deep water operational unit.

Once again the Third World/Communist Coalition (i.e. UNO) will have done the Soviet's dirty work for them, for the surveillance and protection of the Cape Route by the South African Navy will have been neutralised. The argument so often put forward that arms supplied to South Africa would be used to "suppress the natives" holds no water, because South Africa is now self-sufficient in conventional army weapons. What we are talking about are submarines, anti-submarine warfare, maritime aircraft and missile ships. Whoever heard of submarines being used to suppress the natives!

South African Air Force

As the table shows, the South African Air Force with a total manpower of 8,500, including 3,000 conscripts, has 650 combat aircraft, 220 helicopters and is well supported by four transport squadrons, two communication and liaison squadrons and more than 300 operational trainers, some of which are armed.

The Citizens Reserve Force is no less than 25,000 strong, organised into six squadrons.

South African Army

The table shows that the Army is well equipped with tanks, armoured cars, scout cars, armoured personnel carriers, the new Radle Fighting Vehicle, self-propelled guns, and medium and light artillery. The army's strength is 41,000 and of this number the greater proportion are conscripts, the figures being 34,000 men and 2,100 women. This is the Combat Force. The Active Reserve (Citizen Force) is three times the strength of the Combat Force, namely 130,000 Reservists who serve 30 days per year for eight years.

Except for specialist forces and an African regular battalion, there is no regular army, but in South-West Africa five Regular African battalions and one Coloured infantry battalion have been raised. I inspected the latter, now in its ninth month of training, and saw one company being put through its paces in the role of aid to the civil power and another in anti-guerilla warfare. The standard was high, noticeably in map reading. This is no doubt due to the fact that many of the soldiers have passed the matriculation examination.

The Combat Force and the Citizen Force are supported by a home defence Commando Force consisting of 90,000 para-military forces, organised in infantry battalion-type units and grouped in formations of five or more, with the tasks of local industrial and rural protection duties. Members do two years initial and 30 days annual training.

The South African Police Force is 35,500 strong (19,500 White and 16,000 non-Whites).

In the chapter on South-West Africa, I give high credit to the professional performance of the South African Army in the operational area.

Operations in Angola in 1975 consisted mainly of armoured cars and lorried infantry. The objectives were reached on time and Luanda could easily have been captured had not the US Congress denied support just at the time when Soviet reinforcements were being flown in.

Without US support, the South African Government decided that discretion was the better part of valour. Therefore the only alternative to shooting down Soviet transport planes was to retire. An almost exact replica of the Suez operations of 1956!

I had an opportunity to talk at length with the Brigadier who commanded the whole operation and also with one of the task force commanders — and his Intelligence Officer who is a defence correspondent by trade — so I now know the inside story.

Problems of communications and logistics became apparent during the campaign. By NATO standards, the Army is perforce introspective and lacks the latest doctrine and some equipment on account of being denied outside (NATO) staff college and other training facilities. Senior officers are young and keen, but lack practical experience of commanding balanced formations of all arms under conditions of modern warfare against a first class enemy. But this is something that can be easily rectified.

It was that great military genius Field Marshal Lord Slim, who wrote in 1956 in that fine book of his, **Defeat into Victory,** that "stalking terrorists in a Malayan jungle is today, strange as it may seem, the best training for nuclear warfare". Why did he say this? Because whatever form modern war may take, the destruction of bases, disruption of communications, and disorganisation of control, will compel armies to disperse. Dispersed fighting will have two main requirements — skilled and determined junior leaders and self-reliant, physically hard, well-disciplined troops.

"Success in future land operations", went on the Field Marshal, "will depend on the immediate availability of such leaders and such soldiers, ready to operate in small, independent formations. They will have to be prepared to do without regular lines of communication, to guide themselves and to subsist largely on what the country offers."

He then made this pungent pronouncement. "Such land operations, less rigidly controlled and more individualistic than in the past, will not be unlike ours (Burma, in the Second World War) as we approached the Chindwin and the Irrawaddy".

It seems to me that the young soldiers and junior leaders of the South African Army, likewise the Rhodesian Army are, indeed, being well grounded for whatever form of warfare the future may have in store for them. It is the more senior commanders who must keep themselves abreast of modern technology and techniques in the nuclear and non-nuclear fields. I have no reason to believe that the South African Generals are found wanting in this respect, in spite of being denied access to outside (NATO) staff colleges. In February, I read a report which has this to say:

"The South African Army is causing concern to military experts in NATO who regard its conscript men as keen and efficient but insufficiently trained for modern warfare. What really bothers the experts is the apparent complacency of the South African generals who just cannot see the shortcomings of a conscript army which lacks a professional regular core. The South African Air Force and Navy is regarded as being up to standard."

I found that the South African "military" at all levels have a clear idea of the Soviet Union's long and short term aims. They realise that the policy and strategy of their enemies is the expansion of Marxism by fomenting revolution in Southern Africa. They know that the African states by themselves do not possess the ability to initiate a successful aggression against South Africa and that the threat, therefore, is from the militant African bloc supported by the Soviet Union, thereby giving them the ability to wage simultaneously integrated revolutionary and conventional warfare.

I am convinced that the South African Armed Forces possess both the means and the will to defend their country's territorial integrity by fighting a conventional offensive battle against any aggressor. They will not tolerate any aggression against them, but have no ambitions in terms of territorial expansion. Their defence posture is, therefore, defensive but prepared.

Because South Africa does not form part of any alliance with any foreign power, nor can it rely upon such an ally in time of war, the armed forces are being so structured that they will be able to meet the threats against the country without outside help.

They realise that a credible deterrent is the only means of countering the possibility of an attack by any potential aggressor. For this purpose they are building up a balanced army, air force and navy, equipped with the most modern weapons and intend to make use of modern military technology, including, I trust, nuclear technology.

What particularly impressed me was the fact that they understand so well that thwarting insurgency and maintaining the authority of the elected Government requires an indirect strategy, in which military force is but a single facet, for terrorism is only one of the means used by insurgents to achieve their aims. Notwithstanding, the military role is of the utmost importance, and, therefore, the armed forces accord a high priority to the study and implementation of counter-insurgency.

Insurgency is the most difficult problem to counter because it is essentially a political war waged, not only through violence and terrorism, but also through propaganda, infiltration, subversion, strikes and boycotts.

Finally the South African Defence Force as a whole is trained to support the civil authorities in the maintenance of law and order and in the maintenance of essential services throughout the country.

Since writing the above, I was fortunate enough to attend Exercise Quicksilver in May, held near Kimberley. This was the largest army and air force exercise to be held since 1973. I was by myself, conducted personally by the Chief Umpire, and was not inhibited from seeing anything or asking any questions.

The exercise was modern conventional mobile warfare and I can give no higher praise when I say that in many respects the standard was higher than is to be found in NATO. The soldiers looked like soldiers, not long haired shaggy sheep dogs. The South African is a fighter — tough, fit, as hard as nails, well disciplined, with high morale and a tremendous pride in his unit. He know he is fighting for the very survival of his country and that arrayed against him are not only the Soviets and the Third World but the West also. If the country were to be put on a war footing with all White males under fifty years of age being called up, the mobilisation strength would be of the order of 400,000-500,000.

Soldiering to every citizen is now a serious business and military attributes like convoy discipline, dispersal, concealment and camouflage are second nature. Furthermore the South Africans are as proficient at conventional warfare as they are at counter-insurgency operations. Their deep pre-emptive assault into Angola by parachute and armoured columns is proof enough of this, for the resistance they met was fierce and they were attacking entrenched strongholds, and suffered only five killed in the process.

I paid particular attention to their new locally manufactured infantry fighting vehicle, the Radle, which has a good cross-country performance and carries ten soldiers who can use their weapons from portholes without having to dismount. The armament consists of one 20mm gun and one 7.62mm Browning. Then there are their armoured cars which are armed with one 90mm gun and two 7.62 Brownings — one for anti-aircraft and the other in a ground role.

Unless I am mistaken, South Africa is now well advanced in the electronic warfare field, for there were times during the exercise when there was a complete communication black-out, right back to the Ministry of Defence in Cape Town.

I would hazard a guess that the South African armed forces are today in a better position than they were 15 months ago and that there is now no shortage of countries in the queue offering to provide them with hardware, including missile ships. It is, therefore, satisfying to realise that despite the worst endeavours of the Third World/Communist Coalition (UNO), there are those countries which understand only too well that strategically South Africa is the main bulwark against the expansion of Soviet Russia's imperialistic designs in a theatre of power that is becoming increasingly important.

But why is it that America is unable or unwilling to perceive that South Africa is small fry compared to the Soviet Union's ultimate target, which is the USA itself and the destruction of a free capitalist society?

China is only too well aware that if the jugular vein of the Cape route were to be cut, NATO could be brought to its knees without a shot being fired. Therefore, in the face of the mounting Soviet offensive in Africa, it surely behoves China to establish a line of communisation and a new relationship with South Africa. China has much to gain, not only strategically but also in trade, technology and vital mineral supplies. The Chinese Foreign Minister himself has stated that war with Russia is inevitable and that only one thing is holding them back, namely incomplete strategic deployment. America is not only too soft and lacks the will to counter the Soviet Union in Africa, but its policy of appeasement and its supply of credits and technology to Moscow can only rebound in the form of Soviet military aggression and lead to war. The ball is now in China's court and it is up to her Foreign Minister to match his words with deeds before it is too late. Time is running out, for the Soviet naval expansion and deployment show that they regard their navy as a global instrument of Soviet power, with their ships able to lie astride the traditional sea routes. Indeed, in the words of Admiral Sergi Gorshkov, Commander-in-Chief of the Soviet Navy: "For the first time in the country's history, our navy has become a long-range armed force in the full meaning of the word."

CHAPTER 23

The Secret US War against South Africa

IN 1977, the Johannesburg morning newspaper **The Citizen** published a series of articles exposing the US strategy against South Africa. Subsequently it was published as a booklet **Secret US War Against South Africa**[1]. The authoress was Ms Aida Parker, one of South Africa's top investigative journalists who has a high reputation for her writing integrity. Her contacts reach into all parts of Southern Africa and into virtually all political parties and organisations, from extreme radicals to conservatives.

The details revealed in this booklet are indeed shocking. To date, no formal answer or comment has been offered by the US Government, although over 20 top CIA officials were "forced" into early retirement — some referred to this as a "wholesale purge". No connection has, in fact, been proved yet between Aida Parker's revelations and the CIA shakeup.

What are some of the shocking revelations?

The Carter Administration is waging a secret war against South Africa. It is an operation in which:

Opinion against South Africa is being mobilised in the US on a scale of intensity not seen since the anti-Vietnam war crusades.

Foreign governments, through US embassies, are being pressured into withdrawing or reducing investment in South Africa.

Agencies of the US Government are actively trying to destabilise the position in South Africa by generous assistance to resistance movements, Black Consciousness bodies and would-be Black leaders.

The US electorate generally knows little, if anything, about the ramifications of a campaign organised and sponsored by the liberal-internationalist wing of the State Department and its counterparts in the Central Intelligence Agency.

This liberal-internationalist wing is now well-placed in the White House hierarchy and is exercising a decisive influence on the Carter Administration's policies.

These elements have decided that the Whites of South Africa are finished.

---

1. **Secret US War Against South Africa.** By Aida Parker. S.A. Today (Pty) Ltd., Nedbank East City, 120 End Street, Johannesburg 2001. 50c.

The war now being waged is to ensure that the end of White rule, and the substitution of Black majority rule, is achieved as speedily as possible — and that when the Blacks take over, the US will have a special and friendly relationship with them, no matter what their politics.

Ms Aida Parker's inquiries prove that:

1. South Africa is now No. 1 on the American liberal "hit list", ranking higher even than Rhodesia or Chile.

2. Over the past three years, in an attempt to slow or stop the rapid erosion of goodwill between Pretoria and Washington, Pretoria has found it expedient to tolerate gross interference in its domestic affairs, at an ever-increasing rate, by various US agencies.

3. In the US liberal-internationalist campaign to overthrow the Whites, there is a massive and increasing flow of covert State Department-CIA funds into South Africa to support resistance and other anti-government groups and organisations.

4. There is good reason to suspect that much of this money is funnelled into the Republic through the US Embassy in Botswana, an office handling a daily and busy traffic of South African dissidents.

There is evidence that United States Information Service involvement in South African student, labour and political affairs goes far beyond what might be regarded as acceptable.

The USIS was the first (and only) foreign service to establish a Reading Room in Soweto. This may, on the face of it, be regarded as an educational and cultural service, with technical and other works being made available.

However, there are many works dealing with the civil rights struggle which Mr. Andy Young and other US officials are trying to relate to the South African situation, encouraging Blacks to follow the American Negro civil rights example.

At the USIS Soweto facility many inflammatory works are read which try to draw analogies between the American civil rights struggle and Black Power in South Africa.

Court records show that the USIS offices in Shakespeare House, Johannesburg, have frequently been used after hours for duplicating illegal revolutionary pamphlets, although it is not suggested that US officials are directly involved in this.

It was the Johannesburg USIS which arranged a recent Sunday afternoon meeting between UN Ambassador Andy Young and an audience including some of the country's best-known political activists.

Senior Cabinet Ministers claimed this meeting directly contravened the agreed terms of Mr. Young's visit. Presumably, it could not have been held without the knowledge and approval of the US Ambassador.

While rattling the sword of human rights, the Carter Administration does not show the same delicacy about human lives. There is ample evidence that US agents financially back militants who are busy trying to exploit the delicate racial balance by inciting feelings against the Whites and the Government.

A declared tactical aim of the Carter Administration is to promote disaffection in the Republic by undermining the economy, on the assumption that the masses will take affairs into their own hands if life becomes sufficiently difficult. This is the basis of the current vigorously pursued "disinvestment" policy.

South Africa has been so obsessed with the overt danger from the Soviet Union that it has more or less ignored the covert danger from the US posed by the liberal-internationalist element in the American Government.

Because Pretoria trusted the US, no continuous, concentrated effort has ever been made to monitor overt and covert American activities against South Africa.

The greatest tragedy facing South Africa today is Black Power imported deliberately from the US which has been behind some of South Africa's worst disturbances. It is the time bomb ticking away.

Millions of words have been said and written about Black Power. But who asks how this radical philosophy came to South Africa, who was responsible for establishing it, who still contributes the funds that keep the flame alive?

Most Whites and certainly every Black, including the leaders of the constantly proliferating Black Consciousness movements, firmly believe Black Power to be a home-grown, grass roots manifestation, the natural desire of the nation's Black people to develop a pride in their own language, history, culture, ability and awareness of their own racial identity.

These are positive ideals for any group of people. Few would quarrel with them. They are essential to the whole separate development concept.

But investigation shows that:

Black Power is by no means a natural-born South African phenomena.

It was deliberately imported from the US.

It was cynically introduced as a means of inflaming racialist passions and creating a Black-White polarisation, "to achieve social change in the present factual situation." In other words to bring about confrontation.

Ms Aida Parker asked anthropologist Dr. Willie Breytenback of the Africa Institute if he could explain the rationale behind this

USIS "cultural" activity in Soweto.

He said "The pattern was clearly laid down during his visit here by Mr. Andy Young. It is part of the Carter Administration's campaign to relate the experience of South African Blacks to the Americal civil rights movement.

"I maintain there is no relevance whatsoever, culturally or ethnically, in the two experiences.

"The American Negro is virtually detribalised and Westernised, the South African Black is not. Equally, White interests were not really at stake in the US Southern States where Whites were still numerically stronger. In South Africa it is just the opposite.

"Black poetry, Black art, Black literature are all being used in the attempt to transmit the thoughts, modes and behaviours of the American civil rights struggle, so that South African Blacks can accept or take over some aspects of this Negro experience and in so doing be made more and more aware of their Black Negritude".

Old CIA watchers are not too surprised at the Soweto "cultural" development.

"It is a classic case of history repeating itself," one former intelligence officer told Ms Aida Parker.

These extracts are part of the highly successful efforts of American Establishment at destabilising South Africa.

There is not the slightest doubt that this is being done without the knowledge and without the consent of the great majority of American people.

Nevertheless, a certain section is bent on destroying White South Africa — and South Africans must understand this. President Roosevelt once said: "In politics, nothing happens by accident. If it happens, you can bet it was planned that way".

South Africans must now recognise the face of their true enemies, since their country's future may depend on their doing so.

CHAPTER 24

South-West Africa (Namibia)

SOUTH-WEST Africa is the huge mineral-rich territory that South Africa has governed, originally under a 1920 League of Nationals mandate. The map on page 152 shows the comparative size of the country. With London in the top left-hand corner and Berlin in the top right-hand corner, Rome fits into the bottom right-hand corner of Namibia.

At Windhoek, the capital, I had meetings in October 1977 and May this year with Judge M. T. Steyn, the South African appointed Administrator-General. The Judge is an impressive man, highly intelligent, extremely knowledgeable about world affairs; radiates confidence and has all the attributes of a firm leader. Knowing my past history, he opened the serious part of our conversation with this remark:

"The hard fought battle of Kohima was the turning point in the Burma Campaign against Japan in World War II."

I agreed and asked him if he had ever been told what the inscription was on the Kohima memorial. He did not know, so I recounted these moving words:

When you go home

Tell them of us, and say

For your tomorrow

We gave our today.

I added — "What a disgraceful tomorrow. We won the War but have lost the peace." With this he agreed and said one of the main lessons of the Second World War and the numerous conflicts since the end of the war, particularly the collapse of the Portuguese Army in Angola, was the overriding need for really hardy, well-trained and highly disciplined soldiers. He was severely critical of what he called the rabble of 60,000 armed Portuguese soldiers whose one aim was to get out of Angola as quickly as possible, and to hell with the consequences.

We discussed the Soviet Union's long and short term aims and her technique of revolutionary war by proxy. We agreed that the present fashionable French word of the '70's called "detente" was equivalent to an equally fashionable word of the '30's called "appeasement". We also agreed that the Soviet's creed was "Might is Right" and "What is mine I keep; what is yours is negotiable". The only thing the Russians understood was strength backed by the will and determination of a people. It was power, and the will to exercise it, that impresses the Soviets. It is weakness that encourages them to adventure.

I reminded him of two maxims, one by a Norwegian poet who said "Peace is the most ruthless creature in the world. One must fight for it all the time." And the other by General de Gaulle who said "Treaties are like roses and young girls — they last while they last." To prevent war, I said, we must wage peace. It is a battle of information.

Judge Steyn has repealed discriminatory and generally unpopular laws. He has scrapped the pass laws, and established freedom of movement throughout the territory. He has repealed the Immorality and Mixed Marriages Acts. It is no longer necessary to ask permission to hold a political meeting in any of the three northern Homelands of Ovambo, Kavango and Eastern Caprivi. Previously, a permit was needed to hold a meeting of more than five people.

A law providing for indefinite detention has also been scrapped. Now a person may not be detained for more than 96 hours. The judicial power of the tribal authorities in the area has been abolished and sentences for contravening those security regulations that remain in existence have been reduced.

Judge Steyn has emphasised, however, that he would not tolerate force, violence or intimidation anywhere in the territory. He would not hesitate, he declared, to use the powers available to him to uphold law and order whenever necessary.

In October 1977, accompanied by my wife, I flew by a privately chartered light aircraft from Windhoek to Oudangwa in Ovambo. We flew at 10,000 feet and for the last 20 minutes to half an hour we flew at only sixty feet as a precaution against SWAPO's surface to air heat-homing missiles. On arrival at Odangwa, we motored to Oshakati where we stayed overnight at a government rest house. The next morning I visited the army headquarters where I was thoroughly briefed by the South African colonel commanding the brigade in the operational area.

The brigade's total front was about eight hundred kilometres, which gave each battalion an approximate frontage of 100 kilometres and the same distance in depth. The brigade is, of course, able to economise its forces opposite those areas in Angola which are dominated by pro-Western UNITA forces.

I was told — not by the colonel — that when the South African Army launched their offensive into Angola, they inflicted 5,000 casualities for the loss of only 39 of their own troops. The Cubans are not fighting soldiers in the accepted sense of the word. They are road bound and incapable of operating in the bush.

Up to the time of my visit on 13 October, the South African Forces had so far lost that year only two men killed in contacts with the enemy and three killed by mines.

The time taken to concentrate and react to an incident on the spot is about three quarters of an hour, mobility being achieved by the ubiquitous helicopter. The danger of mines is ever present but the problem is being overcome. Of 13 mines detected in the two weeks before my arrival, three had been detonated and ten lifted.

The SWAPO guerillas are equipped with rocket launchers and the most modern Soviet automatic weapons of 1975/76 manufacture. But they do not stand and fight after the initial exchange of fire. Having seen at close quarters the burly and superbly fit and highly trained young South African soldiers, it is not difficult to realise why.

In the operational area that I visited there were three battalions of infantry — one White National Service battalion, one Coloured battalion (Cape Corps) of mixed blood, (two Coloured companies and one White Company) and one local Black battalion. In the Black battalion each platoon of thirty Black soldiers was commanded by a White officer and operations were conducted at platoon strength, unlike a White battalion in which sections of six men are capable of operationg independently under a NCO. The forward troops operate from mobile bases, with their parent static base in the rear. The normal turn-round of troops in a static base is every three months.

A National Service soldier undergoes nine months basic training followed by three weeks intensive training in an operational training camp before being launched into operations proper.

Supporting the soldiers is the Home Guard. With their local knowledge of the area, they are employed as trackers, guides interpreters etc. Special Branch is highly organised and the efficiency of intelligence and psychological warfare officers is also of a high order.

Great importance is attached to the Civic Action Campaign — winning the hearts and minds of the people — and it is in this role that the older Reservists, called up for their annual service play a valuable role. Being mature, experienced and diplomatic they are in a better position to speak to the local headmen and win their confidence and trust.

At first, the colonel at Ashaketi was reluctant to allow me to go any farther forward than his headquarters on the grounds that he was responsible for my safety. However, when I explained that Prime Minister Vorster had told me he would be interested to learn what my candid opinion was of the professional ability of the South African soldier, the colonel readily agreed to put a Puma helicopter at my disposal and he made quick arrangements for me to visit a forward battalion headquarters, followed by a company headquarters close to the border.

The battalion headquarters was located at a place called Ogongo where I was given a highly professional briefing by the Commanding Officer. I was particularly struck by the fact that the average age of the Adjutant, Intelligence Officer and Signals Officer was only twenty-one. The maps in the Operations Room, the layout, and the communications were first class and would have done credit to any British battalion. The vehicles were well maintained and even major repairs were being carried out on the spot.

Forward at one of the company headquarters, at a place called Ombalantu, I found the same high standard of efficiency, the same supreme confidence and excellent liaison with the local administration. I was fortunate enough to see a platoon of young soldiers who had just returned from operations. They were stripped to the waist so one was able to see their magnificent physique and fitness. Their average age was eighteen but they looked about twenty-one, as hard as nails, and every inch a mature soldier. No effeminate long hair in that hot climate, no scruffiness, no bellyaching. Their morale was sky-high and they had the glint of battle in their eyes. They were as keen as mustard to get back into operations and seek out and destroy their enemy. They were cheerful; spoke up well and answered one's questions without hesitation. They were obviously highly trained and every man a marksman. They told me they were fighting for their country of which they were inordinately proud and would repel and smash any attempt by what they called "those Communists" to invade or infiltrate their country. One soldier said to me "We will hit them with all we've got". One came away feeling uplifted at having met such men. These young soldiers, like their Rhodesian counterparts, are certainly second to none.

In October last year, I had a long talk at his headquarters in Windhoek, with Major General J. J. Geldenhuys, who is the General Officer commanding South West Africa and therefore responsible for all the operations against SWAPO guerillas. He is an impressive, young-looking, smart, forthright general who expresses himself clearly and is well informed, a real soldier's soldier.

We found ourselves in complete agreement about the basic principles to be applied in the conduct of anti-guerilla operations. He was able to bring me up to date with the method of applying such principles to suit the type of terrain in which his Security

Forces were operating and against the type of enemy they were fighting.

We were also in complete accord about the threat from the Soviet Union, its long and short term aims and its technique of revolutionary war by proxy. He took a photocopy of my booklet **The Defence of the Western World.**[1] now in its third reprint in the United States, with a distribution of 35,000 copies to date.

If General Geldenhuys is a typical example of South Africa's senior commanders, then Prime Minister Vorster can rest assured that his generals compare more than favourably with those of any super or medium power.

I had a meeting with the retiring Commissioner General in Owamboland who made the following points. What was so essential was that there should be a strong, united, stable Government so as to present a firm front in preparation for independence. All political differences must be resolved under the maxim — "Either we hang together or we hang separately; united we stand, divided we fall." The Commissioner General was adamant that about 80 percent of the Black and Coloured people were anti-SWAPO (South-West African People's Organisation). He also stressed that a strong military presence of South African soldiers opposite the border with Angola was absolutely essential, not only to defend the country from without, but also to defend the country from subversive elements within. He stated that if the South African army was withdrawn before Namibia had raised and trained its own army from the indigenous tribes, SWAPO would take over the country within 24 hours. A UN force would be useless, for the same reasons I stated earlier, with reference to Rhodesia.

One can but hope that Mr. Dick Mudge, who in October 1977, had formed a new multi-racial party called the Republican Party, will rally the country to his banner and win the forthcoming election with an overwhelming working majority. This would put paid to SWAPO's nefarious designs.

However, the UN has its own iniquitous plans to transform Namibia into yet another Red dictatorship. What are these plans?

After my visit in October last year, I wrote the following appreciation of the situation which I believe, subsequent events have proved to be accurate.

With South Africa now so thoroughly in the doghouse, the future course of the negotiations — it has also been called horse trading — about Namibia, must be at best uncertain. In these negotiations the brokers for the United Nations are the Western members of the Security Council, the US, Britain, France, West

---

1. **The Defence of the Western World.** By General Sir Walter Walker, Destiny Publishers, Merrimac, Mass. 01860, USA.

Germany and Canada. Their task is to find a formula under which SWA will be handed over, in some guise or other, to SWAPO, and to persuade or force the South African Government to accept the formula. SWAPO is the "liberation movement" recognised by the UN as the sole and legitimate representative of the people of that country.

The South African Government maintains, quite rightly, that SWAPO is not representative of about 95% of the people, and that it is, moreover, a Communist front organisation. South Africa's claim about SWAPO's unrepresentative nature is unimportant; the UN has ruled otherwise. The objection that SWAPO is a Communist front organisation is irrelevant, because Communist front organisations are perfectly respectable in the eyes of the UN and, therefore, in this case also to the honest brokers.

After all, did not Dr. Kurt Waldheim, the UN Secretary General, newly back from Moscow, where he conferred upon Leonid Brezhnev the UN Peace Medal, just once again laud the struggle SWAPO is waging? He chose a UN meeting of "solidarity" with Namibia to do so. Surely, if Brezhnev's struggle for peace is thus recognised a word of praise for SWAPO is not out of order?

But what is SWAPO's policy? How does it propose to govern Namibia once it is handed control of the territory?

It is a small point which nobody seems yet to have raised with SWAPO, but it is nevertheless relevant. However, Mr. Sam Nujoma, SWAPO's self-appointed leader, has himself now broken the silence on this matter. As soon as he gets control, he has said in New York, private property will be abolished. All land in particular will revert to the nation, and no compensation will be paid for anything so nationalised because, after all it is "stolen property" he said.

One of the proposals being negotiated, or rather, one major demand which the brokers are making on behalf of SWAPO, is that all South African military forces must forthwith be withdrawn from SWA and replaced by a UN garrison to keep peace during the transition period. Mr. Sam Nujoma has now broken silence on this matter too. The UN force, he said in New York, will be ordered to leave the country immediately power is fully in his hands. There will thus be no chance of interference or obstruction when he launches his programme to dispossess all owners of private property. SWAPO's own "freedom fighters" will be adequate to supervise the programme.

For the rest, SWAPO's policy will be to abolish injustice and to "liberate" Walvis Bay, the nearby South African harbour. The "liberation" of Walvis Bay will, of course, require a war, but apart from that SWAPO will work for peace.

The dispossession and nationalisation of all private property have been accomplished in Mozambique and Angola, the latter being the place from where Mr. Sam Nujoma operates and where he has seen the practical application of this policy. He must, therefore, be satisfied with the results achieved.

But is this really the policy that the US, Britain, France, West Germany and Canada have to negotiate for on behalf of SWAPO?

It was made perfectly clear to me throughout my second visit to Southern Africa in April-May, that South Africa does not trust the Timid Five — the United States, Canada, Britain, France and West Germany — because they have shown that they do not possess the moral courage even to stand up for their own proposals in respect of Namibia. In spite of South Africa having agreed to the Western proposals in toto and without reservations, whereas SWAPO had failed to respond, the UN General Assembly proceeded to condemn South Africa for having been "inflexible and intransigent", while praising SWAPO for making "substantial concessions to facilitate a negotiated settlement". The mind boggles at such a blatant distortion of facts and deranged thinking. So fearful were the Timid Five of standing up and being counted that they abstained from voting. Could there be a more pathetic state of affairs?

While I was in South West Africa, Judge Steyn, the Administrator General of the territory, warned that the fighting in Shaba was proof that time was running out in the region and called for immediate action to implement the Western plan for Namibia. He criticised the procrastination of the five Western nations, emphasising that the delay had harmed the credibility of all concerned with the proposals.

Mr. Vorster's patience must have been sorely taxed, for he had leaned over backwards throughout in an effort to achieve an internationally acceptable solution. But on 24 May, he had no option but to accuse Mr. Don McHenry, the United States deputy representative at the United Nations, who was in South Africa the week before, of "transparent attempts to place the blame for a failure on South Africa". He declared: "It is now very clear to me that the foundation is being laid for a recrimination against South Africa that we are to blame because SWAPO has not yet given an answer". He said: "I am not prepared, on behalf of South Africa, to accept the blame."

While South Africa has accepted the Western proposals and is prepared to carry them out, SWAPO has blatantly announced it would continue with violence, and Mr. Sam Nujoma himself has stated that his aim is to establish a single party Marxist state. He is not interested in the ballot box but only in gun-barrel power. If further proof of this is required one only has to read the extracts from the captured documents on pages 155 to 158. South

Africa would be well advised to plan for the worst case, and if SWAPO's methods and Marxist philosophy of order and instability are to be countered, it will be necessary to strike back where it hurts most — at their bases in Angola, again and again.

Walvis Bay, the main port of Namibia is unmistakably and irrefutably constitutionally and politically part of the Republic of South Africa which is determined to retain it.

Legally, there appears to be little doubt to South Africa's claim to Walvis Bay. It was formally annexed by Britain in 1878, incorporated into the Cape Colony in 1884 and consolidated into the Union of South Africa in 1910. It was excluded from the League of Nations mandate on South-West Africa.

Since 1922, it has been administered from Windhoek simply for convenience. The transfer of control to Cape Town puts it administratively back to square one.

The controversy about the status of Walvis Bay is a typical example of so much being said about an issue so little known to so few. This small South African port enclave in the vast Namib Desert, surrounded by South-West Africa/Namibia, has been caught in the crossfire of the various forces involved in settling the political disputes of the southern African sub-continent. The underlying cause of the present debate concerning the status of Walvis Bay lies in the fact that, with South West Africa/Namibia now moving towards independence, the administration of the port and settlement of Walvis Bay has, from 1 September 1977, reverted back to the Cape Province, and therefore to the Republic of South Africa. This terminated a period of 55 years of administration of Walvis Bay as part of the South West African mandate territory.

The accusations raised against South Africa's decision to end this period of indirect administration have been initiated mainly by the South West Africa People's Organisation (SWAPO) and the UN Council for Namibia. In view of the fact that the accusations are devoid of any valid political and legal substance in terms of constitutional and international law, the only inference to be drawn is that the controversy has been raised in an attempt by SWAPO to strengthen its own hand in the process of negotiations over the future of SWA.

SWAPO claims: "Namibians cannot be bound by colonial treaties from the 1880s of which they had no part. South Africa's claim for the bay is an expansionist venture".

It is true that geographically Walvis Bay forms part of SWA: but Alaska, surrounded by Canada, remains part of the USA; Hong Kong, surrounded by the People's Republic of China, is a British colony; Gibraltar, surrounded by Spain, is British territory; and Northern Ireland, geographically part of Ireland and separated by sea from Britain, is part of the United Kingdom.

The argument of geographical contiguity is, therefore, irrelevant. In fact, South Africa's claim to sovereignty over Walvis Bay has never been disputed, and has been formally recognised by the League of Nations, the United Nations and the International Court of Justice.

The town is of commercial and strategic importance. Commercially it is South Africa's fifth biggest port handling some two million tons of cargo a year, including uranium from RTZ's Rossing mine, 40 miles inland. This uranium is essential to Britain's power programme. The fishing, canning and fishmeal industry also represents a £15m investment.

Strategically, it is the most important harbour on the coast south of Lobito in Angola. It guards the trade route round the Cape of Good Hope from Europe to the Gulf and the Far East. It is also easily accessible from the Americas.

South Africa maintains a military garrison in the 350 square mile enclave and one reason it is determined to stay there is that if an independent Namibia turned hostile or fell under Marxist domination, it could be developed into a military bastion.

Walvis Bay commands a fine natural harbour with a sandy bottom which could be dredged to accommodate much larger ships. A development programme already planned calls for the construction of a tanker berth, extensions to wharfs and quays; deepening the entrance channel and the provision of more cargo sheds, cranes and other equipment.

The Bay itself is 5½ miles in length and 1½ miles wide. In this magnificent harbour there is almost unlimited anchorage for merchant vessels and naval ships in tranquil waters secure from the westerly gales to which the whole coast line is subjected.

The harbour is of such strategic importance to Southern Africa and to the West that its transfer to South-West Africa must of necessity depend upon the political stability attained in Southern Africa and the strategic value it holds for the Western powers.

The comparative size of South West Africa

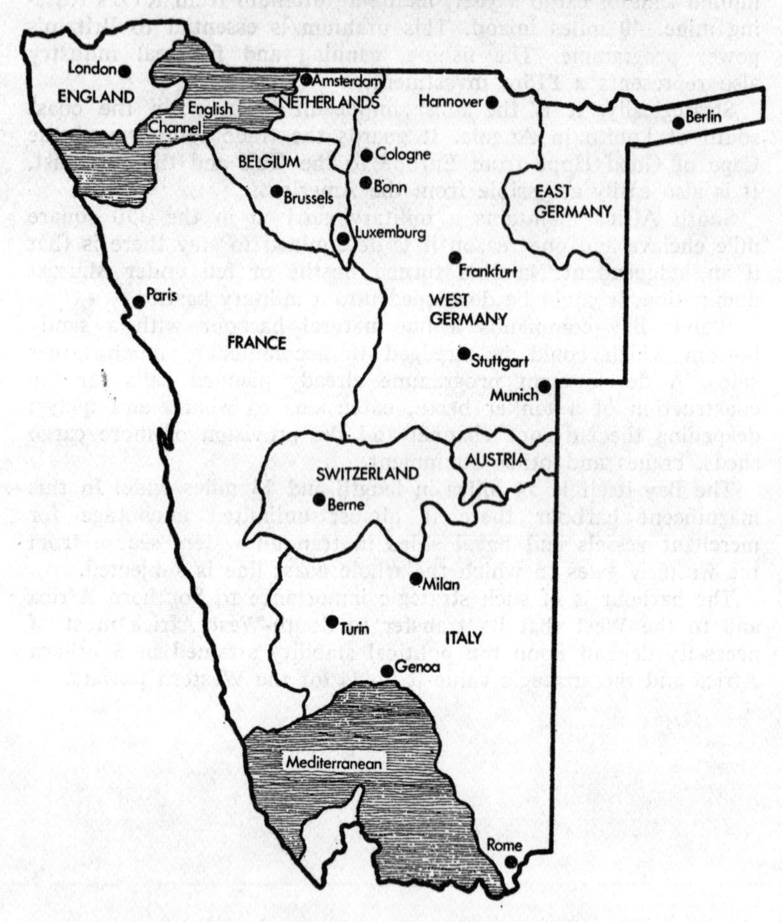

CHAPTER 25

South African Strike into Angola, 4 May, 1978

I WAS in South West Africa (SWA) shortly after the strike into Angola on 4 May. There is no doubt that SWAPO had deliberately created the situation which led to this South African strike on SWAPO terrorist bases. SWAPO had intensified its terrorist activities to a point where the situation had become intolerable and South Africa was forced to strike the terrorist bases to prevent a serious deterioration of the position in SWA. The timing was dictated by the fact that SWAPO was on the point of launching a major assault and to prevent this from happening a pre-emptive strike had to be launched as quickly as possible.

The succession of incidents which preceded the military response from South Africa included the following:—

1. In February, the assassination by SWAPO terrorists of the Ovambo Health Minister, Mr. Toivo Shiyagaya. SWAPO had denied it was responsible for this murder.
2. In March, the murder by SWAPO assassins of Mr. Clemens Kapuuo, the Herero tribal leader and president of the Democratic Turnhalle Alliance (DTA). He might have become the first President of an independent Namibia. SWAPO again denied being implicated in this assassination — Kapuuo's bodyguard had been murdered two weeks before. Unlike Mr. Steve Biko's funeral no Western diplomats thought fit to attend the funeral of Mr. Clemens Kapuuo.
3. In February, the abduction of 190 children from the St. Maria Mission School in Owambo.
4. In March and April, a marked increase in abductions, border violations, the mining of roads and the murder of headmen in order to break down the power of the tribal chiefs.
5. In April, the hi-jacking of a bus and its passengers who were abducted over the border into Angola.
6. At the beginning of May, the attack by SWAPO terrorists on the Ruacana hydro-electric power station near the border between Angola and SWA.
7. An ominous build up in Southern Angola of some 3,000 Soviet-armed SWAPO terrorists who were about to launch a major incursion into SWA, with the aim of establishing a firm base and declaring a revolutionary government. This would be followed by a psychological warfare campaign declaring

the forthcoming arrival of East Germans to assist in the running of the country.

The pre-emptive strike was, therefore, designed to disrupt SWAPO terrorist activities and destroy the supreme headquarters of the SWAPO People's Liberation Army of Namibia (PLAN), at the mining town of Cacinga, code-named "Moscow", and the main operational base in southwestern Angola, code-named "Vietnam".

The attack on "Moscow", about 200 kilometres inside Angola, was carried out by parachute troops, preceded by an airstrike. The strength of the garrison at "Moscow" was normally 800-1,000, but sometimes as much as 2,000, as it was also a transit centre. The Commander-in-Chief and the Chief Political Commissar were located at "Moscow".

The "Vietnam" base, about 30 kilometres inside Angola, was the headquarters of the North West Front with a garrison of about 500, with two forward operational bases of about 150 terrorists in each. "Vietnam" was attacked by armour and infantry preceded by an air strike, and some 200 terrorists were killed and about 200 captured. I was not given the number of terrorists killed at "Moscow". But in an Israeli-type lightning strike of this nature the casualties inflicted must have been heavy. A reliable civilian source told me that 50 dead Cubans had been counted and many wounded.

Each strike was completed within the same day at a cost of only five South African soldiers killed, two scout cars slightly damaged and two helicopters and two aircraft hit, both of which returned to base. The resistance was stronger than expected, with the women in uniform — most of whom manned anti-tank and anti-aircraft guns — putting up the fiercest resistance. The "Vietnam" base was typical of an operational base, complete with underground bunkers and trenches around its perimeter. Large quantites of Soviet arms and ammunition were found in the "Vietnam" base, including sophisticated weapons for conventional warfare, such as 14.5mm anti-aircraft guns, 75mm recoilless anti-tank guns, heavy and medium mortars, machine guns, rocket launchers and the new Soviet sniper rifle, Dragnov.

I personally inspected all these weapons, including a mass of AK-47 automatic rifles, and also Soviet and Rumanian leather boots, blankets and clothing.

An interesting find in the "Vietnam" base was a suitcase which indicated that a Russian soldier had been there, or that somebody with a Russian uniform had been in the base. In the suitcase was a grey fur cap with the red star and hammer and sickle badge on it. With it in the case was a tunic of Russian origin, black shoes, a Russian-English dictionary, a Russian armament reference book and Russian boot polish. One Russian aircraft boarding ticket stamped 4 July, 1977 at Moscow airport was also found.

A few days after the strike, SWAPO terrorists blew up a water tower. This is an example of how they inflict suffering on the very people they profess to liberate. The thousands of people who were dependent on water from the tower now have to rely on limited rainwater. This is typical of how the tenuous thread between civilisation and savagery can snap at a moment's notice.

I visited all those who had been captured, many of whom had been abducted. Those who had gone across the border on their own free will regretted their decision, but will, of course, be powerless to resist if they are again confronted with a rifle held to their head. But at least they will know that all the brainwashing about the tortures they would suffer if captured, is a pack of lies.

I also visited the seriously wounded prisoners who were being treated in the military hospital at Oshakati, having been operated on by the senior orthopaedic surgeon from Johannesburg. There were five nurses and nursing orderlies permanently on duty and one doctor. The patients could not have been better cared for even in a top class hospital. All those I spoke to particularly the women, said they had been told they would be killed or left to die were they to be wounded and captured. They did not have to express their gratitude— one could read it in their eyes.

Judge Steyn, the Administrator General, showed me the originals of four of the captured documents and readily acceded to my request for photocopies. The Press, of course, immediately cast doubt on their authenticity.

One of the documents deals with the assassination of Mr. Toivo Shiyagaya (Ovambo Health Minister) and the other with the murder of Mr. Clemens Kapuuo. So much, therefore, for the denials by SWAPO of having been implicated in these two murders.

The title of the first document is as follows:

MOSCOW 15/02/1978

REPORT ON THE SPECIAL OPERATION THAT LEFT TOIVO SHIYAGAYA DEAD

The report shows that the mission was assigned to two SWAPO comrades on 20 January 1978 and describes how it was carried out. It is signed by:

CHIEF OF INTELLIGENCE AND RECONNAISSANCE
JASON NEHALE.

The second assassination document is entitled:

(P.L.A.N.)

MOSCOW,
27/04/1978

THE MISSION THAT ELIMINATED PUPPET CLEMENCE KAPUUO

The report gives the names of the two SWAPO assassins, their mission and the following description of how the assassination was carried out:

"Kapuuo was eliminated at six o'clock on the twenty-seventh of March 1978 while he was standing near the wall of his shop. He was addressing the old men from the reserves, giving them instructions. He was shot from the distance of five metres, from behind. Credit here is also to be given to the other two comrades who were recruited inside and who gave accurate information."

I visited the exact spot in question and was able to check on the accuracy of the above description.

The third document has the title.

P.L.A.N.

MOSCOW
03/03/1978

MINUTES TAKEN DURING THE TIME OF THE VISIT OF THE PRESIDENT OF SWAPO, COMRADE SAM NUYOMA, AT MOSCOW

Time: 12.40 a.m. SA time.

The first 5 minutes of the visit were taken up with the introduction of personalities and Nuyoma started his speech at "12.45 SA time."

The following are some extracts:

"First I would like on behalf of the Central Committee to extend fraternal greetings and congratulations to the people and all the members of PLAN, who have rendered excellent service for the cause of the struggle on the battlefield."

"The enemy is panicking. He is crying he wants peace — SWAPO must lay down its arms and take part in the so-called peace talks.

"SWAPO is not prepared to lay down its arms and surrender to the enemy.

"It is already the decision of the Central Committee to continue the armed struggle — to liquidate the Boers and for the total seizure of power, we are not fighting to make it easy for the Puppets.

"As you have heard many people are imprisoned, killed, but in spite of this, on the part of PLAN, fight to liquidate the Boers.

"You must not only use your guns against the enemy but also for the Black Boers and the reactionaries.

"Our policy is to establish a socialist state in Namibia. . . . .

"We must all keep in mind that we have these weapons to liberate our Country and to stop and put an end to foreign domination.

". . . . use your guns if there is a reactionary government in the country, to overthrow it, because we have fought that all the sufferings under colonialism could come to an end."

Before I left South Africa on 19 May, I was asked to view a television film taken by a Scandinavian and shown a few days previously on the BBC programme 'Tonight', in which Mr. Sam Nujoma was shown addressing what was alleged to be a SWAPO garrison in a firm base that they were supposed to have established inside South West Africa. Nuyoma's speech appeared to be identical to that made at "Moscow" on 3 March! Furthermore, the so-called firm base was said to be about nine miles north of Oshakati. This intrigued me because I happened to have been flying over that particular area at fifty feet in a Puma helicopter on 14 May! Certainly there was not a single SWAPO terrorist anywhere near Oshakati. Had there been, the pilot of the helicopter would not have been flying me at a suicide height of only fifty feet. Furthermore, Oshakati is the main South African Military Headquarters in the forward operational area and is far too much a hive of activity for even a small party of SWAPO terrorists to be able to remain undetected.

I was asked why the BBC should wish to reproduce such a false picture. My reply was that I had long ago come to regard the BBC not as the British Broadcasting Corporation but as the British Broadcasting Conspiracy. I said that the BBC Panorama programme on Rhodesia shown on 17 April had been another typical example of a distorted portrayal of the true operational situation in Rhodesia.

The fourth captured document is entitled:

(P.L.A.N.)
THE COMMANDING POST HQ'S
PEOPLE'S LIBERATION ARMY OF NAMIBIA
MOSCOW
09/04/1978

THE REGIONAL COMMANDERS
THE REGIONAL STAFFS
FELLOW COMBATANTS OF PLAN!
Dear gallant fighters of PLAN,

MESSAGE OF CONGRATULATIONS

The message is one of congratulations for "capturing a Boer on the battlefield", for performing "the wonder of killing puppet Shiyagaya while walled by a gang of security men", and for performing "the miracle of eliminating the most prominent puppet of imperialism in Namibia Clemence Kapuuo and note, you did marvels by eradicating him exactly in the capital of Namibia."

The message is signed:

DIMO HAMAAMBO

Commander-of-the-Armed-Forces.

Immediately under this is his official rubber stamp with, presumably, his signature across it.

The administrator General of South West Africa, Mr. Justice Steyn, stated categorically when I was in Windhoek that "SWAPO would be hit and hit again until satisfaction had been obtained that it was either prepared to lay down arms or had been rendered incapable of committing acts of violence." I agreed with him wholeheartedly and said that when dealing with terrorists the only medicine fit for them was the 3 H's and 3 R's — Hit Quick, Hit Hard and Keep on Hitting, and be Ruthless, Relentless and Remoreseless.

I said that South Africa should ignore the Anglo-American and UNO protestations because of their hitherto spineless, timid and almost cringing attitude towards the Soviet Union and Cuba. They had been far too intent on sidling up to the Soviets instead of standing up to them.

There had been too much sneaking off and scuttling away from their responsibilities — "chickening out" had now become the popular pastime.

Fortunately, at about this time the DTA chairman, Mr. Dirk Mudge, had rounded on SWA's critics and declared firmly that if SWAPO had adhered to the spirit of the Western proposals — endorsed by South Africa — the strike into Angola would not have been necessary. "If Angola was prepared to allow terrorist bases in its territory and to condone attacks into SWA, then it must also be prepared to take the consequences." When asked whether or not the action would adversely affect the negotiations between the five Western Powers, South Africa and SWAPO, Mr. Mudge replied: "That SWAPO continues with its terrorist activities seems not to have affected the Western powers. Why then should South Africa's reaction to the terrorism influence the Western initiative?"

CHAPTER 26

Transkei

I VISITED independent but unrecognised Transkei, the first-born Homeland of South Africa's separate development policy, just a few days before the country celebrated its first anniversary.

It was impressed upon me at a private audience with the Prime Minister and again at a meeting with the Cabinet, that through no fault of their own the people of Transkei were incorporated in the Union of South Africa by the British Government. Therefore, unlike Botswana, Lesotho, and Swaziland which were British Protectorates and were granted independence by the British Government, Transkei had to negotiate its independence with the Government of South Africa.

The Prime Minister put his country's case clearly in a speech in 1976, when he declared:

"Firstly: We expect recognition of our independence in the world particularly by our brothers in the rest of Africa. Armed struggle, rivers of blood, genocide and resulting famine seem all too often to constitute the entry qualifications of today's community of nations. Where such a struggle and suffering was necessary for a people to secure freedom, let it be so and let the fighters be admired for their perseverance. But where freedom has been gained peacefully who is to say it is less meritorious? If independence by negotiation be a disqualification for membership of the United Nations and the Organisation of African Unity then why are Botswana, Malawi, Lesotho, Swaziland, Zambia, and Tanzania to name but a few, honoured members? Their independence, like ours, came over a conference table and with the loss of no more than a few bottles of ink. No, we shall apply for membership of all relevant international bodies in the knowledge that our cause is just. If membership is denied to us it will represent a grave injustice toward a new nation more populous, larger in area, more advanced and more stable than many states who are already members.

"Secondly: The Transkei will enter into monetary and customs agreements with the Republic of South Africa on the same basis as the ex-Protectorates. We expect in addition that the Republic will continue to assist us as it has done in the past.

"I have no doubt there will be people who will immediately point to both the agreements and the direct aid as being indicative of our economic dependence on the Republic. In answer to such accusations, I can only point to the ex-Protectorates which likewise have such agreements with the RSA and to other African countries receiving aid from the RSA. Even Samora Machel (who receives payment of his mine labourers' wages at the official gold price) has, despite his revolutionary fervour, not seen his way clear to dispensing with this direct grant from the Republic of South Africa.

"Although the Transkei is by no means a rich country, it is not a destitute country and could make do without financial aid. But why should it refuse such aid if there are no strings attached to it. Certainly financial aid, no matter from whom it comes, benefits our development and the fact of its receipt in no way constitutes a disqualification for political independence.

"The Transkei is an independent state of multiracial character with a free economy. It is a sovereign state that will conduct its own affairs as it sees fit but which will have economic agreements and ties with other countries. We feel that this will benefit the Black man not only in the Transkei but also in the Republic. It will also benefit White South Africa.

"It will be a state with a free economy in which investment will be welcomed.

"I am satisfied that we shall fulfil our international obligations — if we are allowed to. If we are not accepted initially by the community of nations, it will be because of the road to sovereignty which the Transkei has followed, namely orderly both through negotiations and peaceful progress within the framework of the policy of separate development. In that event, as I have often said before, we will be the victims of gross discrimination related to the fact that Great Britain handed the Transkei on a plate to the Union of South Africa in 1910 instead of keeping it a protectorate. That our road to sovereignty has passed through South Africa is, in other words, something quite beyond our control and we call upon those who already enjoy freedom, particularly our brothers in Africa, not to visit the sins of the father upon the son."

The Transkei Homeland is no artificial creation of the South African government. The Xhosa people were well established in the region by 1800. Its boundaries have been clearly defined since British colonial days, and the area has been treated as an African reserve since the first portions of the territory were annexed to the British Cape Colony in 1877.

Covering an area equal to Belgium and Luxembourg, Transkei is larger than 22 member countries of the United Nations, has a coast-line of 160 miles and is six times the size of the proposed Arab homeland on the overcrowded West Bank of the Jordan.

Transkei's annual budget runs in excess of £100 million, almost double that of Judea-Samaria (West Bank of the Jordan).

Other comparisons from latest available figures.

	Transkei	Judea-Samaria
Hospitals	31	16
Doctors	136	92
Nurses	4,500	360
Schools	1,820	956
Teachers	8,452	6,831
Pupils, primary	126,802	139,700
Secondary	26,800	18,200

Transkei's Gross National Product was more than £275 million as long ago as 1973-4 compared with Judea-Samaria at £30 million in 1971 (both latest official figures available).

The proposed Palestinian Homeland for up to three million people on the West Bank of the Jordan (Judea-Samaria) would be on lands conquered by Israel in the 1967 war plus the Gaza strip. Apparently it is not the view of the Homeland advocates that the Palestinians should live within its borders. It is rather to be the focus of their national identity.

So, the United States, and the nine Western European nations, and 21 Arab countries now all hold that a Palestinian homeland is necessary for peace in this part of the globe irrespective of its diminutive size or its inability to accommodate all its people.

By a coincidence there are just on three million Xhosa people whose homeland is the Transkei in Southern Africa. Their country is six times the size of the West Bank zone proposed as the homeland of the Palestinians.

Some 1,644,600 Xhosas live in the Transkei which is a one-man-one-vote republic which gained its independence from South Africa in October 1976. Most of the rest of the Xhosas earn their living in the urban areas of South Africa but all have the right to vote in the homeland, the focus of their national identity.

One cannot argue about the fact that gegoraphically and demographically, the Transkei is a state in its own right. Both in size and in numerical strength of population, it is larger than several states already accepted as full members of the United Nations. It is more advanced economically than a dozen or more others. Politically, it is ruled by a party which has contested four general elections conducted along orthodox democratic lines, and in the last of these elections, this party won 95 per cent of the seats — on a policy of separate development and independence. If that is not self-determination, I do not know what is. Yet, not a single country outside South Africa is prepared to recognise the Transkei, and the British Foreign Secretary, for one, has declared that the

Transkei does not fulfil what he called the well-established legal criteria for recognition. Frankly one wonders whether words still have any meaning.

The United States, and the Nine of Western Europe, and the Arab countries all reject Homelands for the Black peoples of South Africa as unjust. The sin of the Xhosas is that they obtained their independence through three general elections for a parliament modelled on Westminster and not through the barrel of the gun. Yet they have been refused a seat at the United Nations.

How can these double standards be justified by the Nine of Western Europe, and the Arab nations, and above all by the US President who declares that he is campaigning for human rights?

It is monstrous that the Transkei should be saddled with a puppet image. These Xhosa people should be permitted forthwith to take their rightful place in the councils of the United Nations.

Despite the lack of recognition, however, foreign investment in the Transkei is substantial. More than 40% of private investment is from overseas with British, American, French, German, Danish and Italian companies showing interest in the nation's economic potential.

The Transkei Development Corporation reports rapid growth with 15 new industries valued at more than £10 million and providing jobs for 2,000 having been establish in the past 18 months.

Umtata, the tiny capital, is burgeoning with new buildings and houses and the population has grown from 21,000 to over 33,000 in seven years. The town has a Black mayor and half the councillors are Black.

At the beginning of May, Transkei, on top of their land grievance decided to breach the Non-aggression Pact with South Africa. The Prime Minister, Chief Kaiser Matanzima announced to the Assembly that: "No military aircraft of the Republic of South Africa shall be accorded a right of peaceful overflight through the air space, or military naval vessels a right of innocent passage in the Transkeian territorial sea or a right to take shelter in the ports in the time of urgent distress." This revokes one of the major clauses of the Pact. The announcement came shortly after the cancellation by South Africa of a proposed course arranged for Transkeian soldiers at the South African School of Infantry.

The cancellation of the course may have been in retaliation for Transkei having announced that they no longer wanted South African officers in command, training or advisory roles in their Army.

Perhaps Transkei feel they are more likely to obtain recognition by an outward display of defiance. Or is the real reason to divert the public's attention away from internal political difficulties?

CHAPTER 27

The Conduct of Anti-terrorist and Anti-guerilla Operations

As I have mentioned previously, I faced two panel discussions on the tactics and techniques of border, rural and urban guerilla operations. In addition, this subject was invariably raised at meetings with both senior military and civilian personnel, and the media also showed considerable interest. I excluded Northern Ireland from the discussions because I have no practical experience of the operations there and, in any case, five years ago I went on record as saying that I thoroughly disagreed with the flabby way operations were conducted at the very ouset of the troubles, as a consequence of which the campaign was bound to be long drawn out, with a heavy toll of lives and material damage.

What I said at the panel discussions, meetings and interviews was based on one's personal and practical experience of anti-terrorist operations, amounting to a large part of one's 39 years' service in the Indian and British armies. In the hope that it will serve a useful purpose to place on permanent record what I said, I reproduce below the views I expressed.

The military tactics of guerillas is something quite new within the accepted pattern of warfare — surprise attack by the enemy against soft targets — withdrawal in the face of opposition to the sanctuary of their side of the border. In the West, the army's training in nuclear and conventional tactics depends for its mobility primarily on roads, railways, water and air. By contrast, in guerilla warfare roads, railways and rivers are the ambusher's paradise, even when convoys obey all the safety rules. But troops who are able to move secretly mostly in small groups, making rendezvous only at the precise moment of battle, cannot be ambushed.

That was the way British, Gurkha and Commonweath soldiers in Malaya and Borneo (now Malaysia) learned to move and they learned to do it better than the guerillas. They were able to out-guerilla the enemy in every department of the game, through sheer good training and tremendous self-discipline, based on continual operational experience. Although such operations are often the platoon and section commanders' wars, nevertheless it is the company commander who has to be able to set the example and do everything that his men can do; do it better and do it longer.

There are four ingredients of success.

First, unified operations between the armed forces themselves, between the armed forces and the police, and between the security forces as a whole and the civil administration. It is this unity, joint planning and joint operations which is the key to success. Joint operations entail control by a triumvirate — civilian, policeman, soldier — all under the single direction of a military Director of Operations. It is the job of the Director of Operations to make sure that the system operates as two blades of a pair of scissors, neither subordinate to the other, but each making it possible for the other to succeed.

Secondly, timely and accurate information. This means a first class intelligence machine. In the Borneo campaign a force of 1,500 border scouts was raised from the various tribes. These became our "eyes and ears". They provided company and platoon commanders with early warning of the movement of enemy on both sides of the border. New battalions sometimes took a very long time to learn the technique of how to use their border scouts properly, but in the end everyone came to realize their worth. This is an example of failing to profit from the lessons of the past, for these same tribes were the very people whom our special forces organized against the Japanese in the Second World War. It was because we won the hearts and minds of these people, that they supplied us with reliable information. Their tribal areas, land, relatives and friends extended on both sides of the border, regardless of the international boundary.

In counter-insurgency operations in urban areas military intelligence should be the servant and not the master of the Special Branch. This is because Special Branch officers and their staff and agents live in the country; speak the language; know the people, and are of the people, whereas army intelligence staffs are here today and gone tomorrow. Good intelligence depends on continuity at every level.

The third principle is the speed, mobility and flexibility of operations, the security of our bases, and the domination of the border and countryside.

In Borneo we dominated and owned the border, the bush and the countryside over a front of 1,000 miles and to a depth of 100 miles against a sophisticated enemy — the Indonesian Regular Army — who had no constraints about cross border operations, and we smashed him every time he attempted an incursion.

It was mainly helicopters that provided the army with the necessary degree of speed, mobility and flexibility. They proved themselves over and over again to be real battle-winners. They flew tirelessly over the mountains and along the valleys, placing men exactly where they would do most good. For example, reconnaissance patrols were positioned along the border to find and report the enemy, and sections were set down neatly in depth to cut off unsuspecting raiders. A clever company commander with a few "choppers" could so block guerillas at every turn that they would think an entire army was on their heels. We hit the enemy so often the moment he put his nose across the border, that we were credited with having some special form of radar. To take the strain off the helicopters and off air dropping, we were always building short jungle airstrips or improving existing ones, for our light fixed wing aircraft.

Anyone who has operated in the bush will know that there is no front in the accepted military sense; and this is even more the case if there are dissident elements within, lying low, prepared for armed rebellion, as was the case in Borneo. Unless commanders take a firm stand, they can very soon have all their forces tied down defending their bases. We dealt with this problem by making everyone responsible for his own protection, wherever he might be, in front or rear areas. Every man in uniform had to be a potential front line infantry soldier. Officers and men of armoured car, artillery, engineer and signals units, were all trained and ready to fight as infantry. The same applied to the administrative services in depth. I use the term "in depth" deliberately, and not "in rear"; for there is no "rear" in counter-insurgency operations.

We made great use of deception and guile, never doing the same thing twice. We used all forms of lethal and warning devices: armoured cars, mortars, dogs, booby traps, claymore mines, trip flares, seismic intruder devices, and so on. Time and time again the enemy tried to infiltrate into villages and towns and to get within mortar range of our airfields. But our intelligence was such that nine times out of ten, we knew his every move and we brought him to battle long before he had reached a point from which he could mortar a village, let alone a town.

In the forward areas, we adopted a mobile defence, keeping our forward posts to the minimum. Such forward posts as there were had to be properly dug in with overhead cover and capable of being held overnight against artillery, mortars, rockets, Bangalore torpedoes, or direct infantry assault. The other two thirds of the garrison was always out in an offensive role, dominating the bush and ambushing tracks by day and night, so that the enemy never knew where we were, and was always liable to be contacted and savaged.

Unlike the American policy in Vietnam of "Search and Destroy" and then return to base, our technique in Borneo was "Clear, Hold and Dominate". Results could not be achieved merely by attacking and shooting the enemy and then returning to base.

He had to be played at his own game; by living out in the bush for weeks on end; by winning the hearts and minds of the people and by planting our own agents in villages known to be unfriendly. In these conditions, the soldier carried his base on his back, and it consisted of a featherweight plastic sheet, a sockful of rice and a pocketful of ammunition. The border, bush and countryside belonged to him, he owned it; controlled and dominated it day and night for months on end.

What, then, is the technique of domination of the bush? It is the individual fighting skill of the soldier which has to make up for the difficulty of providing him with conventional forms of fire support from both ground and air. In Borneo, we made sure he was properly acclimatized and given jungle training at our jungle warfare school. Troops could not be precipitated from Salisbury Plain in England straight into jungle operations against Indonesian regular soldiers (who had been trained as guerillas since 1945) in a tropical climate unless a very great deal of realistic and really tough preliminary training, particularly night training, had taken place.

These Indonesian regular soldiers (the irony of the situation was that it was the British Army who had trained the Indonesian officers at our jungle warfare school in Malaysia and at our school of intelligence in England) were the people we were eventually up against, not the ill-trained volunteers whom we met in the first year. While he was no "jungle superman", he earned his freedom against the Dutch the hard way in 1946, fighting in much the same fashion as he fought in Borneo; but now he was a great deal better trained and equipped than he was in 1946. He possessed a variety of modern weapons, and those of Communist and US manufacture were of high quality. He used such weapons as artillery, medium mortars, anti-personnel mines and rocket launchers with considerable skill. All in all, he was a thoroughly competent adversary. Against him, we established complete mastery by our fierce aggressive patrolling and ambushing — always searching for and hunting the enemy, and ourselves living as guerillas.

Our objective was to dominate and own the bush and the border, week in, week out, day and night. There were no "Prince Rupert" tactics of galloping over the bush in helicopters. We used all our cunning and guile (for example, contour flying) to get within striking distance of the enemy by helicopter, but without being seen or heard. Then we tracked him down, stalking and closing in on our feet for the kill. The sure way to beat a guerilla is to operate more quietly; smoke less, and talk less to possible enemy agents before an operation. In Borneo, it was nearly always the Indonesians who fell into the booby traps and triggered off the claymore mines and trip flares set by patrols. Victory in guerilla warfare goes to the tougher, more resourceful soldier and the more gadget-filled our life becomes, the harder it is to produce him.

I never allowed any of my forward troops into any shop, cafe or bar. When they rested they did so in their operational base away from the bright lights. We avoided tying up troops in static posts. Decentralization was the order of the day. For example, the gunners deployed 30 guns in single gun positions over nearly 1,000 miles. The 105 mm. pack Howitzer could be picked up lock, stock and barrel, with ammunition and detachment, by a Belvedere helicopter: the assembled gun was slung underneath and was switched 20 miles to a platoon post in well under an hour. Our artillery was as mobile and flexible as our infantry. The same applied to the sappers. Heavy bulldozers were air-dropped by Belvederes or flown in by Twin Pioneers and assembled on the ground. Gradually we acquired light air-portable earth moving equipment. We were completely air minded and allowed no obstacle to stand in our way.

It was the ambush which was at one and the same time the guerillas' and our most potent weapon. Whether on a small or large scale, it was the key element. An ambush is merely another word for "fighting from ground of one's own choosing", but with the difference that it depends entirely on complete surprise. The enemy must be unaware that he is walking into a trap. An ambush, requires all the tricks of the soldier's trade: an eye for country, track discipline, concealment, camouflage, silence, alertness, fire discipline, marksmanship, guile, cunning and, above all, self-discipline. It requires constant training and rehearsal. There is no chance of ambushing the enemy if the soldier smokes; chews gum; washes his hands with soap, cleans his teeth; brylcreems his hair; whispers or coughs. In ambush, a man is lying in wait for a dangerous hunted animal whose sense of smell and keen eyesight are phenomenal.

In Borneo, we devised tactical techniques and battle skills which would have done credit to a cat-burglar, gangster, gunman and poacher. The soldiers were able to live in the bush as close to the animal as it was humanly possible to do so, and became so well trained that they were able to fight the guerillas both in the bush and out of it, and to kill and harry them until they were utterly exhausted. The type of fighting, the type of country and the climate called for individual stamina and fortitude, stout legs, stout hearts, fertile brains, and the acceptance of battlefield conditions almost unimagineable in their demands on human endurance.

The fourth but most important principle is "Winning the hearts and minds" of the people and especially the indigenous people.

This was absolutely vital to the success of operations because, by winning over the people to your side, you can succeed in isolating your enemy from supplies, shelter and intelligence. This fourth principle entailed winning the local people's trust, confidence and respect. We set out to speak their language and respect their customs and religion. We sent small highly trained special air service-type patrols to live and work among them; to protect them and share their danger; to get to know them and gain their confidence. These troops were as friendly, understanding and patient to the villagers as they were tough and ruthless in the jungle. We sought to give villagers a feeling of security by day and night, through the presence of phantom patrols and through constant visits by the civil administration, the police and the army. We helped their agriculture; improved their communications and trading facilities; improved their water supply; provided medical clinics and a flying doctor service; established schools; provided transistor radios and attractive programmes and so on.

We went to any lengths to keep our hands clean. For example, our security precautions for offensive air support, for artillery and mortar fire was as fool-proof as it was humanly possible to make them. It was indelibly inscribed on our minds that one civilian killed by us would do more harm than ten killed by the enemy. Every time we defeated the enemy we took every possible precaution to ensure that he could not exact retribution on the nearest village. We gave that village protection, either visible or invisible. If the latter, only the headman was told that we were in ambush nearby. In addition, each village had its own alarm system and local defence plan. At all costs the enemy had to be prevented from capturing a village and digging in, because this would have meant a battle to recapture it and, in the process, its probable destruction. If the price a village had to pay for its liberation from the enemy was to be its own destruction, then the campaign for hearts and minds would never have been won.

Winning the hearts and minds of the indigenous inhabitants is not just a question of direct aid. People must be given the will to help themselves and the necessary expertise to do so. This is something which the British Army is good at, because they have had so much experience and know-how. But this can so easily be lost; and I found that we had to start from scratch because the lessons of the Malayan emergency had been forgotten in a space of three years. Good though our record has been in several insurgency campaigns, on each occasion we have had to play ourselves in all over again.

The lesson to be learned from counter insurgency operations is that terrorists fighting a guerilla-type war can tie up lavishly equipped modern regular forces ten times their number in strength. Moscow and Peking have never underestimated guerilla power.

The money spent arming "nationalist" and "neutralist" movements across the world has paid tremendous dividends, for they have now enmeshed so many countries in their Communist web. The financial outlay that the Soviets incurred by their systematic arming of the African rebels in the former Portuguese African territories, was certainly money well spent.

The lesson of Cambodia, of the French in Indo-China, of the Portuguese in Africa and the Americans in Vietnam, is crystal clear. It is that well-equipped modern armies, sophisticated military operations, and air power, are no protection against guerilla tactics. By contrast our counter-insurgency operations in Malaysia and Borneo were a complete success.

In Vietnam, an over-sophisticated American army and an air force which dropped four times more bombs that they did in the whole of the Second World War, failed to win a limited guerilla war against puny men of a puny nation. That phony and infamous "peace with honour" which earned a Nobel Peace Prize, amounted to nothing more than a fig leaf to cover a scuttle. The Americans were out-fought and outwitted not only in battle, but also at the Paris peace negotiations and in their evacuation plan with their mighty rescue armada. In Washington, they were divided and paralysed as well. The United States poured into the Vietnam War eight years of effort, the lives of 50,000 young men, the good health of another 300,000 and $150 billion of their hard-earned taxpayers' money and the honour and prestige of their nation.

It is easy to see why the Soviets wanted to keep the war going. While America spent $150 billion on weapons that are now down the drain in Vietnam, the Soviets spent an equivalent amount on nuclear weapons to control the world. History will be left to explain America's decision to fight a costly no-win war (or could it not have been won?) that left South-East Asia in far worse condition than it was before American intervention began.

There can be little doubt that television coverage of the Vietnam war was largely responsible for sapping the moral fibre of the American people to continue the struggle.

War is an unpleasant business, and when it is brought into the living room in colour, the ultimate effect on public opinion in an open society is predictable. Blood shows up distinctly and disturbingly on colour television; but the demise of political or civil liberties cannot be flashed on the screen.

In a two-year research of CBS news, 1972-73, one finds that in the NATO environment the attentive viewer would have heard little about the mission of the US Army to defend Western Europe, but much about demoralisation, racial conflict and drug abuse among the troops and about alleged army spying on civilians at home and in Germany.

Whereas the comparison of Soviet-American military capability received one minute of news time during the whole of the two year period, a single item reporting missing table utensils from Pentagon restaurants received 1.5 minutes.

The conclusion is unavoidable: with friends like US television commentators, the US military has little need of enemies.

In both Malaya and Borneo the enemy was at least as formidable as the Viet Cong in the early 1960s, and Indonesia just as strong militarily as North Vietnam. If either campaign had been mismanaged, we too could have had a Vietnam on our hands. The Borneo campaign stands out as being a notable example of how highly trained professional infantrymen can achieve a decisive victory against a well-armed, aggressive and unscrupulous enemy with little bloodshed to ourselves, little destruction of the countryside and with so little disruption of the normal life of the civilian population that reversion to peacetime conditions at the end of hostilities was virtually automatic.

There was no area bombing or interdiction, no napalm or defoliation of the jungle. No wonder the Commonwealth Forces were welcomed for the social and economic benefits they brought to the jungle villages. By mastering the physical conditions, by securing the willing help of the inhabitants, and by the highly skilful use of thoroughly trained infantrymen, the campaign was won without the people at home or the world at large realizing the extent of the fighting soldier's achievements.

Even at this late stage, so long after the successful conclusion of the Borneo campaign, a great deal of unnecessary secrecy still appears to be attached to the cross border operations that we ourselves conducted. We cannot afford to forget the art of hitting an enemy hard by methods which neither escalate the war nor invite United Nations anti-colonialist intervention. Offensive action is the very essence of successful military operations when faced with guerilla or terrorist forces, whether in the Far East, the Middle East, Western Europe, which includes Britain, of course — Yes and Ulster too. A policy of containment is the passport to failure.

CHAPTER 28

Russia's Grand Design

RUSSIA'S grand design is to outflank Europe at sea from the the south as well as the north; take control of the sources of oil supply; dominate the sea routes in the Indian Ocean, South Atlantic and North Atlantic; gain dominance of Western Europe and then dictate to the United States. The West fails to understand that behind the endless Arab-Israeli conflict stands a totalitarian, expansionist, powerful Soviet Union whose relentless determination is to take over Aden and South Yemen, which dominate the approaches to the Red Sea; spread out in the Persian Gulf; join its substantial fleets in the Mediterranean and the Indian Ocean; dominate the whole of Africa; control the Cape route; extend her influence into Asia, and totally change the whole balance of power in the world.

There is no need to argue about the threat in the Horn of Africa when it is crystal clear from a mere glance at the map that Russia's intention is to control the Arabian peninsula itself and the oil **life-line** of the Western World.

Russia's master plan in achieving an overwhelming superiority in global strategy is ten-fold:—

The first step is to control the Red Sea, namely Ethiopia, Djibuti and Somalia.

The second step is to control both sides of the Gulf of Aden. South Yemen (Britain's Aden colony of old) is already a Soviet-Cuban-East German satellite.

The third step is to secure her rear by liquidating the anti-Soviet regime in the Sudan.

The fourth step is to launch the big push into the Arabian peninsula itself by an all-out attack against the Sultanate of Oman.

Oman shares with Iran the guardianship of a vital contemporary waterway — the rock-bound strait of Hormuz that links the Persian Gulf with the Arabian Sea and the seaways of the world. Through this narrow, sinuous channel, super-tankers throb day and night, carying £45,000 million worth of oil a year to refuel the economies of more than half the globe. Whoever rules Oman, therefore, has his thumb on what the Shah of Iran calls the free world's jugular vein.

The fifth step — having subverted and subjected Oman — is to establish its long-cherished foothold on the southern shores of the Persian Gulf.

The sixth step is to spread out in the Persian Gulf from the Iraqi naval base at the head of the Gulf.

The seventh step is to launch the final thrust into Saudi Arabia and the oil reservoirs. Saudi Arabia produces one quarter of the world's oil needs and provides one quarter of American oil imports. Furthermore, she uses her wealth to buttress anti-Communism in the Middle East.

The eighth step is the subjection of Egypt which, by now outflanked, would fall like a rotten orange — bridgeheads having already been established in Libya and Algeria.

The ninth step — which is not ninth in the order of priority since it is already well underway, with Angola, Mozambique, Tanzania and Uganda, and the former French and Portuguese colonies of Guinea already having fallen into Moscow's lap, with Kenya, Zambia and Zaire to follow — is to absorb the whole of Southern Africa and, as described earlier on, deprive the West of vital minerals and key bases, and control the Western World's life-line round the Cape. In the Indian Ocean, the Soviet Union's presence is already felt in Zanzibar, Madagascar and the Seychelles.

The tenth stage in achieving her aim is the complete domination and absorption of Western Europe, including the Mediterranean and the North Atlantic.

The Western Alliance must be reorganised and enlarged to deal with the Soviet global threat. This may necessitate a "South Atlantic Alliance", or an extended charter to include South Africa, Japan, Iran and Australia.

The record of the United States, the United Nations and NATO in the face of the Soviet Union's war by proxy has been abysmal. First, Angola, now the Horn of Africa, Rhodesia, South West Africa and South Africa.

Why did the United States sit paralysed as reinforcements left Cuba by sea and air for Angola, beneath their very nose? The answer is simple. President Carter's political weakness and the fear of sliding into another Vietnam. The US inaction at the takeover of Angola, when Congress merely shut its eyes and waffled, should have showed which way the wind was blowing and what we could expect in the future.

Why do the Americans not assert themselves economically by cutting off their massive programme of credits, technology and grain supplies that support the Soviet Union's war machine?

What about "detente"? Does it only apply to the nuclear field and to the European mainland? It must equally be applied to situations in the Third World and, therefore, should now be cancelled right across the board.

Why did Britain not raise in the Security Council the grave threat to peace caused by this bare-faced aggression by the Soviet Union in the Horn of Africa?

Why did not Britain send even one frigate to the Gulf of Aden or Red Sea in support of the not very credible presence there of three American frigates and one French aircraft carrier?

The answer is simple. In helping to bloc a Marxist takeover of the Afro-Arabian region, there are no votes to be gained, but a lot of Left wing ones to be lost.

The threat is very much a NATO concern. General Alexander Haig, NATO Supreme Commander, warned on 7 February that the Soviet Union had poured more weapons into Ethiopia in the past year than the US had supplied in the past 30 years. He warned that the new build-up was threatening the balance of power.

Therefore, why was NATO impotent to act, even to the extent of sending a small multi-national naval surveillance force to the area?

The answer again is simple. NATO's present southern boundary ends at the Tropic of Cancer. Because defence is indivisible, NATO can no longer afford to shut its eyes to serious threats taking place beyond its present boundaries. One of the great strengths of the Soviets in the Horn of Africa is that they are working according to a global strategy. NATO has no such global strategy and it is high time that it had.

The Soviet Navy Commander-in-Chief, Admiral Grechko, aptly reminded us in February that it is through controlling the oceans of the world that the Kremlin now intends to expand and spread Communist influence. Gunboat diplomacy is the name of the game.

Where stands the much vaunted United Nations? Silent and inactive, because the Afro-Asian cum Third World cum Communist bloc dominate it and desire it that way.

The West must face up to the fact that the right of veto in the Security Council makes the UN a farce, certainly in the military field.

Most of the by-play at the UN is based on hypocrisy. For instance, no one invoked sanctions against the Soviet Union when she invaded Czechoslovakia in 1968.

We should have heeded the warning of Solzhenitsyn four years ago when he pointed out that the United Nations is not a United Nations at all, but merely a United Governments, only a small proportion of its members have ever been elected by the people they purport to represent.

Moscow has seen to it that the UN has become an embodiment of fraud and mischief and a sanctimonious promoter of war in the name of peace.

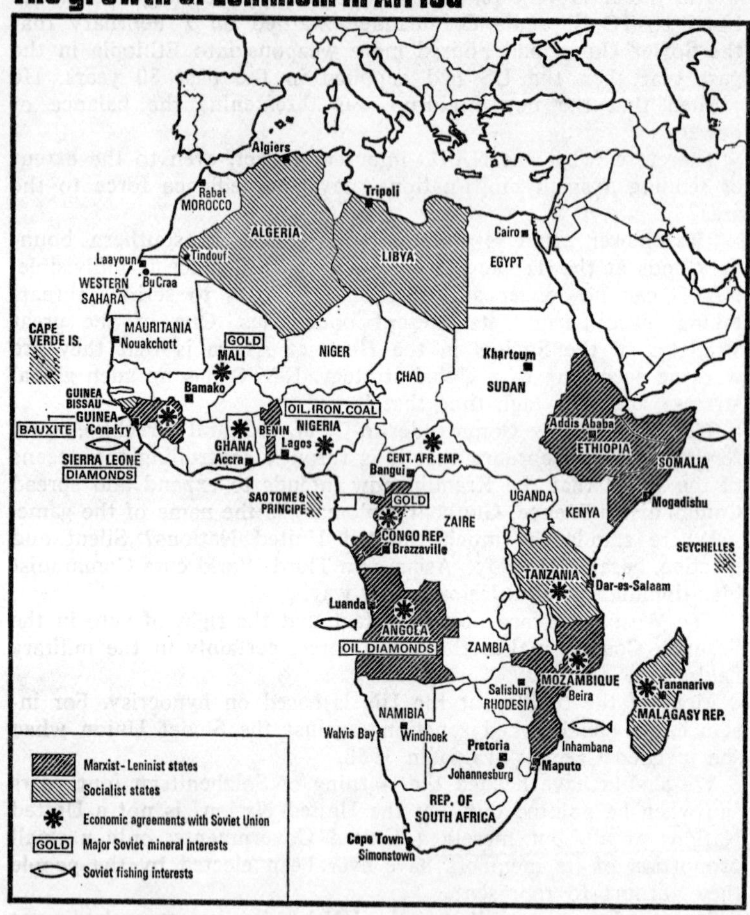

Map by kind permission in the Institute for the Study of Conflict, London.

There are not two Soviet Unions, one a peace-loving Soviet Union and the other a Soviet Union conducting revolutionary war and subversion by proxy wherever the Kremlin can find a soft underbelly. There is only one Soviet Union, an imperialist power still on the move, spreading its tentacles both inside and outside the NATO sphere. The examples of Cuba, Czechoslovakia, Vietnam, Laos, Cambodia, Portugal, the Lebanon, Libya, the Spanish Sahara, Angola, the Horn of Africa, Rhodesia, and South Africa, are proof of the West's impotence in the face of Russia's Cold War Machine.

Britain has now the weakest political team ever to control her defences. Fortunately, Mrs. Margaret Thatcher has shown that she certainly does not indulge in wishful thinking either about the capability or the intention of the Kremlin, which has embarked on a massive armaments build-up without parallel in history. This concentration of military strength far exceeds any conceivable requirement for the Soviet's own self-defence and can only have the most ominous implications for the West in the future.

The weapons and forces that the Soviets are building up have no usefulness except to destroy, or blackmail and dominate, the United States, Western Europe — the whole of Africa and the Middle East — and spread Communist influence throughout the world. The accompanying map illustrates clearly how much of Africa is already dominated by International Communism. This continuing global grab highlights four salient points:

First: How much of the world has already been absorbed by International Communism?

Second: The single-mindedness of purpose of the Soviets in the pursuit of their clearly mapped-out plans.

Third: The relentless determination with which they are pursuing their aim, which is nothing less than world domination. There are now only 30 democracies left in the world.

Fourth: There can be no doubt that the Soviet Union is achieving her aim of establishing a chain of vassal Marxist states around the world.

Meanwhile, the West continues to subsidise its own destruction by providing the Soviet Union with financial, agricultural and technical assistance. Instead of concentrating on improving her economy, the Soviet Union has used the imports of modern technology and large quantities of grain to increase her military manpower and devote more money to the production of nuclear weapons and modern conventional missiles and armaments — on the ground, at sea and in the air.

While the Soviet Union continues to increase her defence budget, the West continues to subsidise her arms industry. We must be mad. Soviet defence expenditure now amounts to between 11-14 percent of her gross national product, compared with less than 6 per cent in the United States.

CHAPTER 29

The Third World War Is Already Being Fought

WHY does the Soviet Union, with half Europe's economic strength, continue to grind out of her people an **offensive** conventional, chemical warfare and nuclear superiority which is about twice as great and grossly in excess of any conceivable legitimate **defensive** needs? Why does this vast Soviet expansionist empire shut itself off; arm itself to the teeth and indoctrinate its people for war?

The answer is that she intends to keep **immediately available — and immediately useable — ready for instant take-off** — that is, without prior reinforcement — vastly superior military forces in key areas, thus giving her a crushing preponderance of conventional forces, plus nuclear superiority, thereby enabling her to dictate from a position of great strength. With this big stick, which is growing bigger all the time, she intends to exert political pressure in the form of threats, intimidation and political blackmail, culminating in an ultimatum.

Because the Soviet Union considers China to be the main long-term threat to her security, she intends to secure her Western frontiers before China can develop her full military potential. The Soviet Union has built up her forces against China in the Far East to a strength of more than 40 divisions without in any way diminishing her capability against NATO. This is a most impressive feat.

In order to secure her Western frontiers, the Soviet Union needs to ensure her domination in Western Europe and this, of course, includes Britain. Therefore, Moscow's strategy is to split NATO; pressure American forces out of Europe, then move on to the total domination and absorption of Western Europe, first by softening us up before having to fire a shot in an international war. They hope that it may be possible to achieve their world wide political aims through the subversion of the West and by the disruption of a plural, democratic society. The Soviet strategy is to gain the dominance of the world by a four-pronged attack, keeping her options open.

The first prong is to be ready to fight and survive a nuclear war if deterrents break down.

The second prong is overt, using her military forces to threaten a britzkrieg attack on land and the severing of the West's jugular veins at seas.

The third prong is political blackmail. The threat of her big stick provides a force for blackmail. She will be able to take us without firing a shot in an **international** war. There is no military advantage in being able to overkill your enemy, but the political advantages are tremendous. Vietnam showed the way; so did the revolutionary war by proxy in Angola. Rhodesia is next on the Soviet's list and then South Africa.

The fourth prong is covert; namely, subversive warfare, the third world war in which we are already engaged. Portugal escaped by the skin of her teeth. It is the war against Communist infiltration of governments, trade unions, industry, law and order, the armed forces and their reduction below the safety limit, thereby breaking the will of the people to resist and imperilling the safety of the home base and the military front.

Subversive warfare is now in operation and we are already engaged in the third world war — the war against Communism — which we are losing. It is an insidious and more dangerous war than conventional, or even nuclear, war because the ordinary man in the street does not realise that we are already locked in such a life and death struggle.

The second prong, military force, will only be used if the third and fourth prongs fail. Meanwhile, Soviet conventional superiority on land, on and under the sea, in the air and upper atmosphere, and in the chemical and electronic warfare field, continues to grow and her strategic nuclear forces to expand.

For the time being, the Soviets do not want war; they want the fruits of war. The Russian bear-hug is not a friendly gesture; it is a fatal embrace. The Russians themselves have said "The role of the Red Army is to stand by ready to shake the tree when the rotten fruit is ripe to fall."

CHAPTER 30

Britain's Defence Cuts

I WAS constantly asked about Britain's seemingly unending succession of savage and crippling defence cuts. I made no excuses for our lamentable performance and went to great lengths to explain the present sorry state of affairs.

I said that at the same time as the British Chancellor of the Exchequer had received a bestowal of praise from the Chairman of the International Monetary Fund, Britain received the first public rebuke ever to be administered by the Secreary General of NATO for weakening the Atlantic Alliance. The irony was that Mr. Denis Healey, who is the architect of Britain's savage defence cuts, proclaimed when he was Minister of Defence — "If we cut our defences to the state where our security is imperilled, we shall have no schools, no hospitals, no houses — we shall have a heap of cinders".

I emphasised that the sinister defence cuts in quick succession were a deliberate attempt by the left wingers of the Labour Party both outside and inside Parliament to encourage other NATO members to follow suit, thus weakening the NATO defence alliance against the Soviet Union and leading to NATO's eventual collapse.

I said whether these people were called crypto-communists, Marxists, fellow-travellers or extremists was beside the point. Their aim was to impose defence cuts that will bring about the dissolution of NATO and cause such large-scale unilateral disarmament that the leadership of all Europe will be delivered to Russia on a plate.

The **Daily Telegraph** published a letter from me in which I stated that it was high time that these parliamentarians — about 80 in number, so we are told — who are alleged to be Communists in all but name, were identified and exposed. Unless they are, the impending disaster will befall Britain sooner rather than later, for the avowed aim of these Fifth Columnists is not merely to disrupt the Atlantic Alliance, but also to secure a vice-like grip on the windpipe of the nation through increased Communist infiltration of the trade unions and other organisations, particularly in the educational field. It will not need a nuclear strike to paralyse Britain.

With each successive cut, the Government tries to bamboozle

the British public into believing that only surplus fat is being removed. The truth is that the fat was removed long ago; the muscle has already been cut and the bone is now exposed. Far from deterring the Soviets, Britain is extending an open invitation to them.

Former and serving high ranking officers of the armed forces seem quite content to watch events with impotent despair. By sitting back and remaining silent in the face of the present grave danger, they are merely contributing to the nation's decline in moral fortitude. It does them little credit to keep their heads firmly buried in the sand. Their weak-kneed resistance to their political masters has been deplorable.

I said that from 1969 to 1972 I spent my time warning NATO politicians about the menace of the Soviet Union's ever-increasing military might and that once more they were gambling with the security of their country. I have continued to warn ever since, but to no avail.

On 28 November 1973, the London **Daily Telegraph** in its leader said — "On this page today General Sir Walter Walker, the former Commander of NATO forces in Northern Europe, provides evidence of the concern felt by senior officers about the West's military weakness. Why will politicians, and the public, not listen more attentively to those who know?".

Defensive thinking is such a British as well as a NATO disease, that it has become contagious and serious discussions are now being based on appeasement, and, when this fails, on the assumptions of an initial retreat and even surrender.

I pointed out that Britain has now fallen from second to sixth place in the military contribution of nations to NATO, and is behind Turkey and Italy. Britain would even be behind Spain if that country were to join the EEC and then NATO. The order of priority, based on cost per head of population, is the United States, Germany, France (at present outside the integrated military alliance), Turkey, Italy, Britain.

I said that disbanding Civil Defence; maintaining inadequate conventional forces in Europe; whittling away trained reserves and leaving the Home Base wide open to attack, does not add up to a deterrent policy, whether it be with or without a credible nuclear potential.

If a country becomes so ill-equipped that it cannot protect itself against attack, or against provocative harassment of its merchant ships and civil aircraft then that country is extremely vulnerable to military, political and economic blackmail.

By failing to provide the country with adequate trained reserves and Home Defence, Britain is indicating to the Soviet

Union that she might not have the will to resist, never mind the capacity.

In the 1930's Britain's politicians gambled with the nation's security. Then, at least, the country was given some warning. Next time there will be no such warning.

Britain, I said, must recreate a citizen's volunteer reserve for three quite distinct roles: first, duties in aid of the civil power, second, home defence; third, as a framework for expansion in the event of war.

If the Atlantic Alliance is to avoid having to meet the terrible costs of war, then it must pay the much more modest costs of peace. NATO represents an enormous net plus to every member nation when its costs are weighed against its benefits in peace and security. Therefore, to preserve that net plus, what is needed is not an attitude of doing less, but one of doing more.

It was Winston Churchill who said: "From what I have seen of our Russian friends during the war, I am convinced that there is nothing for which they have less respect than weakness, especially military weakness. We cannot afford to work on narrow margins offering temptations to a trial of strength."

It is power and the will to exercise it that impresses the Soviets. It is weakness that will encourage them to adventure — and not only in Southern Africa where Dr. Kenneth Kaunda once said: "The plundering tiger, with its deadly cubs is coming in through the back door."

The Royal Navy at its smallest in 80 years, has not only pulled back east of Suez, but east of Gibraltar. The RAF cut back by nearly 90% in the past 20 years, now had barely 100 home-based fighters to defend Britain and the 60 or so North Sea oil platforms valued at more than $500 billion.

Even with full mobilization of its reserves, Britain today has a smaller army than Finland, Sweden or Switzerland. Key armoured units and equipment have had to be removed from the Army of the Rhine, once a bulwark of NATO's central front, for duty in Ulster. The number of British soldiers deployed on NATO's Central Front is less than the number of civilian employees in many county councils.

No wonder, I said, General George Brown, Chairman of the American Joint Chiefs of Staff, called the British military situation "pathetic". But these remarks were taken out of context and were made by General Brown out of compassion and understanding, not criticism and ridicule. General Brown, was in fact, paying us a compliment. He said: "They're no longer a world power. . . . and we're going to miss them. We're going to miss them in the Middle East. They had a way with those people out there that we couldn't acquire in 25 or 30 years". It was in this sense that he meant that the decline in Britain's strength was "pathetic". And so it is.

A current example to hand is Britain's inability to offer any strong leadership in the Rhodesian situation.

General George Brown, who happens to be a fervent Anglophile, was merely blurting out the truth. Britain's armed forces are not pathetic. Indeed, they are highly efficient and professional.

There are far too few armed soldiers on the ground and they have such limited logistic backing, that they could fight very well for only a limited period. There are so few aircraft at the ready that the Royal Air Force would be overstretched to defend Britain's cities even for a few days against conventional attacks from the Soviet Union. There are so few naval vessels that the Royal Navy could maintain only a limited number of ships at sea to keep open a limited number of vital sea lanes for a limited period.

It was certainly pathetic that Britain's stock should have reached such an all-time low, consequent upon the endless and rapid succession of savage defence cuts which, in particular, had weakened both flanks of NATO and also set such an appalling example to Britain's allies. The Soviets may have now won a bloodless victory over NATO on the vital northern flank, due almost entirely to Britain's defence cuts which call for practically the complete winding-up of amphibious forces and halving the number of troop-carrying helicopters.

It was pathetic that British reinforcements will now have to go to "war" by requisitioned car ferries which will be obliged to scuttle into some remote Norwegian fjords, hopefully ahead of the Russians. It was pathetic that the armed forces, the territorial army and the "thin blue line" should be so understrength and overstretched.

The recurring cuts in defence expenditure and the adverse affect they have had on the moral and fighting capability of Britain's armed forces began in 1968, when the Socialists claimed that by abrogating responsibilities overseas and bringing forces home the nation could concentrate attention on Europe and provide a more effective contribution to NATO. The forces were duly brought home, but in recent years our contribution to NATO has been reduced despite the totally unrealistic claims made by the Minister of Defence.

Britain's armed forces, and the country, are entitled to ask why they had to wait six years before any positive action was taken by the Chiefs of Staff. It was not until Marshal of the Royal Air Force Sir Andrew Humphrey became Chief of Defence Staff in succession to Field Marshal Lord Carver, that the right of direct access to the Prime Minister by the Chiefs of Staff was exercised, and then it was too late. Alas, Sir Andrew Humphrey died a few weeks later and Britain is unlikely to see his equal in that important post for a long time to come.

The time is overdue for the establishment of a House of Commons Committee on Defence to which the Chiefs of Staff would be required to give evidence from time to time on the lines of the United States Armed Services Committee. This would fulfil two functions. It would provide an opportunity for the Chiefs of Staff to make their views known and would better inform the British public what was going on in the all-important area of defence. There can be little doubt that the activities of such a committee would encourage the British Cabinet and the Prime Minister to take much more notice of the views of their professional advisers.

I said that a further step in encouraging wider debate on national defence would be to repeal that section of the British Army Act that forbids serving officers to communicate anything but the party doctrine to the press.

The Army had become increasingly aware that it is an integral part of national society and not, as it was in the past, an elite body standing aloof from the day to day political problems of the country. Financial realities, great political consciousness stemming from better educated officers and soldiers, and the arrival of the permissive society forced the change. This process of integration should continue and must be encouraged.

It is an anachronism that any country that jealously guards its own liberties should deny free speech and right of publication to those who could have so much to contribute to the public debate on defence.

The Chairman of Britain's Press Council recently contrasted the alacrity with which the Government imposes restrictions on freedom of information with its slothful approach to the amendment of the Official Secrets Act. Many serving officers hold the view that the Act is misused by the Government, which utilizes it to conceal the gaps in the country's defences, not from hostile powers, but from the British people.

One can take as a single example the intrusion of Soviet bombers into British airspace. Photographs of Royal Air Force Lightnings intercepting a Badger are amusing; less entertaining is the thought of 49 Badgers. Would the Royal Air Force be capable of intercepting them? How many fighters have the Royal Air Force at readiness? The Soviets know the exact number and therefore, why should it be withheld from the public?

A possible answer is that British politicians are willing to mortgage the country's future to obtain their own political presence. The electorate can see and appreciate where the money has been spent. It cannot see the gaps in the country's defences, where money has not been spent. It has a right to be informed of them through the medium of a responsible Press. On the occasions when a senior service officer with courage speaks out directly to the public, he incurs the odium of his political and military masters and thereby sacrifices his career.

The Official Secrets Act is being used not to protect Britain from hostile powers, but to protect politicians from the electorate.

Two-thirds of Soviet industry is directly and indirectly linked with military objectives. Expansionism, totalitarianism, skilful international propaganda and military capability are a formidable combination. The danger is much greater than Western Europe experienced during the rise of the Third Reich more than 40 years ago. These are disquieting parallels between the situation in which Western powers find themselves today.

The only means whereby the great numerical superiority of the enemy could be effectively countered is by the immediate use of tactical nuclear weapons. Constant attention has been drawn to the fact that the warheads of the weapons now available to those NATO nations without their own independent nuclear capability, are kept several miles distant from the weapons and the instant refugee problem is going to make it extremely difficult to marry up the pieces.

Add to this confusion likely to be caused by hostile aircraft and airborne troops, and it would seem unlikely that the tactical nuclear weapons would be brought to bear, even if the President of the United States gave permission in time.

There is much evidence to show that the Warsaw Pact countries are prepared to launch a sudden surprise attack on the march — that is to say without reinforcing their troops on the ground this very day — if they considered that the American strategic response was no longer certain or perhaps unlikely.

I have no doubt in my own mind that Britain would be handed to the Soviet Union on a plate if the present Marxist manipulated and trade union dominated Government is returned to power again, for not only have they already all but destroyed the viability of Britain's armed forces and increased their dissatisfaction and lowered the morale to a dangerously low level, but they have also set us firmly down the road to becoming an East European state.

The latest Defence White Paper (February 1978) can only be described as duplicity remarkable even by the standards of this government. Military assessments cannot be reduced to simple ratios, because a closed society and a unified military machine like the Warsaw Pact enjoys so many additional advantages denied to a free society.

The White Paper's mendacious presentation is a smoke screen

to conceal the criminal neglect of Britain's defensive capability and is designed to play down the true gravity of the threat that NATO faces.

In all three of Britain's armed services there is serious discontent over the contempt with which the government has treated servicemen's living standards — where past pay increases were completely eroded by increases in rent and other compulsory charges.

There is also grave apprehension about future careers, for there is evidence of widespread mistrust about the government's future defence policy under left-wing pressure should it be returned to power at the next election.

As for that political and military pygmy, Mr. Fred Mulley, our "Minister for Disarmament and Disgrace", not only does he fall asleep in the presence of, and at the side of, the Queen at a fly-past by the Royal Air Force but he puts in an appearance — this time very wide awake indeed — on the Grunwick picket line at a time of mob violence. How much lower can a Minister of the Crown sink? And he is by no means alone. Mulley is now not only a laughing stock but, far more serious, he has forfeited the confidence and the trust of the armed forces and of all those of ones fellow countrymen who put the security of the realm and the maintenance of law and order as first priority.

One of Britain's most gallant and highly decorated officers — the retired Major General Bredin — recently wrote an excellent letter to the London **Daily Telegraph** on the disgrace of the present pay of Britain's Armed Services. He reminded us that in the darker days of the Desert Campaign the British Army lost some of its best soldiers because the German 88mm gun was superior to anything we had. Similarly at Dunkirk we suffered grievous losses largely because we could not spare fighter aircraft to cope with the dive-bombers.

These and other shortcomings were due to the short-sightedness and parsimony of those who allocated money to our armed services for many years before the war.

But, as General Bredin so aptly put it, "the greatest munition of war is trained, experienced, professional sailors, soldiers and airmen who can form the basis of a national effort in war. In 1939 we had fair numbers of these".

The present Government is driving them out of the Services that most of them love, not only because they are not being given the tools which are necessary to do the job, but because their rates of pay are now a national disgrace.

The earning position in society of the British serviceman has been allowed to slide down the ladder to such a low position that a fighter pilot's basic wage now equates to that of a bus driver. It costs upwards of £500,000 to train a pilot for one three-year operational flying tour.

A lance-corporal's basic pay equates to that of a civilian on the dole. A heavy goods vehicle driver in the army, with four years' service, on a 22 year contract, takes home less than £40 a week if he is single or £44 if he is married with one child. He could earn twice as much tomorrow as a member of the Transport and General Workers' Union. A plant operator mechanic, with the rank of staff sergeant after 12 years' service, takes home just over £60 a week if he is married with two children.

The commanding officer of an infantry battalion, with 650 men under him and 21 years' of training and experience behind him (roughly the equivalent of the managing director of a substantial industrial company) receives a net salary of £100 a week; and, since the introduction of the military salary, all these officers and men are expected, like their civilian counterparts, to pay for their own food and accommodation.

They have an almost unlimited liability — they are expected to work all hours of the day or night without overtime pay; to go where they are told at a moment's notice; to do the work of striking firemen or transport workers and on top of all that to be shot at as part of a normal day's work.

The unfairness of the situation is what now angers the armed forces, particularly the army. Stretched to their limits by operations in Northern Ireland, soldiers are then expected to act as firemen, carrying out long periods of training and travel to such places as Belize. A more than fair day's work for a more than unfair day's pay it would be difficult to find, and at every step the chance of parity with his civilian counterpart recedes.

Between 1973 and 1977 the average number of officers applying for premature release from the Royal Air Force in each financial year was 482. In the first three quarters of the current financial year alone it was 537. The army figures are even worse — an annual average of 562 officers from 1973 to 1976 compared with 646 between April and December 1977.

A letter from one of these 646 officers was published in the **Times** newspaper on 8 March this year. He described the mood within the Army as angry, alarming and depressing and said the reason for the present unrest among soldiers and officers was "the deplorable financial reward offered to those who serve. Nothing brought home to me more the appalling decline in the prestige of the profession of soldiery than the sight of a very senior army officer trying, lamely to justify the curious reasonings behind the last Armed Forces Pay Review Board's recommendations. The real danger here is that officers and soldiers have lost the trust which they used to have in their most senior officers' ability to fight for a 'better deal', and this opens the door to the frightening spectre of the intervention, or creation of a soldiers' trade union.

A pilot who volunteered for redundancy from the Royal Air Force wrote a letter in similar vein to the **Daily Telegraph.** He said he left "along with hundreds of my colleagues, many volunteers, many not, most of whom had between 15 and 25 years of service yet to give. Most of the volunteers would readily admit that they left not because they were disillusioned with service flying, but because they were sick and tried of being treated as political pawns by inept politicians, the Civil Service lackeys and senior RAF officers whose only loyalty appears to be to their pensions.

"Things have never been worse for the British Serviceman in relation to his civilian counterpart; he no longer has job security, his conditions of service are often appalling after successive cutbacks in the 'tail', his pay has been grossly eroded, and all the time he is being asked to do more with fewer resources. Recent events have made that very clear.

"Those who feel able to make a success of a second career are opting to do so in increasing numbers (always at Her Majesty's discretion), and inevitably it is those with ability and initiative who leave."

Recently the Minister for the Army was made to realise how unpopular his policies were when, at the Adjutant General's conference, he was heckled and derided in a scene which would have been unthinkable five years ago. It should be entirely unnecessary for it to happen and surely must be a portent for all to see. As General Bredin so rightly said: "We do not want a Cromwell to arise nor do we want trade unions in the services".

Most officers and soldiers acknowledge that, despite manning reductions, lessening career opportunities and the pressure on them, service in the army could be a satisfying and worthwhile job, but not so long as they are treated with the contempt at present being displayed by their political masters as far as pay is concerned. Members of Her Majesty's Army are just not prepared to carry on serving their Queen and country unless their contribution to that country is fairly assessed. The departure of those who after such a long time, have given up hope of that ever happening presents a disturbing threat to the effectiveness of the armed forces and Britain's national security.

The deficiencies in service equipment could be put right, though late in the day, by a stroke of the pen, but a very heavy long-term responsibility devolves on the Armed Services Pay Review Board.

There are perfectly feasible ways of bringing service pay up to reasonable equality with comparable employment (including the firemen) by more use of the X-factor (compensation for restrictions such as the inability to earn overtime, the inability to strike, frequent moves, etc.) without breaking the 10 per cent rise rule, provided the Board are not intimidated by political factors. If the Board fails to rise to the occasion, we shall be dangerously short of manpower: the greatest munition of war and the one that is irreplaceable save in the very long term.

The Board should look at the food and lodging charges levied on servicemen. In May 1977, they were given a five per cent pay rise that did not even keep pace with inflation. At the same time board and lodging charges were raised so that in some cases the actual rise was a miserable, insulting 3p a week.

After paying their charges, some Servicemen are left with no more than £35 a week.

Why not reduce these charges drastically — and immediately.

That would not conflict with any wage policy. And it would be better than a pay rise — it would be tax free.

General Bredin ended his letter with these words: "Lest people should ask why a time-expired soldier with a nice pension should bother, may I quote from a letter recently received from a Royal Engineer corporal in Northern Ireland who had seen a letter of mine in a national newspaper?

" 'It is people like yourself who I and my comrades rely on to fight our battles with our political leaders who always tread on us because we have no powerful union to speak for us."

"These soldiers realise that their own senior serving officers are hamstrung because they are not allowed to tell the public let alone the soldiers what is going on".

Personally, I do not agree with the last sentence. Senior serving officers have a loyalty to the servicemen whom they have the honour to command, and should not be concerned about risking their pensions and alienating the Establishment. Loyalty does not consist of running with the herd, but rather of having the moral courage to fight when the normal channels have been exhausted. We do not want trade unions in the armed forces, but we must now face the fact that there are those who certainly do.

There is an international organisation specialising in agitation in the armed forces of the West. The task of its agents is to turn the troops against their present democratically elected political leaders in order to install a one-party Marxist dictatorship.

This subversive strategy starts with an apparently innocent demand to form soldiers' committees and the formation of independent trade unions in the army — linked to the trade union movement outside the army. These are then used as a rival power base to the existing military hierarchy to manipulate the army for revolutionary purposes.[1]

In the case of Britain, this politically motivated campaign was started from the top by politicians. It reached its climax early June 1976, when 54 Left-wing Labour MPs, during the debate on the annual Armed Forces Bill, voted in favour of the creation of such independent trade unions within the armed forces against the wishes of the Labour Government.

The Socialist Charter Movement, a Trotskyist tendency within the Labour Party, urges the Labour Government "(to) guarantee . . . trade union rights to Soldiers, Sailors and Airmen, giving power to arrest officers engaged in anti-Government activity. Arming of the working classes . . . defence of ex-propriated property with barricades, workers' defence units, etc., as and where needed."

This organisation has published a pamphlet aimed specifically at troops, **The Soldiers' Charter,** and it reads: "We demand the absolute right for all servicemen to form soldiers' committees and to join a trade union".

The organisers claim that they "help the only working-class organisation inside the Army — the still miniscule Soldiers Trade Union Rights Movement".

In volunteer professional forces morale tends to be much higher than with conscripts, and the scope for subversive activity much smaller. Therefore the immediate threat to the volunteer, professional forces of Britain is slight. But there is no room for complacency in view of the increasing internal security role of the army, the growing importance of key installations in a highly centralised technological society, and the vigorous propaganda of Leftist groups.

In October 1975, four articles were printed in the **Morning Star** the newspaper of the Communist Party of Great Britain. Three quotations will suffice to illustrate the hostile propaganda and incitement to hatred of the armed forces of the British Crown:—

"There is also a lessening distinction between fighting Left-wing insurgency abroad and **protecting** the **capitalist** status quo at home."

"This is the major **threat** posed by the British Army today — that it is a tightly-knit band of **politically motivated** men capable of being used to break strikes and otherwise protect the political and industrial interests of the State."

"The armed forces are a vital part of the State. They are its **coercive** arm, its **last resort,** its **repressive** apparatus.

(The bold type above is mine).

---

1. See **The Destruction of Loyalty: An examination of the threat of propaganda and subversion against the Armed Forces of the West.** By Anthony Burton. Foreign Affairs Pub. Co. 1976.

Finally, as 43 percent of Britain's defence budget is already spent on manpower compared to only 40 per cent on equipment, many civilians see the answer to the pay problem as a return to some form of National Service.

Britain would learn discipline and the rudiments of some branch of the service. And it would absorb some of the unemployed school leavers.

But those senior officers who experienced National Service after the last war are deeply opposed to the suggestion, on the grounds that the small professional Army spent too large a proportion of its time training the recruits who returned to civil life as soon as they were useful.

Personally, I agree with the Bishop of London, Dr. Ellison, who told the General Synod of the Church of England on 1 February, that some form of compulsory National Service might have to be introduced eventually to deal with "the unemployment gap" that faces school leavers. Dr. Ellison said: "It would seem self-evident that there must be some connexion between the prevalent gangsterdom which is so widespread and the lack of work and occupation which afflicts so many, especially among the young".

A period of National Service would not necessarily be military it could be spent on socially useful activities and could teach a cross-section of society how to live together in community.

We all need a spot of discipline in our lives. Research by the Manpower Services Commission shows that Britain's school leavers are so rude, scruffy and badly educated that many of them may never find work. Many employers would rather take on housewives than employ youngsters.

There must be plenty of self-rewarding work waiting to be done by the young on the neglected inland waterways of Britain; on farmland to make the country self-sufficient; on the restoration of condemned buildings and the clearance of slums; on converting every available spare space into playing fields and recreation areas; on providing regular help to Old Age Pensioners, particularly War Widows; on conservancy of the countryside, the re-opening of public footpaths, the elimination of eyesores, the restoration of historic monuments.

CHAPTER 31

A Credible Scenario for a Warsaw Pact Surprise Blitzkrieg Attack

THE Soviet Army is a formidable machine with 170 divisions, 45,000 tanks, 55,000 armoured personnel carriers and nearly five million men.

Since 1965, the Soviets have supported a military manpower increase of 800,000 men — almost as large as the entire United States Army.

Military service is compulsory. In general, all Soviet men serve two (formerly three) years in the armed forces after leaving school. They are liable for military service until they are 55.

Military training forms part of the curriculum in schools, universities and institutes. Civil defence — about which there has been hot debate in the West — is given high priority with a chief of staff for civil defence in each of the 15 republics, and regular exercises in factories and institutes.

No expense is spared for military research and equipment. The Soviets have already, according to NATO, developed the tank that will face the American XM1.

The T80, as it is designated, has a huge 125mm gun, is built of toughened steel with layers of synthetic material that can keep out the most modern missiles, and has a remarkable suspension system to allow fast speeds over rough ground. Eventually, it may be armed with anti-tank missiles and laser target illuminators.

Tanks are still the backbone of Soviet tactics. Soviet military doctrine places heavy emphasis on massive firepower, and a quick advance against intensive defensive fire. It expects heavy losses in men and material.

Design, training and maintenance, therefore, require a large number of tanks and weapons, as battlefield maintenance is limited and a large proportion of troops in a Soviet division are assigned to combat.

Soviet land warfare doctrine is an adaption of the German blitzkrieg. Forces are organised to provide shock power; engaging the enemy with high speed manoeuvres; supported by massive artillery, missiles and air bombardment in a very brief time.

Soviet forces are designed for offensive warfare, and the doctrine emphasizes the importance of initiative through surprise and preemption. The Egyptian attack in Sinai in 1973 was a classic example of Soviet tactics.

The crack Soviet units are all on the Western flank. There are 58 divisions stationed in Ukraine, Byelorussia, the Baltic Republics and the Leningrad region — facing NATO's central region.

The Communist Party has an absolute grip on the armed forces. Roughly 90 percent of the officers are Party members.

There are 20,000 Soviet undercover agents and fifth columnists inside West Germany, ready to seize and sabotage early warning radars and communication installations, headquarters, radio and television stations. also, there are Soviet paratroopers and amphibious Commando Units trained to penetrate deep into West Germany.

There are Soviet trawlers in British and NATO ports every day, with Marine Commandos and a helicopter on board. How easy would it be for them to carry out a coup de main? How many "teeth arm" soldiers of ours are there, stationed this very minute at barracks at our main ports?

Deployed on the ground, this very moment, are vastly superior Warsaw Pact ground and air forces which are immediately available and immediately usable in key areas, capable of striking with hell for leather speed, with little or no warning under surprise conditions "off the march" — that is without prior concentration of forces — under the guise of manoeuvres and exercises, and at the same time blinding us with their electronic warfare capability.

If the Soviet Union were to decide to resort to the second prong — namely, outright military aggression — a credible scenario for a brief blitzkreig war in Europe would be something on the following lines.

The Baltic is an inland sea, dominated by the warships of the Warsaw Pact. The cork in the Baltic bottle is Denmark. The shallow and narrow straits which provide the only exit from the Baltic are within sight of Danish territory.

Within the Baltic, Western naval forces are outnumbered by something approaching six-to-one. In recent years, the Soviets have taken to conducting large amphibious exercises, in which their troop transports and warships head directly for the Danish coast, only to turn south at the final moment and then land on East German beaches, which bear a striking similarity to the Danish beaches. Soviet attack aircraft have made simulated runs.

At 5 p.m. on a Friday evening, under the guise of manoeuvres when NATO forces have stood down for the weekend, a combined Soviet airborne and naval assault is met by a standing Danish army about half the size of the New York Police force. Neither Denmark nor Norway, the other Scandinavian NATO ally, allows the stationing of Allied troops or nuclear weapons on their territory in peacetime.

Airborne, land, and amphibious assaults are launched to occupy the northern tip of Norway and Denmark, which dominate Soviet sea passages to the Atlantic Ocean. Norway's and Denmark's relatively feeble local forces are quite incapable of holding off the greatly superior Soviet air, airborne, amphibious, land, chemical, electronic and sabotage attacks before the arrival of Allied external reinforcements.

Simultaneously, on the Central Front across the North German Plain, the Warsaw Pact forces, employing their "meat-grinder" tactics crunch their way forward, regardless of casualties, at a speed of 70 miles a day, supported in depth by airborne troops, armed helicopters, air attack and chemical attack. Their doctrine regards the tactical use of chemical weapons as a normal form of conventional warfare, and in this field they are better equipped militarily and psychologically prepared than any other country in the world.

The speed, devastating power and velocity of the Soviet onslaught is such that NATO is not able to resort to the use of their tactical nuclear weapons for the simple reason that there has not been sufficient time for the necessary political decisions to be taken. In any case, the missile sites have already been overrun. It would be surprising if the Soviet General Staff did not know the number and location of every nuclear bomb site in Western Europe.

The Soviets offer the Germans, the Danes, and the Norwegians a cease-fire and peace agreement — in exchange for withdrawal from NATO, disarmament, neutrality and unlocking of the naval gates to the Atlantic.

Would the densely populated countries of West Europe prefer to be overrun by Soviet troops, and their homelands made conventional or nuclear battlefields rather than opt for concessions, peace and neutrality? Would an American President reject negotiations and engage in atomic war in Europe, which could rapidly escalate to strategic war with the Soviet Union, which has probably established nuclear superiority? Soviet conventional superiority continues to grow, her strategic forces to expand. There is no precedent in history for such a build-up of naval and military power where that power was not eventually used.

The Soviet Union has developed an air force which is capable of launching a devastating attack into Western Europe in the form of massive air strikes to destroy NATO air bases — particularly those in Britain — and nuclear storage depots. This would deprive NATO of its nuclear response option and enable Soviet ground forces to advance rapidly through NATO territory.

Satellite coverage has recently revealed a newly discovered Soviet biological factory. The Soviets may well be considering the possibility of "a disabling war" in which weapons such as the neutron warhead, chemical and bacteriological weapons which could disable — not kill — people while leaving structures undamaged would achieve the Soviet's political aims at less cost to themselves and enormous gains in any post-war occupation of Europe.

The only safe prediction today is that the unexpected must be expected. With spies in the sky, you can photograph the enemy's capability. But you cannot photograph his intentions, particularly when his forces are deployed and pre-positioned under the guise of an exercise. The one thing that will **deter** the Soviet hawks from flexing their muscles is the sight of soldiers on patrol on the ground in combat dress, in sufficient numbers, with modern weapons. And the same applies at sea and in the air.

Our failure to maintain a sufficient level of **conventional** forces has now jeopardised NATO's whole strategy of flexible response, or graduated deterrence, which is based on the three deployment options of conventional, theatre nuclear, and strategic nuclear forces. This strategy depends for success on four essential ingredients.

First, sufficient warning. Such is the overwhelming strength of the Warsaw Pact conventional forces on the ground this very day that we shall be lucky to get more than a few days warning.

Second, timely political decisions. In their present disarray the NATO politicians are unlikely to reach vital decisions in time.

Third, the physical presence of sufficient conventional strength to deter aggression.

NATO is now so outnumbered, outgunned and outstripped in every direction that the Soviet Union may well be tempted to flex her muscles.

Fourth, our forces must be combat ready (they are not), at the right place (they are not), at the right time (at present they cannot be), so as to ensure there will be a vigorous response to any aggression or threat.

We simply must succeed in getting across to our people that flexible response requires not less conventional strength, but stronger conventional forces than did the previous NATO strategy of massive retaliation — the old trip-wire strategy.

CHAPTER 32

The High Seas

DURING my visit to Southern Africa, I made a particular point of emphasising that the sea is not only a right of way for the world, but the one arena in which the Soviet could, at low risk, and at a time and place of their own choosing, probe the strength and weaknesses of the West's ability to defend its very lifelines.

The opportunities are numerous and the Soviets are renowned chess-players. Ships can be stopped for inspection on a dozen excuses; they can be hijacked or sabotaged and perhaps even sunk without trace or without concrete evidence of their fate.

Those who argue that the powerful Soviet fleet offers no threat, should read the lessons of history and the use of sea power.

This massive projection of sea power by a largely self-sufficient, continental totalitarian state, can only have a sinister purpose. It constitutes a mortal danger to the countries for whom the seas are vital lines of communication. The purpose behind this naval build-up is to challenge the Western powers at sea.

People are not yet sufficently aware of the fundamental change in the Soviet use and employment of sea power. The margin of safety in the Atlantic is wearing thin and in some places, is wearing through.

The Soviet fleet is no longer a fleet of defence, but an ocean fleet with a three-dimensional challenge — air, surface and submarine. For eight years I had watched the Free World's reaction and, regretfully, its inaction to the growing Soviet naval fleet.

On NATO's northern flank, it is the intention of the Soviets to push their naval defence line outwards to Iceland and the Faroes. If this is a likely development then it indicates that the Soviets would, to an increasing degree, come to regard the Norwegian sea as a Soviet lake behind which, of course, Norway will lie.

When the Suez Canal route is fully operative, the major oil producing countries of the Middle East would be effectively ringed by the Soviet Navy. Israel's survival is the major obstacle to the Soviet domination of the Eastern Mediterranean. If we forget this, we do so at our peril.

The position of South Africa is a vital link in any defensive Western chain because its strategic location makes it the guardian of the West's oil route round the Cape and a counter weight to the Soviet naval build-up in the Indian Ocean.

Because defence is indivisible, NATO cannot shut its eyes to events taking place beyond its present boundaries, which is what it tried to do during the Arab-Israeli War of 1973. In future, the Alliance must be far more outward looking and realise that the defence of the Mediterranean cannot be divorced from the security of the Middle East, Africa and the Indian Ocean. Nor can NATO's Southern boundary end at the Tropic of Cancer.

In spite of the political implications involved, there is an overriding case for NATO's boundary to be extended below the Tropic of Cancer, to include joint defence of the Gulf. Inasmuch as 66% of world oil reserves lie near the Persian Gulf, stability must be safeguarded in that theatre otherwise the continuing access to energy by the US, the NATO countries and Japan will be at grave risk.

It is imperative that top priority is given forthwith to the global nature of the Soviet threat and the vulnerability of the lifelines to the West and to Japan. This means that the charter of NATO must be extended to include South Africa, Japan and Spain in the NATO defence concept. Iran, Israel, Brazil, Argentina and Australia should eventually be added to this concept.

If the Soviet Union's strategy is global as, indeed, it is then NATO's strategy must also be global.

The political implications and the divergencies of national interest of this concept may severely strain the solidarity of NATO. But the Soviet global threat is advancing so relentlessly and ruthlessly that it is futile to suggest that it can be met by an informal agreement on the exchange of information on the security of the Gulf, Indian Ocean, the South Atlantic by representatives of the Western-oriented states concerned.

The Alliance can no longer afford to continue to take such a myopic view of the overall threat — a threat which is by no means confined only to the sea rights in all oceans, but also war by proxy in distant countries — with Rhodesia and South Africa now high up on the list.

If the NATO problem is set in a truly global perspective, the strategic location of South Africa and the Cape route stands out as a prime target for our enemies. By putting the thumbscrews on South Africa, the West is merely playing into the Soviet's hands and handing the prize to them on a plate. Fortunately for civilization, the South Africans are made of sterner stuff and have no intention of committing suicide, even if it means being driven, in desperation, to resorting to the use of the ultimate nuclear deterrent.

Watching Russia's deep penetration of strategic areas one can see that the Soviet Merchant Fleet calls at 600 ports in 91 countries on regular trade routes — and only 13 of these countries are Communist.

On any day in the year, 2,800 merchant ships are alongside in the ports of NATO Europe while 800 are loading or discharging on the East Coast of North America. Moving to and from these ports are some 3,350 merchants ships, while a further 750 are underway in the Mediterranean. Nearly 60 percent of the huge volume of shipping rounding the Cape of Good Hope belongs to NATO and, on the same day, 200 Western tankers are at sea in the Indian Ocean.

These are the ships unseen and unknown to the vast majority of our citizens, upon whom every one of us depends for his or her life and livelihood. It is the thought of how vulnerable these trade routes are to any nation opposed to us which should shock public opinion.

No shots need be fired. If the Soviet Union sees us weak and unprepared, the mere presence of large numbers of powerful and operational ships could so easily disrupt the West's communications and bring NATO, and Britain in particular, to a halt.

The Soviet's merchant ships, like their warships, are under one central control in Moscow. Their merchant navy is now able to establish a global maritime presence corresponding to their naval strategy of control of the seas. The Soviets regard their merchant navy as a 4th arm of defence, and officers and ratings of the Soviet navy serve in their merchant ships which visit ports all round the world every week. It is not difficult to imagine the scale of espionage that is being carried out all the time and it could well outweigh that posed by Communist bloc diplomats.

The British public is not aware of the Soviet submarine and spy trawler activity off Ireland and Scotland, whose sole purpose is to keep a close watch on British and American Polaris nuclear missile submarines, moving between their Clyde bases and Atlantic patrol areas. Releasing only minimum details of Soviet sea power serves merely to keep the public in ignorance of the real level of the threat at sea.

Soviet spy "trawlers" snoop on Polaris submarines off the Firth of Clyde. These trawlers, at least one of which is on station at all times, are packed with electronic intelligence gear to track the entry and exits of the Polaris submarines based at Holy Loch and Faslane.

Their immediate purpose is to secure information about the patrol patterns of the British and American nuclear deterrent fleets. They are also in communication with Soviet chaser submarines lying offshore in the hope of following the Polaris vessels. The object is to test new underwater tracking equipment designed to enable them to lock on to a Polaris vessel and trail it throughout its patrol.

Just before leaving Johannesburg airport on my return journey to England, I was amazed to be asked the following question by South African Broadcasting Corporation:

"General, this week has seen the conference taking place in Pretoria on marketing of South Africa's image abroad, and during this conference various delegates including Mr. Reginald Maudling said that the Cape Sea Route had no real strategic value to the West any longer. People who said it was were 10 years out of date, and also that South Africa's minerals such as titanium, vanadium, iron ore, etc., were of no real use. Any comments on this?"

I said that there came a time when an ex-Minister of the Crown would be well advised to turn in his tongue and withhold his opinions. Ministers are only politicians temporarily in office. If I, as an ex-NATO Commander-in-Chief said the Cape Route was of great strategic importance, then presumably one had good grounds for saying so, and would be privy to information not necessarily made available to even a Minister.

Since this radio interview, a Royal Navy nuclear-powered submarine has been refused passage through the Suez Canal. This reinforces the importance of the Cape Route.

No nuclear powered submarines have transit rights through the Suez Canal for reasons that are understandable. Why Britain was so stupid as to try to pass one through is not known publicly.

This particular submarine, **Dreadnought,** 4,000 tons, is not armed with nuclear weapons. She is a hunter-killer and is merely powered by nuclear engines.

Experience of more than a decade has shown that nuclear-powered ships present not the slightest hazard to the harbours they use.

In the event of war, the canal would be closed within hours by one side or the other. It would require just one nuclear weapon in the 200 kiloton range to destroy it. The Cape route is therefore vital not only in war but in peace. Britain has painful practical experience of how easy it is to put the canal out of action and the totally unpredictable Arabs are liable to close it at any time.

Mr. Maudling would be well advised to read the book by Admiral Gorshkov who has been Commander-in-Chief of the Soviet Navy for 22 years.

Entitled **Sea Power of the State,** this top-level official document is nothing less than a literal blueprint for the destruction of what the author calls "American Imperialism". It certainly is a hair-raiser and minces no words in making the following key claims:

— Today's Soviet Navy can saturate US military-industrial complexes such as San Diego with nuclear weapons from platforms on and beneath the sea.

— It has the capacity of blockading US ports and isolating outlying islands and territories in case of war.

— The Soviet fleet can flag down and cripple the flow of oil and other strategic materials to the US and Western Europe. (The US, remember, depends on imports for 87 of its 93 strategic materials.)

— In preparation for possible war, the USSR is now engaged in placing task forces on strategic locations throughout the world's oceans and building elaborate overseas bases in friendly countries to support them.

—The Soviet Navy is being expanded as rapidly as possible as a major instrument in the Kremlin plan to communise other nations. It is planned to have a critical role in eliminating what the writer calls imperialist attempts to control the world's oceans and their natural resources.

Gorshkov concludes: "Our seapower will determine the success of future political measures and the accomplishment of strategic missions. Its development is the outstanding event which has shattered the illusions of the imperialist aggressors that they had no strong opponent in the sphere of naval warfare."

One of the most frightening aspects of Gorshkov's writing has been the reaction of Pentagon officials. Although they have been deploring the decline of US seapower relative to the greatly growing naval power of the Soviets, almost invariably they refuse to discuss his sinister book, even off the record on a background basis.

The only official comment was made in a speech by a US Navy Secretary who said:

"Like **Mein Kampf**, which spelled out Hitler's intentions, when the history of the age is written, Gorshkov's book may have been the most prophetic statement over the last part of the 20th century."

In fairness to Mr. Maudling, one has to admit that his views would appear to be in accord with those of Dr. Owen. An illuminating conversation took place between a South African and a member of Dr. Owen's staff who he had known at a university in England when they had a reunion during the Owen-Andrew Young visit to South Africa.

The Foreign Office man explained that the determining factor in the Western policies was the United States' flat refusal after Vietnam to become embroiled with the Soviets in Southern Africa.

"Does that mean that you recognise Southern Africa as a Russian sphere of influence?" asked the South African.

"Yes", said the Foreign Office man.

Questioned about the effect of this abdication on the security of the Cape sea route which at present carries about 60 per cent of the West's oil imports, Dr. Owen's aide replied that this route was no longer important because oil supplies will in future reach Europe by pipeline from the Middle East fields. He also shrugged off the dangers of losing Southern Africa's vast resources of strategic minerals to the Russians. The West could acquire these minerals from the Soviets in exchange for wheat, he said.

Since comparable arguments hold good for almost any region in which there is a risk of embroilment with the Soviets, is there any reason to assume that Australia, South America, or for that matter, even Western Europe will be defended?

Where will the line be drawn? A moral issue on which to join battle with the West can always be produced for the occasion by the Soviets and their dupes.

These views are completely contrary to those expressed so strongly by this year's North Atlantic Assembly of 15 Nations and to which I have drawn attention earlier in the chapter headed 'The Free World Would do Well to Listen to the Voice of NATO.'

NATO and Europe depend on their sea lines of communication for their very survival and unless they can keep them open they will starve, and their industry and fighting forces will grind to a standstill.

57 per cent of the oil supplies of NATO-Europe and 25 per cent of its food come round the Cape of Good Hope and through the South Atlantic. In one month, 2,000 NATO-European ships pass the Cape of Good Hope, and in one year about 13,000 call at South African ports. In 1970, the Soviet Naval Attache in Colombo, asked the Second-in-Command of a British frigate how the Royal Navy was enjoying the Soviet Indian Ocean.

The ending of the Simonstown Agreement for naval co-operation with South Africa was strategic folly and highly suspect. It was a frightening victory for Left-wing agitation in Britain and Soviet maritime strategy.

The opposition to apartheid was the excuse for it, rather than the reason. It was an appalling state of affairs when Ministers could contemplate such a strategic sacrifice in the interests of party dogma and appeasement of their left-wing in preference to the security of Britain and the defence of the Free World.

Britain got out of the Persian Gulf to save money. Hardly a smart economy move seeing what we are having to pay for oil now.

The United States, Britain and the NATO Allies need Simonstown to support anti-submarine patrols in times of tension or war. Of 5,150 allied merchant ships sunk in the Second War, 559, or one ship in nine, were sunk in the South Atlantic or Indian Ocean.

When I visited the underground Communications & Surveillance

Centre at Silvermine, I was able to pinpoint the exact position of every ship sailing the southern hemisphere, and identify its country of origin, type and cargo or armaments carried. Silvermine is not only equipped with sophisticaated electronics, but also with a world-wide radio communications network which gives immediate contact with aircraft, ships and submarines from South America to the Indian Ocean and as far south as Antarctica. We have reached a sad state of affairs when the Cape Sea Route now remains the most unguarded strategic region in the world.

Accurate assessments are kept of the Soviet fleet strengths in the Indian Ocean and South Atlantic. Intelligence reports on every ship that passes the Cape are available to both Washington and the NATO alliance. But if the ageing Shackleton planes that do most of the patrol work are not replaced, the Cape watch will be rendered ineffective. The irony is that it is the West that will suffer and the Kremlin planners who will gain so much.

On average, there is one ship every 25 miles along the Cape Route carrying cargo for Britain, and more than two million tons of oil is shipped round the Cape each month, of which 90 per cent goes to European ports. In a conventional war, the Soviet Union would be able to prevent oil from reaching the West if it controlled South Africa and the Suez Canal.

It will be futile to base plans on the assumption that NATO's six-nation naval task force will be activated in time to protect the West's shipping lanes beyond the NATO area's present southern boundary — The Tropic of Cancer — for the simple reason that there will not be enough ships to go round, even in the unlikely event of the member-nations of NATO being able to reach unanimous political agreement in time.

In any case, the protection of the shipping routes within NATO's present boundaries, particularly the sea lanes across the North Atlantic between Europe and the United States and Canada, will already have absorbed all of NATO's already totally inadequate naval resources.

The Mediterranean Sea is no longer a NATO lake, while the Atlantic Ocean is now prowled by twice as many Soviet submarines as German U-boats in the darkest days of the Second World War, each capable of raining havoc on a distant continent, not a nearby convoy.

For anyone in a position of authority to say that the Cape sea route is no longer important, because in future oil supplies will reach Europe by pipeline from the Middle East fields, manifests the appalling ignorance and apathy that exists in high places and the inexcusable failure to have the feasibility of such a mammoth project properly researched before passing judgement on it. One never ceases to be amazed by the ignorance, irresponsibility and impenetrable self-righteousness of such men.

What are the facts?

According to the experts, any scheme to pipe oil from the Arabian oilfields to Britain, thus avoiding the long haul round the Cape is merely a pipe dream.

Physically it would be possible to lay pipe across land or through the Mediterranean, but two overriding conditions would have to be fulfilled. First, complete co-operation on the part of every country concerned, and second, guaranteed peace in all the territories crossed by the pipe line.

The complete agreement of eight to ten governments would be involved, plus the full support of the political parties and trade unions in each territory.

The vulnerable areas would not only be countries like Yugoslavia, Greece, Turkey and Italy but also in the volatile areas of France and other nearby countries.

Any government on the route would be able to interfere at any time. Even if the whole region was at peace the pipeline could be used as a blackmailing weapon. It would certainly be a soft target for extremist groups such as international terrorists. One British expert reminded me that in uninhabited areas like Alaska the pipeline had been sabotaged several times, so what would happen in hot-blooded populated areas?

A pipeline laid under the sea would be fraught with similar dangers and problems. With the Soviet Union having more than a toehold in the area, it would take little effort to put the whole pipeline out of action. The guarding and protection of both land and sea lines would make the cost almost prohibitive, compared with the long sea haul by oil tanker.

Initially the basic cost of a pipeline would work out at around $5,000 per mile per inch — that is, if the pipe was the normal 42 inch diameter it would cost approximately £105,000 per mile for the whole route. To this must be added the annual maintenance, plus the rental agreed with the governments of the countries through which the line passed. It is impossble to estimate what this figure would be.

Finding the necessary finance would present a real problem. The financial backing of the countries at each end of the line would be easier to obtain than from the other countries involved. Costs might be reduced by running "spurs" in the various countries through which the pipe passes and so pump oil to them .But this would again require a great deal of negotiating and argument. With "spur" lines, the country through which the pipe passes would almost certainly demand an almost prohibitive rental, plus guarantees of the safety and protection of the line.

There are lessons to be learned from other pipeline projects, but none of them have the same international repercussions.

For example, the National Iranian Oil Company (a State enterprise) planned in 1970 to build a line 1,150 miles long from Ahuaz on the Persian Gulf to the Turkish Mediterranean port of Isjenderum. The cost was then estimated to exceed £306 million and unavailing efforts were made to raise two thirds of the money from the US, Britain, France and West German finance companies. International banks were also approached. The cost at today's figure would be greatly in excess of £306 million.

Saudi Arabian oilfields, under another scheme in 1969, were to be linked to the port of Yanbu on the Red Sea. This was to have a 48 inch diameter pipe running 1,370 km and capable of carrying two million barrels of oil a day. The cost in 1969 would have been £900 million.

The Italian State oil company planned in 1976 a Sumed pipe — 42 inches in diameter — to run 200 km and link Suez with the Mediterranean. Work has not yet started.

CHAPTER 33

What is the solution if the West is to survive?

WHAT is the solution if the West is to survive? The United States must close the strategic nuclear missile gap, for nothing in the world can defend freedom against the Soviet nuclear arsenal except the nuclear power of America. In particular the new generation of cruise missiles could prove a most important technological advance. Therefore, on no account must America forego its ability to develop this weapon.

Meanwhile, the European nations of NATO must build up their conventional forces. They cannot possibly match tank for tank, soldier for soldier, ship for ship, or aircraft for aircraft. But what they can do is to **standardise** their weapons and equipment and use their **technology** to close the numerical gap, by increasing their mobility and fire power with the new range of very accurate conventional missile delivery systems against tanks, against aircraft and against ships.

To stem a Soviet blitzkrieg assault, there are revolutionary advances in mini-nuclear weapons technology, such as the neutron bomb and shell — a miniature battlefield nuclear warhead — which kills by lethal gamma rays and not by blast and fire. The neutron warhead, about the size of a cricket ball, releases up to 80 per cent of its total power as an intense burst of nuclear particles and gamma rays, so penetrating that they are lethal to soldiers even in heavy tanks. But they do minimum damage to buildings and leave so little radioactive fall-out that troops can enter a combat zone within minutes.

This is the most powerful battlefield **deterrent** today. It would slaughter hundreds of thousands of Soviet troops in the first wave of a blitzkrieg attack without inflicting casualties to civilians and massive destruction of buildings and devastation of the countryside.

In a letter to the London **Times** newspaper published as long ago as August 1977, I wrote:—

"The brutal truth is that owing to the criminal negligence of politicians and the weak-kneed resistance of Service Chiefs, our conventional strength has been allowed to fall to such a parlous level that the neutron bomb will be the West's only salvation.

"Were the Russians to mount a massive tank attack against Western Europe the neutron bomb would be the best known way to stop them, causing the loss of far less lives and destruction than the old fashioned 'dirty' nuclear weapons which have been employed in Europe for the past decade,"

The Soviets have craftily made a big fuss about the neutron weapon in order to direct attention from their own deployment in Eastern Europe of the far more devastating medium-range SS-20 missiles aimed, not at the United States but at NATO targets.

Mr. Brezhnev's concern is that neutron weapons could bring the new Soviet T72 tanks to a speedy halt should they attempt to invade Western Germany. Indeed, there is now little else to prevent the Soviets from overrunning Europe. The neutron warhead would have considerable value as a deterrent, for it can be used with the Lance missile, which is already in service in Europe by the United States, Britain, Belgium, Holland and West Germany.

The neutron warhead is one of the most effective **deterrent** weapons yet invented, assuming that we in Europe still wish to deter the massive tank and motor rifle divisions of the Warsaw Pact from taking over Western Europe. If deterrence should fail, and the Soviets decide on an adventure into Europe, they must first provide new shielding protection for all their armoured vehicles and for troops in the open. Current armour is not proof against high energy neutrons.

The neutron warhead is no worse than any other weapon of war designed specifically to kill men on the battlefield. The idea that some well-intentioned body meeting in Geneva could succeed in drawing up a set of rules for war after the fashion of a football game, specifying what weapons may be used, when and under what circumstances within a strict time limit, ignores the weaknesses of human nature and the harsh reality that the Soviet Union plays by its own rules which it makes as it goes along.

The ideal is to **prevent** war, and the deterrence provided by nuclear weapons of all kinds has been successful in Europe for more than 30 years. The neutron warhead reinforces that deterrence and may be the one weapon that will persuade the Soviet Union that the time has come to engage in meaningful discussions on a reduction of arms in Europe.

If the Soviets themselves have not already got the neutron weapon, it is only a question of time before they add it to their stockpile as a valuable weapon for use against troops in the field, in the same way as they regard their deadly nerve gas (B gas), which has the same effect on humans that DDT has on insects. It demolishes their nervous system and they curl up and die. It does not destroy buildings, but, once released, it is at the mercy of the elements and will kill any living creature that comes in contact with it.

The next weapons to be exploited by NATO, particularly on the Northern flank, in Norway, are atomic demolition mines — known as ADMs — of the new "clean" mini-nuclear type of device. They should be pre-positioned in depth in vital and vulnerable areas, not only to act as a deterrent, but also to counter a surprise Soviet attack. ADMs would save countless lives on the battlefield. They can be fired by remote control by being pre-positioned in concrete chambers and made completely safe, by fitting each mine with an electronic lock operated by a coded signal.

There is far too much waste and duplication in NATO. We want much more co-operation in arms purchases. The jargon is called rationalisation. In other words, interdependence, and not independence. With far more NATO standardisation of weapons, equipment, logistics, training and tactics, we would get twice as good defence at half the present price. What we want is value for money and not jobs for the boys. There are far too many over-staffed and over-stuffed headquarters.

Another word of warning. To over-depend on the nuclear deterrent is just as much an illusion as the over-dependence of the French on their Maginot Line. What is wanted is a "public deterrence," a kind of territorial guard of citizen soldiers trained in anti-tank and anti-aircraft units. The Yom-Kippur War showed how single men, using hand-held weapons of devastating power, can inflict incredible losses against tanks.

How is a neutral country like Switzerland able to provide itself with such a strong defence? The Swiss militia system provides a well-trained, part-time army that would be thoroughly dependable in defence. I am convinced there should be a Swiss-type militia covering the whole territory in great depth throughout Europe, and being essentially complementary and additional to, and certainly not a substitute for, regular forces. Such a militia force would release regular army formations for use in an essentially mobile and hard-hitting role.

The key to the success of such operations is for regular and territorial forces to operate to a single, co-ordinated and mutually supporting plan. In other words, territorial commanders would be responsible for all operations in their area, but would answer to the commander of the tactical formation within whose boundaries their area lies. Such areas would be covered by a lattice of small territorial teams, each of about six men, equipped with modern hand-held stand-off anti-tank and anti-aircraft missiles. Their tasks would be the neutralisation of enemy tanks, armour, convoys, aircraft and parachutists, through kills and through the destruction of bridges, petrol supplies, ammunition, food etc.

Modern sensors now enable a very few men to watch and patrol a front, particularly at night, and to have a night vision of up to

1,000 yards. The tactics are those of "shoot and scoot". Having struck, the team disengages before the enemy has time to react, and lies up in a prepared hide until the dust has settled and another attack is undertaken.

I do not know to what extent NATO plans may have already been developed in this direction, but what I do know is that this concept of special and regular forces operating to a single, co-ordinated and mutually supporting plan, has not been accorded the importance and pride of place that it now justifies.

Finally, NATO must have a global strategy and must also exploit its economic strength.

Why are Western statesmen so weak-kneed as to bail the Soviet economy out instead of putting on the thumbscrews? What sort of conspiracy is this? Whose side are they on? Have we not had enough lying, spying, cheating, double-dealing and corruption?

If the United States wants the Soviet Union and Cuba out of Angola and the Horn of Africa, then why restock Soviet granaries? If the United States is serious about Jewish emigration from the Soviet Union, why grant the Soviets commercial benefits and credits. Cuba is on the very doorstep of America and yet this tiny island is allowed to deploy a quarter of its army in indirect aggression in Africa — some 45,000 men — with impunity.

By supplying the Soviet Union police state with food, machinery, plants, mills, technology, know-how and credit, the taxpayers of the West are enabling the Soviet Union to pour more and more money, faster and faster, into her vast armaments industry. They are assisting her not only in getting a foothold in Western Europe, the Middle East and Africa, and to rule the waves and dominate the skies, but also to communise the world and establish herself as the leading world power.

Russia, industrialised by 1917, is a ghastly economic failure. Though the richest agricultural country in the world and a pre-revolution grain exporter, her agriculture is now so abysmally inefficient that she cannot even feed herself, let alone assist the hungry elsewhere.

I have already given sufficient emphasis to the importance of the West having a global strategy. I believe that such a strategy is well within the economic and military ability of the Western Allies. The solution is to have a multi-national mobile presence at sea, on land and in the air. At sea, NATO already has the standing Naval Force Atlantic, consisting of warships of several NATO nations. A similar multi-national naval presence is required as a deterrent in the Mediterranean, and another such standing naval force in the South Atlantic and Indian Ocean. The nations of Northern Europe would each contribute one warship to the Northern task force. Likewise the countries of Central and Southern

Europe would contribute a warship to the Mediterranean task force and to the South Atlantic and Indian Ocean Task Force. Both South Africa and Australia and, indeed, Iran, should be included in the Standing Naval Force South Atlantic and Indian Ocean. The Shah of Iran has a large fleet, by Middle East standards, in which Britain plays a large supplying role. There is a new Iranian naval base at Banda Abbas in the Persian Gulf and the Shah is known to be interested in procuring nuclear-powered submarines for his own navy. A Royal Navy hydrographic team are already at work surveying the shallow waters of the Gulf with a view to future Iranian submarine navigation.

NATO already has a multi-national Allied Command Europe (ACE) Mobile Force — Army and Air Force — to deploy to either the Northern or Southern flanks. The rub is that it cannot deploy to both flanks at the same time in a flag waving deterrent role. What is, therefore, required is a second ACE Mobile Force. Such truly multinational, integrated forces, ready to deploy at the drop of a hat, would be a real deterrent to the Soviet's expansionist ambitions. Furthermore, they could provide an almost permanent presence because of the need for constant exercises. Such a demonstration of multinational presence at sea, on land and in the air would be practical proof of NATO's will and determination to deter Soviet aggression.

CHAPTER 34

What is the State of Play in Britain Today?

ONE of the questions I was asked by Prime Ministers Vorster and Smith and invariably by most of those with whom I had interviews — whether the media, politicians, the business community, etc. — was "What is the state of play in Britain today?"

I said that as a former public servant of perhaps a little prominence: I had a duty to support my country's policy unless I believed that policy to be definitely wrong. In my view, the country's policy was positively disastrous and I had been saying so publicly for the past five years. The country was committing hara kari and inflicting on itself what Napoleon, Kaiser Wilhelm and Hitler failed to do.

I said the gravity of Britain's internal situation could not begin to be appreciated unless it was seen in the context of the pernicious threat of the Soviet Union's subtle and insidious strategy of subversion. There were all too few who realised that it was Moscow's hands which were manipulating the strings of anarchy in Britain and everywhere else.

I said the authentic voice today of that good natured, lazy, half afraid, half asleep mass, which goes by the name of the British public, could be summed up as: "Tell us what to do, but do not tell us anything we do not want to hear." "Give us leadership, but do not ask us to do anything — no trouble please." This was the sign of a once great nation that had suffered a nervous breakdown and was under sedation.

The silent majority, I said, was, not merely silent but also deaf, blind and paralysed. We had become a sick nation, with industrial anarchy, national blackmail, a perpetual state of industrial unrest and the rule of the bully boys.

I emphasised that we were now poorer than our former foes and our defeated allies. Most of our wounds were self-inflicted and our reputation was in tatters.

The trade unions, I said, seemed to be above the law and by abusing their power had been likened to mediaeval barons. People were afraid to run foul of the unions for fear of losing their jobs. We had reached the stage where trade union policy was government of a section of the people for a section of the people by a section of the people. I quoted Mr. Dan Jones, a Labour M.P., sponsored by the Amalgamated Union of Engineering Workers (AUEW), who had stated: "On 11 July, 1974, in the House of Commons, the Trade Union Council accepted the surrender of politicians after a hard battle that had lasted five years."

In answer to questions about Britain's economic situation, I said that Mr. Denis Healey had received a public accolade for becoming such an apt pupil of the IMF that the ordinary man in the street tended to forget that Britain had about 1½ million unemployed, a huge national debt that could mortgage North Sea Oil for some time ahead, the highest inflation rate in Europe, and the value of the pound was less than half what it was when the Labour Government came into power. North Sea Oil had arrived just in time to subsidise a standard of living which we no longer earned.

When I was asked to amplify this I gave the following explanation.

If some economic factors appeared to be moving temporarily in favour of the Labour Government — if Government it could be called — the credit was due entirely to the International Monetary Fund which, in bailing Britain out of economic collapse, imposed stern guidelines and stipulated that the Government should abandon its plans for yet more nationalisation and slash public expenditure. In effect, what the IMF had demanded was that the British economy should be run on the severest Tory principles for the period throughout late 1976 and 1977. In no way, I stated, had we emerged from our debilitating malaise.

I warned that the British public had to realise that the Labour Party's Left Wing — the Socialist wolves temporarily in sheep's clothing — was biding its time in the wings, consolidating its power base, and that if a Labour Government was returned to power, Mr. Callaghan and his so-called moderates would be forced to dance to the tune of Mr. Benn and the extreme left-wing Labour Members of Parliament. In other words, I explained, a vote for Labour would be a vote for a Marxist State.

I pointed out that Lord Wigg, in his autobiography, recalled asking Mr. Callaghan what was his "recipe for political success". He had received the answer "Wait till the trade unions decide their line, and follow them".

I said that the trade unions had long since lurched to the Left and accepted Marxist penetration of their leadership as a fact of life.

To emphasise how far Communist infiltration had penetrated, I gave as an example Mrs. Thatcher's challenge to the Prime Minister in July 1977, about the pro-Communist opinions of one of his back-benchers, when Mr. Callaghan sought to make a joke about the matter by accusing the Opposition leader of lacking a "sense of humour".

Nothing, I said, could better illustrate this Government's incapacity to judge the mood of the nation. The truth was that most people did not regard Communist infiltration as a laughing matter. Nor, in reality, did the Prime Minister. But instead of meeting the challenge, he preferred to hide his embarrassment behind a giggle.

Was there any other country in the world, I asked, where such frivolity could pass for statesmanship?

I emphasised that the programme, **Labour 1976,** of the National Executive Committee of the Labour Party, spelt out a programme of further nationalisation, regulation and confiscation far to the Left of, for example, the Italian Communist Party's election programme. Britain's Labour Party's sharp shift to the left wing was, I said, a sinister lookout for the country's freedom, prosperity and jobs. I had no hesitation in ramming home the point that a Labour Party victory at the next election would take Britain a long way down the road to East European style serfdom.

I was always asked about Britain's state of unemployment and poor production. One could not deny that, already with more than a million and a half unemployed, Britain was proportionately the worst in Europe. The figure when the Tories left office was 600,000 out of work.

As for production, one could not deny that it was so sluggish and low that Britain had one of the lowest levels of industrial productivity in Europe. We were producing less than we did in the three-day week of 1974. If this was not an absolutely and appalling industrial performance, then what else was it?

In answer to close questioning, one had to admit that Britain was plagued by overmanning, restrictive practices, wilful absenteeism, spinning out jobs to get overtime, working to rule, refusing to man new machinery without exorbitant pay increases, and the endless inciting of class warfare by Marxists and their Socialist fellow travellers. Meanwhile the closed shop was spreading its tentacles through the sprawling ranks of Britain's industrial giants. While the penalties for indolence were waived, the rewards of diligence had largely disappeared. Little wonder was it, I said, that our trade figures were bad.

I was questioned on bogus productivity deals being the order of the day. I had to concede that on one pretext or other the giants were able to circumvent the ten per cent pay limit, whereas the smaller firms which attempted to break the guidelines were blacklisted.

I acknowledged that the British Steel Industry and British Leyland were both a shambles, and that as both were nationalised there could not be a worse reflection on the advocacy of public ownership. I gave the British Steel Corporation's vast losses as running at £10 million a week — every penny of which was taxpayer's money.

I agreed that the pound in our pocket today was worth little more than half what it was worth when the Tories left office. The cost of living was rising, I said, the standard of living falling, the taxes were almost the highest in Europe, while the chances of being unemployed were increasing.

Since my return from Southern Africa, the Government's cynicism has only been exceeded by it incompetence. The British taxpayer now has to subsidise Communist Poland, Communist Vietnam and India to take our ships which will then be used to compete with our own shipping lines and shipyards and put them out of business. These ships deals are, of course, designed to win the votes of workers in Labour constituencies.

I was at pains to point out that the Soviet Union regarded Britain as a soft touch. The present industrial chaos, plus the assault by left-wingers on defence spending was, I explained all part and parcel of the Soviet Union's carefully co-ordinated orchestration of subversion by remote control — using left-wing militants in the trade unions, the universities, schools, the Church, television, and Parliament itself, to achieve their nefarious designs. The Soviets' aim was to move Britain towards the Eastern Bloc and erode our military credibility as an ally of the United States and NATO. We were rolling down the slope towards the cliff and what was now needed was not the brake, but the reverse gear. The arrogance of the militants in the unions was such that they were causing untold suffering on their fellow citizens. This was more than industrial blackmail and intimidation, it amounted to industrial terrorism.

The rank and file people of Britain did not seem to realise that the Marxists and Communists in their midst had no interest whether wages were £125 or even £220 per week. Their aim was to cause maximum havoc to the national economy by work stoppages and demanding unrealistic wages.

I said that what was so chilling about the success of Marxist brainwashing was the present bland acceptance by so many people that life in Eastern Europe was really not much different from life in Britain. The sort of complete mental blur and support for the Communist cause which led Mr. Clive Jenkins (when the TUC were welcoming Shelepin) to claim that, as a political institution, the KGB was no different from the House of Lords, or Jack Jones to claim (as he did at a recent TUC conference) that there was no comparison between the tyranny of South Africa and the regimes of Eastern Europe. Since then we have had Mr. Alex

Kitson, a member of Labour's National Executive Committee, saying how pleasant it was to be in the Soviet Union where there was no unemployment and a continual growth in living standards.

There was nothing very surprising, I said, in these people saying such things; they were no more than would be said by many of their fellow members of the Labour Party and by 80 or so people who described themselves as Labour Members of Parliament.

Britain was being subjected to a slow drip of subtle propaganda and the way in which the television services — both BBC and ITV — celebrated the beginnings and subsequent history of Soviet Communism on the 60th anniversary of the Bolshevik Revolution was an example of this softening up and brain washing process.

On many occasions, I had to answer the criticism that Britain had now become a nation of strikers, high and low, doctors, teachers, taxmen, miners, powermen, firemen, etc. Was I not alarmed, I was asked, at the frequency, magnitude and seriousness of strikes in a sophisticated, democratic society?

I confirmed that I was. I said the whole morale of the nation was in jeopardy when society had sunk to such a level that the strike weapon was now being used in the first instance instead of as a last resort. Industrial action was deliberately made to "bite" so as to hurt innocent people and thereby force the Government and/or employers to toe the line.

I agreed that the strike weapon had become so commonplace and so successful that it was now part of Britain's way of life. The militants were not interested in the size of a settlement, but only in a demonstration of their muscle power for political purposes.

I was asked about Mr. Jack Jones's "Year of the Beaver". This, I said, had produced the biggest crop of strikes for four years. The number of working days lost through strikes in the first eleven months of 1977 was nearly three times higher, at 8,976,000, than in the same period of 1976.

I was questioned on why we did not change the rules when it was so obvious that workers in essential services were able to dislocate the country simply by working to rule. Power workers, for instance, could inflict black-outs on the public and cause grave harm to the elderly, the young, the sick and the disabled. Did they not give a damn about the public, I was asked?

I said that in my opinion, these people were nothing less than industrial terrorists and the public were therefore entitled to give them a double dose of their own medicine by blacking them from shops.

I was asked if a Tory Prime Minister would be prepared to do what Briand did in 1910? When faced by a strike on the Chemin du Fer du Nord in 1910, he mobilised the strikers and sent them back to work as soldiers under military discipline. I said that if the public were told the brutal truth they would support the Prime Minister of the day. Since then we have had the firemen's strike and surely the lesson to be learned is that the fire services should be brought under the control of the Ministry of Defence, particularly in this age of terrorism, and industrial anarchy.

The question that was invariably put to me was — "In a serious national emergency, what steps could be taken to ensure that essential services would be maintained?" I replied that a statement of principle had in fact been laid down by a British Labour Cabinet as long ago as 1946. This statement had made it clear that:

"It is the elementary duty of the government of the day to ensure that the community is not deprived of the essentials of life. It follows that if the normal means of supplying those essentials break down, whether as a result of industrial disputes or as a result of an attempt by a political faction to coerce the community, the government must provide alternative machinery of its own".

I said that in my view, this meant that it was the duty of the Government of the day and the local authorities, as well as the community as a whole, to prepare, not only for the consequences of every sort of emergency, natural, technical, political, military, or whatever was likely to render the country's essential services to be overstretched or impotent in the time of need.

Unfortunately, I added, Britain's Civil Defence was disbanded by a Labour Government at the stroke of a pen. Thus, the members of Britain's community were now denied the very means whereby they could play their part in a voluntary self-help organisation designed to provide an essential back-up in any emergency situation.

I stressed that it was the public's right and duty to help others as well as themselves, and the best method of giving them the opportunity to help in emergency situations of all sorts would be to resurrect Civil Defence in an updated and extended version, perhaps in the form of a "National Service for the Community", supplemented by a skilled volunteer reserve. This would certainly serve to release the already overstretched armed forces.

Obviously, I said, there would be howls of rage from the left-wingers and the bully boys about strike breaking. These would simply have to be ignored because any strike is troublesome enough, but on no account must a strike be allowed to cripple the country economically; endanger life, limb and property, or hazard the sick, the old, the weak, the vulnerable or, for that matter, the community as a whole.

That ace journalist, Mr. Chapman Pincher, confirmed my worst fears in a brilliant article in the **Daily Express** of 7 November, entitled "Whose Finger is **Really** on the Blackout Button?". Mr. Chapman Pincher warns that from the heart of the Soviet Union there is now a new bid to provoke industrial chaos in Britain.

It was suggested to me that the behaviour of some of Britain's Socialist MPs should bring to mind the words of Dr. Johnson: "It has been observed that they who most loudly clamour for liberty do not most liberally grant it . . . . ".

I said that there were many in the Labour Party, and even further to the Left outside, who saw an independent judiciary as a major barrier to the creation of a centralised Socialist state.

Therefore anything that impeded centralised Socialist authority must be systematically attacked.

As more and more power came to be concentrated in the hands of government, an independent judiciary was the last line of defence of the citizen's freedom. Throughout history, I said, interference with courts of law had been a first step in a dictator's march to power.

I was questioned on the alarming increase in crime and the state of law and order in Britain. I said that I did not believe that law and order would be restored until the understrength, underpaid and overworked police forces — now stretched as tight as a violent string — were treated as a corps d'elite. Far too many experienced police officers were leaving the force on premature retirement because they were thoroughly disillusioned and dissatisfied with their lot.

The first responsibility of government, I said, was to maintain law and order. But what did we get instead? Politicians supporting lawbreakers. Criminal violence stalking Britain's cities. Marauding louts and hooligans rampaging in their eagerness to provoke the police and indulge in a trial of strength. A softy, softy, namby-pamby, pussy-footing approach to vicious elements who had never had it so good. This was the result of years of leniency and years of psychiatric rubbish. The grave issues involved had been relegated by politicians to the day-to-day cut and thrust of party politics. A referendum would soon show that the will of the people is that corporal punishment should be reintroduced, and the penalty for waging war against the state and the killing of policemen should be capital punishment.

I said the police should be given first call on the public purse and first call on the public's support. The steady decay of police power should be halted; particularly in the Courts where trials were degenerating into a battle of wits between lawyers, instead of a battle for the truth.

I was asked for my views on corporal and capital punishment. I replied that I was convinced that a referendum would show that the people of Britain were in favour of the reintroduction of corporal punishment for those convicted of crimes of violence and vandalism. The threat of physical pain had always been effective in preventing certain crimes.

Punishment should wherever possible, be swift, exemplary, painful and detract as little as possible from the self-respect of the punished.

I said that corporal punishment not only fits most crimes; it also meets the requirements of humanity and the instincts of natural justice far better than terrible and corrupting incarcerations.

As for capital punishment, I gave it as my opinion that here again a referendum would show that the country was in favour of the reintroduction of capital punishment for acts of terrorism, waging war against the state — as in the case of Northern Ireland — and the killing of policemen. I said we had abolished capital punishment and put no deterent in its place.

Far more consideration should be given to the victim than to the criminal. In Northern Ireland, I said, too much cant was talked about the so-called glamour of martyrdom and too little attention to the brutal murders of innocent civilians and the dreadful maiming and suffering of women and children. I reminded my listeners that in Northern Ireland we were not dealing with disciplined soldiers but with ruthless terrorist killers who should be treated as such. It was the will of the people that should prevail and not that of a conceited, over-optimistic Minister who so blatantly misinterpreted the capabilities of the IRA and by making imprudent and boastful forecasts merely provoked them into activity.

I was asked about immigration. At that particular time Mrs. Thatcher had not reopened the debate on this vexed issue. I said that 83 per cent of the coloured immigrant population gave their votes to Labour in the October 1974 election and gained them the vital votes which put them into government.

I mentioned that under the Callaghan Government the unemployment of young blacks had quadrupled. The House Improvement Campaign that was doing much to improve the old houses in which they lived had been cut by two thirds by Mr. Callaghan's ministers.

I said I had done some research on how the sinister weapon of subversion was being used to incite certain sections of the coloured population of Britain to racial violence and to stir up hatred for the police. A significant portion of coloured immigrants, particularly youths, had already been deeply penetrated and subverted. A campaign of hatred of the police was now constantly being whipped up by at least three publications I could name. They were widely read by the coloured community but were only otherwise available at left-wing bookshops.

I mentioned that of equal importance to immigration was emigration — the exodus of highly and expensively trained and skilled British people, whether they were doctors, scientists and so on. They were leaving because they were insufficiently rewarded and grossly overtaxed.

I was asked to give my opinion of the Lib/Lab Pact. I explained that the point of the pact was to put off the evil day of a General Election. Mr. David Steel and his friends realised that the only way to avoid electoral catastrophe was to sustain Labour's Prime Minister in office. Mr. Callaghan was only too relieved to have the Liberal Party as his poodle.

Why, I was asked, was Mr. Heath brooding in the wings? All I could say was that when Edward Heath attained the premiership in 1970, he received unfailingly generous support from his predecessor, the then Sir Alec Douglas-Home. Mrs. Thatcher had received neither warmth, good will, co-operation nor an appearance of allegiance from a man who, in my view, could best be described as a frustrated prima donna.

I was invariably asked what chance Mrs. Thatcher had of wining a General Election with a working majority. I said that if Gallop Polls were anything to go by, Mrs. Thatcher's lead had fluctuated. But a few weeks in politics was a long time, especially when the Labour Government was obliged to rely so much on the lobby fodder — the Lib/Lab Pact.

I mentioned that the Labour Party had suffered a number of important defections because of the extent of Marxist infiltration and trade union domination. The instances I gave were Rt. Hon. Reg. Prentice, Mr. Woodrow Wyatt, Mr. Paul Johnson, Lord Chalfont, Mr. Christopher Mayhew and Lord George-Brown. I said if anyone should know how bad the cancer was, these people should, and Mr. Woodrow Wyatt had gone as far as saying "If Labour stay in power, it will bring much closer the day when democracy will cease to exist in Britain".

I said that Mrs. Thatcher had recently scored a hat trick: her "love, set and match" on the BBC television programme **Panorama;** wiping the floor with the Treasury Bench in the economic debate in July, and her masterly performance on the television programme **Face the Press,** which resulted in the Press facing her. I added that she gave an equally polished performance in mid-September on the television programme **Weekend World,** when she explained that if the militants forced a confrontation on a Government led by her, she would, in certain circumstances, be obliged to resort to a referendum so that the voice of the people could be heard loud and clear and the will of the people prevail.

What did I think of Mrs. Thatcher's Shadow Cabinet, was another frequent question? I said it was a wobbly team of too many fainthearts who were conspicuously listless and lacklustre. There would have to be changes, with some big guns brought in — men with real fire in their bellies.

Notwithstanding, I emphasised that there could be do doubt that the salvation of Britain, a country which had sunk to an all time low, lay in the early return of a Conservative Government, with such a strong working majority that the will of the people — and not that of a comparatively small but immensely powerful clique of extreme left-wingers — would prevail.

This always steered the conversation towards the inevitable question — would Mrs. Thatcher really be able to compete with the situation in which Britain now found herself?

I had no hesitation in saying that Mrs. Thatcher was the one ray of hope and deserved well of her party and the country. I reminded my audience that she took a degree in chemistry but her real ambition was to be a lawyer. After Oxford she had been refused a grant, so she studied law in her own time and became a barrister. Her Tory Front Bench jobs had included education, transport, power, housing and treasury.

I described her as a tough-minded lady with a sure grasp of all the important issues. She was confident, cool, ambitious and brilliant and could certainly provide the Tories with a winning strategy for the forthcoming General Election. She stood for self-reliance, personal independence and freedom from state interference, which was what the country yearned for after so much creeping Socialism and state control.

Without doubt, I said, she would be Britain's next Prime Minister and it was high time her senior colleagues said so, loud and clear.

This always led to the next question, which was — what, then, can Britain expect from Mrs. Thatcher when she becomes Prime Minister?

In my reply I said I could only give my personal opinion but I would be surprised if her policies did not include the following. Restoring and upholding the rule of law and order; building up the police and the armed forces — both were understrength and dissatisfied because they were underpaid; giving the army a freer hand in Northern Ireland and taking a tougher line; getting bureaucracy off industry's back; pulling government out of constant intervention in the economy; rewarding enterprise, hard work and risk-taking; reducing taxation; pegging increases in pay to increases in production — without this there can be no prospect of economic recovery; cutting excessive controls, rules, regulations, orders in council and the massive red tape which is strangling the economy; encouraging private enterprise; having the courage to come to grips, firmly and decisively, with the immigration problem about which the British public is gravely concerned; loosening the grip on Parliament and Whitehall of overbearing and unrepresentative trade union leaders, whose proper job is to look after their members at their place of work, and not usurp the job of politicians; introducing compulsory postal ballots, and union elections to be held in "firm's time" so as to stop small groups of extremists controlling the unions; making all union bosses subject to periodic election — some union leaders are elected for life; and last but by no means least, stop dictating to South Africa from several thousands of miles away how she should solve her internal problems, and persuade NATO to get its priorities right, one of which is that South Africa is the last bulwark against the Soviet Union's intention to absorb the whole of Southern Africa and control the Cape Route — thus a global strategy must be evolved and the Simonstown Agreement reactivated.

The Communist Bear is not only at Africa's back door but also breathing down Britain's neck. Mrs. Thatcher made a trenchant statement in August 1977, when she said she regarded as "Left" all those "who use force to get their own way, who want to destroy our way of life". She added for good measure: "The only sense in which I regard it as Left or Right is that Communism is the left foot of Socialism and Fascism its right boot, using Socialism in the sense that it is total regimentation and control by the state".

In addition to Mrs. Thatcher being the one ray of hope on an otherwise bleak horizon, Britain is in the enviable position of being served by a sovereign of outstanding devotion to duty and professional skill who arouses respect and affection throughout the realm. During the Jubilee Celebrations of June 1977, there was a vast outpouring of emotion when the nation — misgoverned at home; despised abroad — gave thanks for 25 years of peerless service by a well-loved Queen.

But the motives ran far deeper.

Here was the one time when the famous silent majority, frustrated and buffeted and battered by the failure of the politicians, was able to speak with its true voice.

That voice whether it emanated from a regal state ceremony or from the humblest street party or the humblest suburb was unmistakable.

The British people, in their millions, still have faith and burning pride in their country. Another Britain emerged: self-disciplined, loyal, patriotic, generous, wholesome, dignified and proud. Thus, Britain has two Nations: the magnaminous one of Jubilee

Week is the true one. The other one is the creation of malevolent and unrepresentative minorities.

The true Britain yearns for unity and for the leadership that can restore Britain's place in the world.

Mrs. Margaret Thatcher can give this leadership, for she is a leader of world class who can put the name Great back in Great Britain once again and restore the realisation that neither material prosperity, nor welfare, nor social advancement can be ours unless the country once more pays its way in the world.

The whole of the Free World stands in greater danger than at any time since the dark days of the Second World War. From the West, clarion call comes there none, except from Mrs. Thatcher whose call to the nation "Britain awake" earned her the title of "Iron Lady" from Moscow.

The road to peace and the defence of freedom has never been through appeasement or negotiation from weakness. The entire recorded history of mankind is precisely to the contrary. Among the great nations **only the strong survive.**

EPILOGUE

THE second battle of Kolwezi has been won by the Soviet Union. Through their agents the Cubans and Angolans, they skilfully exploited a complex combination of tribal and national rivalries.

The object of the attack was to destabilise black Africa by causing the Whites to leave and to deny the West copper and other minerals. The situation was neatly summed up by two London newspapers. **The Times** observed:

"The expulsion of the Portuguese from Angola not only wrecked its major productive industries, but then delivered them and the administration into the hands of the Cubans, Russians, East Germans and other brotherly colonialists.

The Times concluded:

"The bill for Kolwezi — financial, economic and political — has not come in but it will be stiff. This should suit the enemies of the West admirably."

The **Daily Telegraph** commented that . . . "The Russians must think there is nothing they cannot get away with under detente and concluded:

"If Russia is allowed brazenly to continue to upset the global balance by direct or indirect conquest, then Europe's fate is sealed."

If Black African nations are to preserve their independence and sovereignity against Russo-Cuban intrusion, they must create the mechanism and means to set up an organisation of collective security. This should take the form of a Pan-African peace-keeping mobile force. The role of the West should be limited to economic aid and logistical support.

Recently a delegation of the United States House Armed Services Committee spent ten days in the Soviet Union. The Soviet First Deputy Minister of Defence, Mr. Ogarkov, told Congressman John D. Breckinridge: "The United States has always been in a position where it could not be threatened by foreign powers. That is no longer true. Today the Soviet Union has military superiority over the United States and henceforth the United States will be threatened. You had better get used to it."

In a nutshell the situation can be summed up as: External encirclement, plus internal demoralisation, plus thermonuclear blackmail, equals progressive surrender. The United States general — Major General John K. Singlaub — who was recalled from Korea in 1977 for calling into question the planned troop withdrawal from South Korea, resigned from the Army in May rather than "be part of a cover-up of the truth." He regards the neutron bomb as "another arrow in the quiver of NATO, and we seem to be short of arrows." He has criticized President Carter for "making decisions relating to the national security without consultation with his military advisers," and regards the President's national security staff as inexperienced, leaderless and without direction. "Many of America's allies" he says, "have expressed some concern that we do not live up to our obligations as a leader of the Free World." We shall hear more of Major General Singlaub, for he is planning a campaign to carry his warnings to the American public.

Finally, I wish to end with my own warning about one particular aspect of the situation in Rhodesia.

What will the inevitable reaction be if there are more unspeakable atrocities committed in Rhodesia on the scale of the June indiscriminate massacre of innocent, unarmed Umtali white missionaries and their families, including three little girls and a three week old baby, Pamela Lynn, who were hacked, clubbed and bayonneted to death with hideous mutilation by brutalised savages, and the women were raped as well?

The answer is that a repetition of such carnage might not only spark off a savage backlash from exasperated Whites in Rhodesia, but there could also be backlash by people in Britain who are no longer prepared to see their kith and kin slaughtered with such ultimate bestiality.

Another shock of such barbaric slaughter coinciding with the run-up to an October election would not be tolerated by the British electorate and could well result in the Rhodesian situation becoming a vital election issue.

As I have described elsewhere, the black criminal henchmen of the Soviet-supported phony Patriotic Front have been massacring and committing appalling atrocities against black civilians for a long time now. But the killing and mutilating of Black by Black does not produce the same shock and outrage as does the slaughter of Whites by Black African terrorists, any more than does the grisly carnage of White by White in Northern Ireland.

There can be few in Britain today who would not agree with the sentiments expressed by the Editor of the London **Sunday Express,** who wrote on 2 July:

"It is moving and fitting that in the same coffin in a graveyard in Umtali, three week old Pamela Lynn will lie for evermore in the arms of her mother — in those same arms which, when their murdered, outraged bodies were found, were outstretched as if in a last desperate bid to protect her.

"Would it be too much to ask that Dr. David Owen thinks of that coffin and of that baby the next time he shakes hands with the savages who murdered her?

"May God help Rhodesia. And forgive us for what is being done in our name."

APPENDIX 1

Biographies of Leading Nationalists in Rhodesia

JOSHUA NKOMO (ZAPU)

Born—June 1917, Semukwe Reserve, Matabeleland.
1941—Enrolled at Adams College, South Africa.
1944—Enrolled Jan Hofmeyr School of Social Science in Johannesburg where he completed his matriculation and obtained his diploma.
1947—Returned to Rhodesia and employed by Rhodesia Railways as a Social Worker; the first African to be given such a post. Graduated Bachelor of Arts in Economics and Sociology by correspondence.
1951—Appointed Secretary of the Railway Workers Association.
1952—Elected President of the African National Congress, also in 1952 attended a London Conference on the proposed Federation of Rhodesia and Nyasaland.
1958—In December he travelled to the All African Peoples Conference in Accra. Whilst there, his Party was banned. He remained in London for the next 18 months.
1960—Formed the National Democratic Party and was elected President. NDP was banned and ZAPU was formed in December 1961 with Nkomo as the President.
1962—In September ZAPU too was banned. A split between him-
1963—self and Ndabaningi Sithole occured in August, and during the next six months there was violence and strife between the supporters of these two groups.
1964—On 16 April 1964, Joshua Nkomo was arrested and restricted for the next 10½ years.
1965—During this restriction, he attended a conference with Mr. Harold Wilson on 29 October 1965, and in November 1968 he met Mr. George Thompson in Salisbury.
1972—On 10 November, he was interviewed by members of the Pearce Commission.
1974—In November, he was flown to Salisbury prior to moving to Lusaka for the Conference of Nationalists to form a unified voice for discussions with Government, and was at this time finally released from restriction.
1975—He attended the Victoria Falls Conference on 25 and 26 August. Towards the end of October 1975, he started a series of meetings with Mr. Ian Smith, designed to prepare the ground for a full Constitutional Conference. He signed a Declaration of Intent on 1 December, to hold a constitu-

tional Conference with the minimum delay. These talks
1976—eventually collapsed on 19 March.

Following Mr. Ian Smith's acceptance of the principle of majority rule on 24 September, Mr. Johua Nkomo returned from extensive travelling around the world to prepare the ground for the conference that lay ahead. On 9 October, he, together with Mr. Robert Mugabe, announced the formation of the Patriotic Front and said that they totally rejected the Kissinger proposals.

He attended the Geneva Conference in October/November 1976.

Following this conference Mr. Nkomo remained outside Rhodesia.

Personal Details

Joshua Nkomo married in 1959. His wife is the grand-daughter of Magwegwe, the Chief Counsellor of Lobengula.

He has four children, his only son has been in Budapest since 1973.

ROBERT GABRIEL MUGABE (Leader of ZANLA)

Born at Kutama Mission in the Zwimba TTL in 1928.

He was brought up in the Roman Catholic faith.

Qualified as a Primary School teacher and taught in the 1940's in various schools throughout Rhodesia.

Commenced studies for a degree, with the University of South Africa, and in 1949 won a scholarship to Fort Hare, South Africa, where he graduated BA in 1951.

1954—Obtained his B.Ed by correspondence.

1955—He moved to Zambia and taught for three years, obtaining a B.Sc. from the University of London by correspondence.

1958—Accepted a teaching post in Ghana.

1960—Asked by Nationalists to return and in November was elected Publicity Secretary to the NDP. He organised the Militant Youth Wing of the new Party.
After the banning of NDP, Mr. Mugabe was elected to the same post in its successor Party, ZAPU.

1963—He was suspended by Mr. Nkomo in August and moved with Mr. Ndabaningi Sithole to form ZANU where he became the Secretary-General.

1964—In 1964 he was arrested and remained in detention until November, 1974. Whilst in detention he successfully obtained three more degrees, including an LL.B.(London) and a B.Admin (London).
Deposed Mr. Sithole whilst in detention as the President of ZANU.

1974—On release in November, he received a frosty reception from both President Kaunda and President Nyerere, and was forced to abandon his pretensions and accept the leadership of Mr. Sithole.

1975—He slipped out of Rhodesia in March and started to assert himself as the only political leader in whom the terrorists still had trust.

1976—On 9 October he joined with Nkomo in the formation of the Patriotic Front.
He attended the Geneva Conference.
A committed Marxist whose stated aim is the creation of a Marxist state in Zimbabwe.

Personal Details

Married to a Ghanian who is reputed to be a vigorous activist. They had one son who died in 1966.

NDABANINGI SITHOLE (President of ZANU)

Born — 21 July 1920 at Nyamandhlovu, North of Bulawayo. His father was an Ndau and his mother an Ndebele from Nyamandhlovu.

1933/34—He worked as a kitchen boy but continued his education by attending a night school.

1935—He attended Dadaya Mission where he studied under Garfield Todd.

1939—Obtained a bursary and trained at Waddilove Training Institute for two years and qualified as a Primary School teacher. He later taught at Dadaya where he obtained his Matriculation Certificate.

1948—Moved to Tegwani Mission where he did intensive Bible study and became accredited preacher for the British Methodist Church.

1950—He joined the United Methodist Church.

1953—Appointed to the teaching staff at Mt. Selinda, an American Methodist Mission, and while teaching there, obtained a B.A. degree by correspondence.

1955—The church leaders sent him to Newton Theological College, Boston, Massachusetts. Here he studied theology and wrote **African Nationalism.**

1958—Returned to Southern Rhodesia and was ordained at Mt. Selinda and appointed Principal of Chikore Primary School.

1959—Entered politics and became President of the African Teachers Association.

1960—In January the NDP was formed and Rev. Sithole soon moved into prominence. He was elected Treasurer and in December was part of the NDP delegation at the Federal Review Conference in London. He and Mr. Joshua Nkomo walked out of this conference.

1962—ZAPU was banned and Sithole remained outside Rhodesia from where he broadcast propaganda from Dar es Salaam to Rhodesians.

1963—In April the differences between the leaders came to a head and the rift between Mr. Nkomo and his Shona supporters became unbridgeable.
On 28 July Rev. Sithole returned to Salisbury and created ZANU, with himself as President and Mr. Mugabe as his Secretary-General.

1964—He was arrested, together with many other Nationalist leaders.

1968—He was tried and convicted on a charge of plotting to assassinate Ian Smith and other Cabinet Ministers and sentenced to six years in prison. During his detention, he wrote two other books.

1974—Released from detention following his depostiion as leader of ZANU and the appointment of Mugabe in his place. In December was a signatory to the Lusaka Declaration.

1975—On 4 March, he was arrested and brought before a special tribunal on a charge of plotting to assassinate African political rivals. After South African pressure, he was released and flown to Dar es Salaam to attend a meeting of the OAU Foreign Ministers. He became progressively more militant.

In August he attended the Victoria Falls Conference.

Denounced Mr. Nkomo as a sell-out because of his negotiations with Smith.

Published **In Defence of a Birthright** in which he stated that there was no alternative to bloodshed and claimed that the armed struggle had brought about the release of detainees and that no reconciliation was possible between the guerillas and Smith.

1976—In October, he was not invited to the Geneva Conference but eventually attended.

Pensonal Details

Married at Dadaya Mission in 1946.

6 children, 2 boys and 4 girls. All are studying overseas.

He has revealed a strong penchant for violence, his capabilities for intrigue and political manoeuvre make even his political colleagues nervous.

He is acknowledged as an intellectual. He confesses that politics and the pursuit of power are inseparable.

BISHOP ABEL TENDEKAYI MUZOREWA (UANC)

Born: 14 April 1925 at a United Methodist Church Settlement in the Eastern Districts of Rhodesia.

Attended Missionary primary school and then went to Nyadiri Mission. Taught as an evangelist before studying theology in Umtali where in August 1953 was ordained as a Minister of the Church. Became Pastor of the Chiduku Circuit until 1957.

1958—Muzorewa was awarded a scholarship to study for a theological degree and spent 5 years at the Central Methodist College, Fayette, Missouri where he obtained a BA and at Nashville University, Tennessee, where he gained his Master's degree in 1963.

1964—He returned to Rhodesia and was appointed National Director of the church's Christian Youth Movement.

1968—Was consecrated a Bishop of the United Methodist Church, the first black member of his church to receive such a distinction.

1970—The Central Methodist College in Missouri awarded him an honorary Doctorate in Divinity.

1971—In September he came to general public notice when Internal Affairs banned him from entering the Tribal Trust Lands. Two months later, he found himself pitchforked into active politics. He was approached by a delegation of ZAPU and ZANU factions and asked to lead a united effort to oppose the Smith/Home constitutional proposals, and the African National Council was formed with Muzorewa as the leader.

1972—In May, the ANC was completely successful in opposing the Pearce Commission.

1973—In July, Mr. Ian Smith invited the Bishop to talks on the constitutional issue. After a promising start, the talks dwindled. In October, Muzorewa was awarded a United Nations prize for "outstanding achievements in the field of human rights".

1974—In December, at the ANC's first congress in Lusaka, the Bishop was appointed the leader of the ZAPU/FROLIZI/ZANU/ANC organisations. His pleasure at this election was short-lived. Vicious faction fighting broke out in Zambia, leading in March 1975 to the murder of Mr. Herbert Chitepo, and the imprisonment of many other Nationalists in Lusaka. At this time, Rev. Ndabaningi Sithole was arrested for plotting to assassinate the other leaders.

1975—In April Muzorewa addressed a Commonwealth conference in Jamaica. In August, he attended the Victoria Falls Con-

ference. A few days after the conference, the ANC unity died. Following the reorganisation of the split factions the 'Muzorewa ANC' and 'Nkomo ANC' were formed.
In October Muzorewa moved his headquarters to Dar es Salaam, but was denounced by the terrorists in Tanzania and Mozambique.

1976—On 3 October saw the triumphant return of Muzorewa to Salisbury. He attended the Geneva Conference from 8 October.

Personal Details

Married with five children, all of whom are studying outside Rhodesia.

JOSIAH MAGAMA TONGOGARA (Military leader of ZANLA)

Born in Selukwe in 1938. Obtained his Primary education at an Anglican Mission School.

Went to Zambia in 1960 and studied Bookkeeping. Was employed at an African Golf Club as the Secretary.

1961—He became a militant nationalist and travelled extensively throughout the Middle East, the Far East and Eastern Europe, studying politics and training himself as a military leader. He underwent training in China with President Samora Machel with whom he is understood to have a close relationship. A **Daily Telegraph** report of 12 April 1976 stated that he fought alongside Machel in the Tete Province of Mozambique.

1972—He became the Military Commander of ZANLA. He headed the 18-man military high command.

1973—He escorted the abducted Gerald Hawksworth from the Rhodesian border to Tanzania.

1974—In December, in Lusaka he stood out firmly against detente, maintaining that the military struggle must be continued.

1975—In March, following the death of Mr. Herbert Chitepo, Tongogara was detained by the Zambian Government and brought to trial in Lusaka.

1976—On 21 April he was imprisoned for the murder of Chitepo. Was eventually released in time to join the Geneva Conference.

Personal Details

Greatly admired Patrice Lumumba and Mao-Tse-Tung and is a committed Marxist. Married with three children. The reference I am referring to states "for relaxation, he likes to watch soccer and Kung Fu films".

REX NHONGO (ZANLA)

Aged about 30.

He was originally a ZAPU supporter but joined ZANU in 1971. During the detention of Tongogara he acted as Commander-in-Chief of ZANLA.

Attended the Geneva Conference and is currently No. 2 to Tongogara.

He has entered Rhodesia on many occasions as he was originally a comparatively low-grade Section Commander in 1973.

His most recent entrance into Rhodesia was an abortive attack on a Police Post in the Eastern Districts in April 1978.

Senator Chief JEREMIAH CHIRAU (ZUPO)

Chief Chirau was born in the Zwimba Tribal Trust Lands, Sinoia, on 6 June 1923. He attended school during the years 1935 to 1939, attaining a Standard IV Certificate.

Between 1942 and 1946, he served with the Rhodesian Air Force Air Askari Corps (RAAC) and took his discharge with the rank of Corporal, returning to his kraal thereafter. During 1948 he joined the Rhodesia Prison Service and served with this Department at various centres until he took his discharge in 1958 when he joined the Lusaka Fire Brigade (Zambia) as a Station Officer. He holds the 1939-1945 War Medal.

1960—He returned to Rhodesia and became the Chief Cashier at the Sinoia beerhall.

1961—As a result of his father's death, was appointed acting chief. He became a substantive Chief during 1971.

1964—He took part in a 'Chief's tour' during which he visited Pakistan, England, Italy, South Africa and Mozambique. He was elected to the Council of Chiefs during 1966 and became President of this body in 1973.

1970—On 28 April Chirau was elected to the Senate and in that year was awarded the Independence Commemorative Decoration.

1976—On 28 April he was sworn in as a Minister Chief in the Rhodesian Cabinet, later to take up the portfolio of Minister of Development in Mashonaland West and Central.

He later resigned from the Government to form the Zimbabwe United People's Organisation (ZUPO). He is a member of the Executive Council of the Transitional Government.

APPENDIX 2

A Brief Operational History of Rhodesia, 1972-1977

ON 21 December 1972, the current war really started. Anything prior to that date can be considered as falling into the prepartory phase of guerilla warfare and no incursions to this date posed any major problem to Rhodesia. However, on 21 December 1972, an attack took place on a farm homestead in the Centenary District in which an 8 year old white girl was injured. This attack was meant to be part of a simultaneous co-ordinated attack on five homesteads but one group got its instructions wrong and attacked 24 hours prematurely. This allowed the Rhodesian Security Forces to get into the area and counter these intended attacks. However it was the start of a new situation. Instead of having the tribesmen willingly coming forward to report the presence of terrorists, the terrorists had prepared the ground carefully before an overt act of terrorism took place. Generally speaking, the tribesmen gave passive support to the terrorists by not reporting their presence and by being unco-operative with government agencies. Within a matter of weeks, the war proper had started as more farm attacks took place and more and more terrorists entered Rhodesia in the north-eastern area.

Operation **Hurricane** started and slowly, mainly because of complacency, Rhodesia's war machine began to work.

In July 1973, Rhodesia had the first major abduction of school children by terrorists. St. Alberts Mission on the escarpment was attacked by a gang of terrorists who abducted 295 pupils and staff and force-marched them down the escarpment into the Zambesi Valley and north towards Mozambique. Luckily, the Security Forces intercepted them and recovered all but eight of the abductees but it was the forerunner of things to come, as since this incident there have been many others, with hundreds of school children being taken across the borders for terrorist training. Because of the involvement of the tribesmen, it was rapidly apparant that the Security Forces could do little without an adequate means of controlling the population. Accordingly, the protected village (PV) programme was instituted to divorce the tribesmen away from the terrorists; protect him and deny the terrorist a source of food, intelligence and recruits.

In mid 1974, the first protected village programme was instituted in a Tribal Trust Land (TTL) when 50,000 people were moved in a three-week operation into 21 PVs. Immediately after another TTL was tackled in the same way. This effectively drove away the terrorists, who were well exconsed in those TTLs, and the Security Forces started to get the upper hand.

By being able to concentrate the entire country's resources in a relatively small area of Rhodesia, the Security Forces were able to have large force levels deployed, an improvement in the communication network and the construction of excellent airfields. With the assistance of the South African Police who were mainly engaged in border control along the Zambesi, although a number were involved in hot operations, the kill rate increased considerably. In October and November of 1974, the Security Forces killed more terrorists than they had killed in the total period from 1972 to October 1974. By 11 December 1974 there were only 70 terrorists left within Rhodesia. These 70 were, of course, hard core terrorists.

On 11 December 1974, Rhodesia accepted the South African initiated detente exercise or ceasefire. Militarily, this may have been a mistake. With only 70 terrorists left it would have been a matter of weeks, possibly months, before they were totally elminated. However, the ceasefire was accepted which meant that the South African Police (SAP) were confined to their camps and were not to do anything other than patrol the immediate vicinity of those camps for their own protection. The Rhodesia security forces were restricted to non-offensive patrolling. What this meant was that the 70 hard core terrorists were able to move out of Rhodesia with impunity, visiting all kraals en route out, stating that they had won the war and had brought Ian Smith to the negotiating table. 11 December 1974 also saw the release of all the nationalist leaders from detention to engage in talks with the government. Psychologically, therefore, Rhodesia lost a tremendous amount of face with the tribal people who were influenced by the terrorists and, of course, with the majority of the law abiding black population of Rhodesia who saw the rabid nationalists being released from detention. Rhodesia now knows not to enter into these sort of negotiations with terrorists unless they have guarantees that they will abide by the rules. For example, on 16 December 1974, five days after the ceasefire had been accepted, a group of terrorists, (under the leadership of one Mr. Herbert Shungu now a "top" terrorist training commander) sent an emissary to a South African camp with an invitation to them to come and talk surrender terms. The SAP, somewhat naively, accepted the invitation and were ambushed on the Mazoe high level bridge where six of them were killed. So much for the ceasefire.

It was in April 1974 that the coup in Portugal took place. It had no immediate effect on Rhodesia because Samora Machel took a considerable time to move south to Maputo. During this period Rhodesia had good relations with the local Frelimo commanders who pledged their support to eliminate ZANU from Mozambique. However, once Machel was safely installed, the attitude rapidly changed. Late 1974 and 1975 saw a faster turn round of terrorist recruits than had previously been possible. They started to be trained in Mozambique and were assisted in their movement by Frelimo placing vehicles, railways and ships at their disposal.

The terrorist sectorial commanders became disillusioned with the conduct of the war following spectacular security force successes in 1974. No re-supply or reinforcements were able to enter Rhodesia. In addition they had learned of political moves taking place in Lusaka. They, therefore, left Rhodesia and went to Lusaka. In Lusaka, they arrested a number of commanders for the mess they were making of the war. At least 14 hardcore veteran leaders were executed. This set CT efforts back considerably until 1976. Rhodesia was able to gain the upper hand in 1975 because of the inexperience of the field commanders.

The South African Police were totally withdrawn in February 1975.

The ceasefire was well and truly over when a group of 60 ZANU terrorists infiltrated Rhodesia in mid-January. For the rest of 1975, the Rhodesian security forces had to regain the pyschological, and therefore the military ground that they had lost during the ceasefire period and it was an uphill struggle. However, with the continuing pattern of protected villages and by again concentrating all their resources in one small area, they were able to estimate that by December 1975 there were only three groups of 10 terrorists each operating in Rhodesia. However, they were not complacent because they knew that there were still large numbers of trained and semi-trained ZANU terrorists outside Rhodesia.

On 21 January 1976, a crossing of 90 terrorists took place south of Nyamapanda. Rhodesian security forces contacted that group the morning after they crossed. Four were killed and one was captured. The story this CT gave was that they were part of a simultaneous three-pronged assault on Rhodesia. However, their plan did not work in that the second assault in the Melsetter area by 130 terrorists took place some five weeks later and the third assault in the south-eastern area took place seven weeks later i.e. three months after the first assault. This meant the Rhodesian security forces were able to deploy troops accordingly. In February 1976 Operation Thrasher started and in May 1976 Operation Repulse began.

During this period, ZPA was created, a so-called amalgamation of ZANLA and ZPRA under the leadership of an 18-man Central

Committee. The Soviets now took over a major control of the war in view of the influence they exerted over Mozambique. ZPA never really worked because ZPRA were numerically inferior to ZANLA and, of course, had not been involved in the war for a number of years. Therefore, the ZANLA terrorists usurped positions of authority and command to the detriment of ZPRA. The effect it had was that in the training camps in Tanzania inter-faction fighting took place. In one of these clashes 400 terrorists were killed and in another 200 were killed. It had a side effect such that when these combined groups normally consisting of eight ZANLA and two ZPRA terrorists, entered Rhodesia, the ZPRA element would desert and head back for their home areas. Of course the same thing is happening today with the myth of the Patriotic Front.

In mid 1976, therefore, there was a gradual drift of these ZPRA elements through Rhodesia towards Francistown. The more dedicated of them collected recruits as they went through the country and committed various acts of terrorism. At this time, ZAPU had been told in no uncertain fashion by the OAU Liberation Committee that unless they took a more active role in the war they were to be cut off from all sources of funds. As a result ZAPU, led by Soviet trained intelligence agents, started to infiltrate across the Zambesi. This lead to Operation Tangent being opened in August 1976. The abortive Geneva Conference took place in late 1976 where the Patriotic Front became the "force to be negotiated with" in the eyes of the British and American Governments.

In 1977, the pattern of increasing infiltration from Mozambique continued. Rhodesia instituted a number of defensive measures, one of which was to increase the commitment to the protected village programme which has now spread throughout all operational areas. They also increased recruiting for their own security forces. During 1977 there was increased ZPRA involvement, with a number of incursions across the Zambesi.

APPENDIX 3

Steve Biko Speaks his Mind

BEFORE he was detained, Mr. Steve Biko was on record as stating that the "Westminster type of Parliamentary rule was a completely artificial thing." He said his aim was "a one party state" with "no place for opposition politics" and "no guarantees for minority groups." He believed that "opposition parties would die as in Zambia and elsewhere," and that he would be able to reach his "ideal in an evolutionary process without having to legislate."

He wanted South Africa to be "self-sufficient" and "independent" and was "against foreign investment" because a country like "America would wish to safeguard its investments" and in doing so would thus become "interested in the stability of government," "Now for an activist like me" said Biko, "I am in-interested in the instability of government so the two just don't go together."

"Blacks", he stated, were to be the "vanguard of the whole liberation process" and there would be no place for whites in the "front line", though there could be "useful coalitions with White individuals and/or groups. My particular point against participation by Whites", said Biko, "has been the extent to which it dulls the natural growth of Black leadership, because of the superiority/inferiority complex that exists throughout society. It is almost natural for Whites to want to participate in leadership roles and almost natural for some Blacks to want to accept inputs from the articulate leftist Whites who get involved in these movements. And it has got no relevance to solutions which must relate to the actual problems that the Black man faces in everyday cases and I think can only spring from the minds of those who have got the necessary experience."

Mr. Biko went on — "So I tend to conclude then that Whites are not important as a factor in the change process at the front line level. They certainly are important in a faciliatory role and the only role they can fulfill is coalition at that level; to facilitate the change process which is spearheaded by the Black led movement which is essentially a Black movement.

"Now, I feel this is beginning to be accepted by the most leftist Whites," said Mr. Biko. But "certainly not the liberal Whites. I think of Donald Woods, for instance, who is always in the war with me about this one — that he can't be a member of Black Peoples Convention and so on. But I think he is now sufficiently aware of the favoured. No one means to hit at him necessarily because he is White. We don't really hate him, except that we're saying to him: 'You might just put a spanner in the works at a crucial moment because your cousin lives in that house we're planning to bomb?"

When Mr. Biko was asked how much support he thought he had and what percentage of the population knew what he was trying to do and if they did know, with what did they sympathise, he gave this reply:

"Its not as difficult as all that actually. One could make it purely on the basis of age. We invested and still do invest heavily in youth. We made up our minds long ago and certainly I made up my mind when I began to be involved."

Mr. Biko went on to explain that the support "is attributable to the Black Consciousness movements which teach them to be and live for what they are, rather than to play the kind of role expected of them by a White society." He went on: "I'm saying that the Soweto disturbances certainly started off spontaneously They were a manifestation of the mood which the White man couldn't read clearly, because they were not talking to the youth but to the oldies. When the Whites want to negotiate they call the teachers and the Urban Bantu Council, both of whom are irrelevant . . . They are themselves defeated elements in society; defeated by a new force in society — the forces of youth which are much stronger in their commitment to the cause. The parents are aware of this, so that in a sense the parents are as afraid of their kids as of the government, except that morally they feel they should be on the side of the kids. So", said Biko, "in answer to the question, if I had to put it in the terms of numbers the influence is tremendous — there is no doubt about it."

Mr. Biko elaborated on this: "I mean the township where I stay, I've never for a moment preached. And when I came out here there was sufficient in that township to create a very strong feeling. I'm a bad man, but I move in that township up and down. I can get into any house, at a party, but I'm absolutely sure in my mind, not one person's going to sell-out. Even those who'd want to sell-out are afraid of the reaction of the others to their selling out, and I've never preached to anybody. You know, I just live there."

Mr. Biko continued: "Since then the population in universities has grown heavily and of course ipso facto the government also has turned down central affiliation to SASO (South African Stupdents Organisation) by students so that a head count would be difficult now. I mean there is no doubt that SASO controls the minds of all students. Black students at universities — well in scientific terms I would say the main part. You are likely to get virtually about 90% students on campuses being supporters if they're not necessarily members.

"The South African Students Movement works hand in hand and SASO has I think, contributed a hell of a lot to the growth of that organisation. It came about because SASO does not admit high school kids, it takes university students only. So they said, well, we want to align ourselves in this kind of thing and form our own thing, which we call South African Students Movement."

Mr. Biko then talked about the spectrum from a peaceful situation to violence and said: "You know it just depends on the forces at play at the given moment. I can say to you by the way that we don't have any armed struggle wing at this given stage in Black Consciousness Movements. We have a lot of exiles, possibly up to about between two hundred and fifty (250) and three hundred (300) who are really on a limb because they don't quite know what to do. They can't operate by instructions; certainly not in our name. But our view at the moment is, you know, we don't want to get into that area. We'll leave it to PAC (Pan African Congress) and ANC (African National Congress) for the time being. We operate purely on an assumption that we can bring the White man to his knees through confronting him with an overwhelming Black demand. (Of course you can say that's a very infantile view). But it's sufficient to recover our activities right now. We haven't contemplated violence. In the first instance because we operate above board and therefore can't debate it. Its illegal to even debate the moralities so freely, so that we are confined in fact to operating peacefully precisely because we exist above board in this country. But that doesn't necessarily mean that other options are not open and even before you get to violence, there are other ways of operation, which in themselves are still illegal anyway without being violent. You know, mass strikes, and that sort of thing.

An interviewer asked Mr. Biko "I was surprised that that hadn't been done yet in South Africa. It seems such an obvious form of resistance. But I suppose that you do have to move slowly and carefully. That might sort of destroy every bit of progress that you had already made?"

Mr. Biko replied: "It is a question of when to strike. I won't put it strictly into some kind of timetable. But I can point out a sequence of events which I think has been crucial to development:

"1. Rhodesia must go, Zimbabwe goes and Namibia goes. This widens the border, it frees Botswana and it stamps itself in the minds of Whites out here as being so much more nearer the heart which is Cape Town and Pretoria.

"2. You have got that much more moral boosting effect of the Blacks.
"3. You are going to be in a situation where there will be sporadic outbursts of resistance by Blacks, like Soweto. In time they will change from being sporadic to being organised.
"4. You get the crucial period now where Whites must decide whether it is going to be negotiation or force. Some people think that Whites are going to decide to negotiate and therefore prolong the whole change process. I think there will be a sufficiently strong conservative wing who will want to opt for force. And what happens thereafter will be decided by whichever of those two alternatives the Whites take."

Mr. Biko then proceeded to elaborate:

"I think you know, what I call sporadic outbursts by the Black community are going to increase in significance and the White community which so far have been feeling very well protected is going to increasingly realise just how thin their security is, as more and more of these things happen with greater significance and sometimes closer home. Possibly I think much closer home. Blacks will be moving into White suburbs and White towns to destroy anything that is to make a real impact. I think this is going to happen you know; they are going to move out of the townships into White suburbs to destroy out there. I think at that stage you will get a gross panic. I mean the amount of panic even now amongst the propertied people — white people. You must be aware of this shipping out of money, you know to countries outside and far away. But I think that's going to grow and is going to become more generalised with time."

The following is the pamphlet that Mr. Biko had in his possession when he was arrested:—

AUGUST 18th — COMMEMORATION DAY

All Black peoples must show unity in their rejection of this racist regime. Only when we stand united against the enemy can we hope to achieve victory. Students must show solidarity with their fellow students, the workers must show solidarity with the students and Black parents with their children. It is high time that everybody should take a stand especially our parents, they must not be neutralists, they must either identify themselves with the struggle or with the enemy. OUR Black parents have seen their children being brutally murdered and others maimed for life — all this happened in front of their own eyes!

The oppressed masses of Mozambique and Angola have shown us the way of over-throwing an oppressive regime despite its overwhelming supply of arms.

Here at home we have seen freedom flicker and then beaten down but NOT EXTINGUISHED — by masses of hippo trucks and troops. We have seen young students who have seen nothing but life under oppressive rule die for a freedom about which they had heard from others or from their own hearts. We have seen unarmed children, old people, our brothers and sisters being blown to pieces by the racist regime's sophisticated weapons. NO, SOUTH AFRICA WILL NEVER FORGET THOSE DAYS.

This is an appeal to all Black people to show solidarity with the exiled and the jailed, to show sympathy with those who lost their brothers, sisters, children and parents, during this period last year, by mourning. All workers, shopkeepers, students, teachers, clerks, nurses — the entire Black community — must show solidarity with the cause by STAYING AT HOME on the **18th of AUGUST.** On this day everybody **must** wear BLACK CLOTHES OR MUST HAVE AT LEAST A BLACK CLOTH, DOEK or HANDKERCHIEF. On the 19th Aug. at 14h00 (2.00 p.m.) a commemoration service will be held at the field near the GREAT CENTENARY HALL.

Wherever you are, organise yourselves into groups to deal with those who do not heed this appeal. BEAT THEM, burn their books, burn their cars and shops. Show no mercy to informers and other collaborators — they must be KILLED!

THERE MUST BE CRIES, BURNING HOUSES, PEOPLE WITH CLENCHED FISTS, BODIES LYING ON STREETS, BRUISED AND BLEEDING PEOPLE — THEN THERE WILL BE **FREEDOM — YES FREEDOM** THE BLACK PEOPLE ARE GOING TO GET THEIR FREEDOM, THERE IS NOT ENOUGH POWER ON EARTH TO STOP THEM!

LONG LIVE THE REVOLUTION!
POWER TO THE PEOPLE!

APPENDIX 4

Is the Foreign Office Orchestrating the Media?

I WAS shown a report which said: "There are many indications that a calculated campaign has been mounted by Dr. Owen (or members of the Foreign and Commonwealth Office acting on his behalf) to rig news reports from Rhodesia to reflect support for the Foreign Secretary's contention that the Internal Settlement will not work".

"The first of these indications was the BBC Panorama programme of 17 April, wherein an interview in Salisbury with Dr. Owen was beamed direct to London by satellite. This interview made the Foreign Secretary's reservations regarding the Internal Settlement quite clear, and the contents of the feature by the BBC TV team of Mr. Lindley and Mr. Deneslow on a ten day attachment to a Fire Force in Rhodesia was palpably designed to reinforce Dr. Owen's contentions."

The report went on to say: "The doubtful ethics employed by these two BBC reporters are well known in Rhodesia, so much so that when they first made application to do a feature for Panorama they were refused clearance. Both Mr. Lindley and Mr. Deneslow have a history dating back to the mid 1960s of anti-Rhodesia bias in their reporting and of subterfuge in obtaining their information. However, they found an unexpected ally in the Rhodesian Ministry of Information who made a special plea on their behalf for them to be cleared for the programme. Accordingly, a limited clearance was granted."

The report then listed four pages of "glaring misrepresentations and blatant statements of unsubstantiated opinions in the TV feature as well as the articles in the Press." For example, the Fire Force to which Mr. Lindley and Mr. Deneslow were attached was described as '52% mercenary', the inference being that Rhodesia is relying heavily on mercenaries. The facts are that 78% of the Rhodesian Army is black, so it is a little difficult to see how 52% of the Force can be 'mercenaries'. "Or," said the report, "did he do a head count in one isolated sub-unit and try to apply that to the whole force?"

The description of the Selous Scouts can only have been based on hearsay, otherwise they could not have been described as 'black

Rhodesian Soldiers', as they happen to be an integrated Black/White force.

The article in **The Guardian** of 17 April by Mr. Deneslow entitled 'The double-cross pattern of the Rhodesian war' immediately indicates bias, suggesting a lack of integrity on the part of Rhodesia. The article states that "the Commandos and pilots at Shabani were mostly foreign. They were professional soldiers (mercenaries many would call them) from Britain, America and South Africa, their main motive being simply that they enjoyed fighting."

The White population of Rhodesia comprises, in round figures, approximately one third Britons, one third South Africans and one third born Rhodesians. The term "foreign" can, therefore hardly be applied to Britons and South Africans and the use of the term in this context is intended solely to emphasise the suggestion that the war in Rhodesia is being fought by "mercenaries".

The article in **The Listener** of 20 April, by Mr. Lindley entitled 'The boys in the bush', followed by the quote "The whites have now allowed Africans to discover — that power can, indeed grow out of the barrel of a gun . . . . the lesson to the Patriotic Front is plain: if you want to keep up the pressure for more radical change, keep hold of your guns."

This opening quote reveals an immediate bias, the punchline of which is "more radical change" — precisely what Dr. Owen is trying to bring out of the Transitional Government in Salisbury. "The link", says the report, "is obvious".

The report refers to an article by Mr. Ashford in **The Sunday Times** of 22 April, and lists a number of observations that "are pertinent in the context of the assertion that Dr. Owen has deliberately rigged press reports".

The report concludes "One cannot read these reports without being drawn to the inescapable conclusion, that there is a conductor in the background who is orchestrating them. It seems more likely from many of the reports that the conductor is Dr. Owen — or his representatives in the Foreign and Commonwealth Office. Ethics aside, the problem being faced is complicated enough already without resorting to this type of tactic."

A Reminder of Britain's

Murder by Radio Propaganda

The decision of the United Nations Organisation to beam anti-apartheid programmes to the Republic of South Africa brings memories flooding back to Rhodesians. Immediately after Rhodesia declared it independence in 1965, the Zambian Broadcasting

Corporation began systematic broadcasts by former leaders of the banned Rhodesian black nationalist parties inciting blacks in Rhodesia to commit acts of violence aimed at breaking down the rule of law and order.

At about the same time, the BBC arranged with the Zambia BC to recommence the relaying of BBC news and talks programmes, beamed to Rhodesia. These relays had stopped shortly after Zambia became independent in 1964. Thus the BBC began involvement with the Zambian BC in programmes aimed at Rhodesia and which provided, in fact, a daily reminder of Britain's part in the incitement of murder, arson, sabotage and destruction in Rhodesia.

Zambia was then receiving massive aid from British taxpayers and if there had been a warning by Britain of stopping such help, Zambia would certainly have stopped the vicious broadcasts. Instead, the British Government gave every indication of condoning Zambia's activities in what was dubbed at the time as "Murder by radio".

Britain showed further vengefulness at this time when it began to pour propaganda into Rhodesia from the newly established broadcasting station at Francistown in Botswana, just across the border from Rhodesia. That station was guarded by British soldiers — a belittling role for men of some famous regiments. Whilst these broadcasts drew the line at openly advocating murder and maiming, the tone of many of them was such as to underwrite by skilful implication the radio filth coming from Zambia. It was not Francistown Radio advocating that blood had to be spilt — it was merely Francistown Radio furthering a Zambian suggestion that blood had to be spilt. It need hardly be stressed that this nice difference would not be appreciated by unsophisticated Black African listeners. One had only to imagine the BBC beaming similar quotes to the delicately poised multi-racial communities in Britain, especially Northern Ireland. The Francistown radio station was unquestionably there for propaganda purposes, for in addition to carrying BBC world news bulletins, the station broadcast regular commentaries clearly designed to sap Rhodesian morale.

It must be clearly understood that the Francistown station was not a BBC undertaking. It was — like Zambia Radio — an outright government-owned and government-controlled instrument. Radio Francistown was a cloak-and-dagger affair. It was built by the Diplomatic Wireless Service for the British Information Service and it was, and probably still is, a British Government agency whose job is to install and maintain radio transmitting and receiving stations for British missions in foreign countries.

Following official denials that (in addition to its broadcast programmes) the station was being used to eavesdrop on the internal radio communications of countries on Bechuanaland's borders, permission was sought for a combined Rhodesian Broadcasting Corporation and Rhodesia TV team to visit the Francistown establishment. On orders from London, permission was refused point blank. The conclusion is inescapable.

The decision of the UN to beam anti-apartheid programmes to South Africa has resulted in a prompt response from the BBC to the suggestion that its services might be asked to co-operate. Self-righteously a spokesman said the Corporation was not a government organisation and he said: "We don't broadcast propaganda on our own behalf or on behalf of others." The declaration will get a mixed interpretation. There will be engendered in African states an ardent desire to bombard South Africa in a radio offensive. If that happens will Britain wish to remain aloof from the wishes of the United Nations representatives who voted by 140 raised hands to nil for the resolution? If not, how will the Labour Government set about a practical participation in the radio war and has the BBC in fact said the last word on this particular issue?